In His H...

In His Hands

IN HIS HANDS

"...a compelling autobiography"

of life lived as

'clay in the Potter's hands'

Donald G. Karsgaard

Available from Amazon.com, from other various retail outlets, and from the author's website: www.Donald-G-Karsgaard.com

Library of Congress Cataloging-in-Publication Data
    Karsgaard, Donald G., 1947 –
    In His Hands / Donald G. Karsgaard
    ISBN-13: 978-1986599115
    ISBN-10: 1986599116

Especially for my family and friends
who may have always wondered
what motivated me to do
all that I have done
over the years.
I love you.

In His Hands

Contents

In His Hands

Acknowledgements

In appreciation

My wife, Lorraine, has been very patient with me during the writing of this book, for which I am thankful. It has taken much longer for me to write, edit, and publish than I ever imagined, and so I also appreciate the patience of all to whom I promised that this book would have been published before now.

This book is not only about me, but much of it also includes Lorraine. Therefore, I again want to thank her for all she has done for me throughout our fifty-plus years together, for all the wonderful times we have shared together, and also for the not-so-wonderful times we have had together. In retrospect, I do not know how we could have managed life without each other.

I also want to thank each of our three children—Jason, Deborah, and Nathan—for the wonderful memories I have of them from before they were even born. Each one was loved more than they will ever realize, and I cannot imagine what life would have been like without them. They added a wonderful dimension to our lives in so many ways.

I wish to thank each of those who have contributed to my life in various ways. Some of these people are mentioned in this book, but many are not. In any case, I wish to thank each one for their involvement in our lives. Many have been a special blessing to us, as well as a few who have helped in my/our character development, if you know what I mean. Whatever their involvement has been, we have benefited from knowing all these people, and I know their involvement was orchestrated by our wonderful Lord, who has proven His love to us over and over again. So I am thankful for each person I have had the privilege of knowing.

In addition I would like to give my special thanks to Bobbie Helland who has worked alongside me doing much of the editing of this my first book – helping to make it literarily correct and fluently understandable. Her skills and her many hours of dedication to this task are truly appreciated.

If I were to sum up how I feel when looking back over these seventy-plus years, I would say, *"So many people, from so many places, have been involved in the enrichment of my life, that it is just not possible to thank each of you. In my heart I do appreciate having known each one, and I thank you all for the contributions you have made to my life. May you be blessed as you read this book, and see how wonderfully the Lord has used you and others in my life, as well as how He has blessed many other people as a result."*

IN HIS HANDS

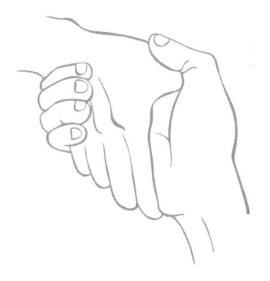

In His Hands

In His Hands

An example of a life lived "as clay in the Potter's hands"

Preface

There are different events and many things in our lives that we remember well, and then there are many that at some point we subconsciously deem insignificant enough to forget. But when we are reminded of those events, we find that they are no longer forgotten. So really nothing has ever been erased; everything has a part in the tapestry of our lives.

What does your tapestry reveal about your life? What does the tapestry of my life tell you? These questions are the essence of this book.

God is at work in the lives of us all, whether we recognize this or not. Many popular and strategic people in our world today, and in history, are great examples of this. But what about the 'average' person, or the 'common' people? Are they important or significant in God's universal plan? And what if a person has been following their own desires, instead of living according to God's plan? Does God care? Can things be changed?

As we read the Bible, we see this in the lives of the people of Israel. Jeremiah 18:1–6 says,

> This is the word that came to Jeremiah from the LORD: "Go down to the potter's house, and there I will give you my message." So I went down to the potter's house, and I saw him working at the

wheel. But the pot he was shaping from the clay was marred in his hands; so the potter formed it into another pot, shaping it as seemed best to him. Then the word of the Lord came to me. He said, "Can I not do with you, Israel, as this potter does?" declares the Lord. "Like clay in the hand of the potter, so are you in my hand, Israel."

As I look back over my life, I cannot remember everything; but it is apparent that God has had a plan. From an early age it has been my desire to conduct my life according to my Creator's intentions—and so this book gives testimony to what God has done in the life of an 'ordinary' person.

Several things described in this book were difficult to write about; but the real purpose for including them is to illustrate how the Lord can take us through all kinds of situations and prove Himself to be faithful and merciful, as well as loving, with the dispensing of His wonderful grace.

I trust that the highlights of my life which I have chosen to share will be a help to you, wherever you happen to be in your life. I trust you will be encouraged to follow God's guidance, so that you, too, can experience the joy and satisfaction of being "clay in the Potter's hands."

You, Lord, are our Father.
We are the clay; you are the potter.
We are all the work of your hand.

Isaiah 64:8

Who Am I?

An Introduction

I am a Canadian citizen, born and raised in Canada. However, I have also lived in the United States and become a naturalized American citizen, and have lived in Mexico and become a Permanent Resident of Mexico. So I have had the opportunity and advantage of trying to speak three languages: English, (my native language), French, which seemed very hard to learn, and Spanish, which seemed much easier.

In English we often say, *"I am tired, I am hungry, I am sick, or I am happy..."*—but really, that is not who we are. The Spanish language is more accurate, because we say (when translated to English), *"I have fear, I have hunger, I have thirst..."*

In English I say, *"I am Donald Gordon Karsgaard,"* but in Spanish (when translated to English), I say, *"I am called Donald Gordon Karsgaard,"* or *"My name is Donald Gordon Karsgaard."*

When people are introduced to each other, they say, *"Who are you? Tell me about yourself..."* and we reply by giving our name and what we do or have done in our lives. And while this may be helpful in getting to know each other, it does not really answer the question, *"Who are you?"*

When you ask someone, *"Who are you?"* what is it you are really asking? Are you simply wanting to know their name and maybe their citizenship or occupation? Or do you want to go further and learn what activities they like, what hobbies they have, or what they have accomplished in their lives? Maybe you are hoping to discover what they did to become successful, or what struggles they have had in life and how they were able to overcome such difficulties.

The reason we ask this question is usually to discover whether or not we could benefit in some way by getting to know the other person better. For example, if both people discover that they play tennis, then they might become tennis partners. Or if one person has some knowledge or experience that the other is searching for, then they might start spending time together to learn from each other.

When you picked up this book, you were probably a little curious to know what I have done in my life. I am sure it was not just to learn my name, my citizenship, and how good life has been to me. Rather, I hope it was to learn something from what I have done, or possibly how I have handled things in my life. Therefore, I have chosen to share with you not only some of the wonderful things I have done, but also some of the struggles and difficulties as well.

I trust you will be encouraged by and learn something from how I have handled certain situations. The Lord has been very good to me, and I hope that your life will be enriched in many ways from reading my story.

But really ... who am I? Not unlike you, I am a creation of God, made for a special purpose according to His plan, and chosen by Him to be a positive influence in the lives of many people. This is what His Word states:

Ephesians 1:4, "Before he made the world, God loved us and chose us" (NLT).

Jeremiah 1:5, "'I knew you before I formed you in your mother's womb. Before you were born, I set you apart and appointed you'" (NLT).

Isaiah 49:1–6, "The LORD called me before my birth; from within the womb he called me by name. ... (He) formed me in my mother's womb to be his servant. ... (He) commissioned me" (NLT).

1 Peter 2:9, "You are a chosen people. ... You are royal priests, a holy nation ... for He called you out" (NLT).

Ephesians 2:8–10, "God saved you. ... We are God's masterpiece. He has created us anew ... so we can do the good things   He planned for us" (NLT).

John 15:16, "I chose you. I appointed you to go and produce lasting fruit" (NLT).

Although God has good intentions for us, we all learn early on that we object to His interference in what we want to do. And whenever these thoughts come to the surface, we have a choice: to continue with our objections and do what we want, or to give in to God's plan for our lives. In my case, I came to realize that my ideas and plans did not truly satisfy me. I also learned at an early age that trusting God and following His guidance brought purpose to my life, success to my endeavors, peace to my mind, and joy to my heart.

Even so, these lessons did not keep me from doing things I would prefer not to remember. I knew it was necessary to put into practice what I was learning, realizing that just knowing these lessons would not guarantee me success. Yet it was not always easy to apply these basic life principles to my life, and later I found there were more principles that would also need to be applied. I had frustrations and challenges.

But I am so glad to be able to report three things: First, God has never given up on me. Second, when applying these first two principles to my life, I was able to overcome many of my challenges and difficulties. And third, because I have sought to make these two principles my foundation, God has used my life to bless many people whom I have had the privilege of knowing.

Perhaps you have a similar testimony, or maybe you have had doubts about allowing God to take control of your life. In either case, I hope you will enjoy reading this book and be blessed in the process.

PHASE ONE

My Early Years

I grew up in a 'Christian home.' My parents took us to church every Sunday, and most times it was for two services on Sunday morning and another one on Sunday evening. We read the Bible and prayed at breakfast and at dinner every day, and we prayed again before bed each night. I knew that God was the Creator of everything, and that every person needed Jesus Christ to be their Savior if they wanted to go to heaven when they died. I accepted all this as fact at an early age, and as best as I was able, I understood that I was what the church I attended called a 'believer' or a 'Christian.'

When I was in grade four, I was hit broadside by a car as I rode my bike to school one day. I flew about twenty feet but only ended up with a scrape on my knee. I thought, *"This is a miracle!"* And my mind raced on, knowing that God had already saved me spiritually and now I had been saved physically—probably because God had something planned for my life. From then on, I wondered what God had in mind for me.

When I was twelve years old, I heard there was going to be another baptism in our church (we had them every few months), and so like the Ethiopian eunuch in Acts 8, I asked my parents, *"Why can't I be baptized?"* I met with one of the elders in our church, and he asked me some basic questions about the Bible. He also wanted to know if I trusted Jesus Christ as my Savior. I replied, *"Yes, of course. I want to go to heaven when I die."*

So on Sunday, July 5, 1959, Dr. John Elder baptized me along with four or five others.

PHASE TWO

High School in Vancouver

A new phase of my life began when I entered grade seven at Point Grey Junior High School in Vancouver, British Columbia. What I liked best at that time was attending the young people's group activities at our church and being involved in the Christian Club at Point Grey. The following year I became president of the Christian Club, and I was elected president the following two years as well.

In my first year as president, one of the highlights for me was bringing a champion boxer to our school to speak about his life as a boxer and how his relationship with Jesus Christ had affected the way he lived. In my second and third years, I rented Christian movies and arranged to have them shown in the auditorium during lunch hours. I also spoke to the students about how the life principles shown in the movies could benefit those who would take the time to come and watch them.

Despite this, I was struggling emotionally. One day, while walking home from Point Grey with my girlfriend, I shared my feelings of not being loved. It wasn't that I wanted more from her; I just expected more out of life in general. At that time, I had a younger brother (age twelve) and three sisters (ages seven, five, and newborn), and I didn't feel like my parents had any time for me. Also, everything I was doing with the Christian Club was not as well attended as I had hoped. And because I was living openly as a Christian, encouraging others to consider accepting Jesus Christ as their Savior and then share their faith, some students were making fun of me.

I was dealing with classic rejection. I told my girlfriend how I was feeling and that I was actually considering suicide. Her response saved my life: *"Don, you've been such a great influence on so many of the kids at school—more than you'll ever realize. You just can't walk away from what God has called you to do. He loves you, and He also has a great plan for your life. I'm sure of that."*

Not only had she saved my life, but my life became more focused because of her encouragement. I knew that God indeed loved me; but what I needed to learn was that God would be with me—not just in the good times, but also in difficult times.

In the months that followed, one of the youth leaders at our church asked what our names meant. I did not know what *Donald* meant, so I went to the school library. There I found this: *"Donald means world leader or world changer."* That confirmed for me that my girlfriend was right. *God does have a plan for my life that will impact others*, I thought. *I need to keep being obedient to whatever He desires me to do. I'm important to His plans for the world.*

A few weeks later in Sunday school, the Lord spoke to me through our teacher, who was teaching on John 15. As we read verses 11 through 17, I could sense the Lord saying to me (in my own abbreviated paraphrase), "I'm telling you these things in advance, so that you will be filled with My joy. Yes, your joy is going be greater than you can imagine! You did not choose Me, but I have chosen you, and I am appointing you, commissioning you, to go and bear fruit—fruit that will last. In fact, this is not only your responsibility—it is My command to you. So stay together and love each other. When the world hates you, remember that it hated Me first. The world would love you, but you do not belong to the world anymore. No, I have chosen you to be separate from the people in this world, and so they will hate you—and because they have persecuted Me, they will also persecute you. ... They will do this to you because of Me. ... But be encouraged: I will send you a Helper, the Spirit of Truth. He will teach you about Me. ... And then you must go and teach others about Me."

That reassured me that God had plans for my life. I was 'chosen,' I had been 'appointed,' and I was being 'commissioned.' So despite what others were saying about me and what I might do in my life, I knew God had a plan different from what the world recommended; so I needed to listen to Him and do whatever He asked. I believed deep inside that I was chosen and qualified to do important things according to God's master plan. God had told me so.

In one of my daily Bible readings, I read John 10:7–11, where Jesus says (my own abbreviated paraphrase), "I tell you the truth: I am the gate for the sheep. All who came before Me were thieves and robbers. But the true sheep do not listen to them. ... Those who come in through Me will be saved, and they will come and go freely, and they will find good pastures. The thief's purpose is to steal and kill and destroy. But My purpose is to give My sheep a full and satisfying life. I am the Good Shepherd."

At fourteen years old, I knew deep in my heart, from what I was reading and from the lessons I had learned, that when I was obeying Jesus Christ, all my needs would be met. I believed that I was embarking on what would be—for me—the greatest life possible, and that I would experience real joy in doing whatever He would lead me to do. He would be my Good Shepherd throughout my life.

I also knew that some people would challenge me, trying to lead me in other directions. They might even try to take away my joy, and possibly even my life. But I knew there would be no better place than in His sheepfold, and that nothing could harm me or prevent the fulfillment of God's plan for my life.

A year later, Mr. George Rich, one of the men in our church who went regularly to speak at some small churches, asked if I would like to go along with him to the Vancouver City Mission (a place where the homeless went to get a meal). So I went, not really knowing what I was getting into.

As we drove home that first night, Mr. Rich asked me to speak the next time he was going to the City Mission. With my voice trembling, I said, *"I would be glad to."* Inwardly, I knew it was not Mr. Rich asking me, but God speaking to me through him. So the following month I again went to the City Mission, and delivered a message to the men (a preacher always spoke to the men before dinner was served). I knew I was not a great preacher; I was just being an obedient servant of God—despite that in John 15, Jesus said I was not to think of myself as a servant, but rather as His friend.

So I gave the message I had prepared, telling the men they could live forever in God's heaven if they accepted Jesus Christ as their personal Savior. Afterward, one of the men who reeked of alcohol and stale tobacco said to me, *"How dare you come here and tell us that we should accept Jesus so that we can live forever. I don't want to live like this forever! Living like this, on the streets and not having a great place to sleep or have good meals all the time, is most certainly not what I want to do."*

I went home dejected, wondering what I had done wrong. I asked God to help me—to show me where I had failed—and He told me that 'His love' had been missing. So I asked Him for 'His love'. When Mr. Rich asked me to go with him the following month, I agreed, not knowing if anything had changed

There I was, back preaching at the City Mission. But this time, after I had given the message I had prepared, one of the men came to me asking some questions, and then he and I prayed together—with my arm around him, no less!

Later that night, I asked myself, *How did that happen? How was it that I prayed for a man, with my arm around him— one of those detestable 'men who reeked of alcohol and stale tobacco'?* Then I realized that God had given me 'His love.' He had answered my prayer, just as it said He would in John 15:16 (my own abbreviated paraphrase): I could "ask the Father for whatever Jesus would do, and He will give it" to me.

Wow. I was again sure that God had called me to "go and bear fruit"—that I was to help people according to the meaning of my own name, and according to Matthew 28:19–20. "To go around the world teaching people about Jesus" meant to me at that time that I should not be afraid to go to any place that I might not normally go or to places that I might be uncomfortable with, or to even do things that I might not think I was qualified to do. God was telling me that He had His plan for my life and would provide everything I would need to be a part of it, including 'His love' for people I might not otherwise love. God had started to guide me, because I had chosen to obey Him.

After my time at Point Grey Junior High School, I went to Magee Senior High School, also in Vancouver. In my first year there, all students had to take an aptitude test to help us determine what our future occupation would be, and what courses we should take over the following three years.

The results showed that I should become a social worker, a psychologist, or maybe even a psychiatrist. But I did not think any of these fields would be where I was headed, because in my heart I knew I was going to be in some kind of full-time Christian service. *Maybe I'll even become a missionary*, I thought.

However, I was never a great student. I received a C- in most of my classes, no matter how hard I studied. And I did study, often for hours before an exam, but my grades did not get much better—except in bookkeeping and mathematics. I got a B in math one time, and I was so proud. Still, I struggled particularly with French, English literature, and history.

I did not appreciate the mannerisms of the older woman who taught French class, and I simply could not understand why she thought we needed to know about the subway trains in France. I also did not understand the messages my English teacher said were being given by the authors of the books and poetry we were studying. And when my history teacher tried to get us to memorize various dates in history, I thought, *When am I ever going to use this in my adult life?*

In my second year of high school, I failed all three subjects—French, English, and history—but I wanted to graduate, so I went to summer school and retook history. To my surprise, I passed, allowing me to proceed to my next year without having to repeat the whole first year of high school.

Even so, the school principal said I was on probation. I needed to do better in my English class this next year, and I needed to choose and pass a language course. Because French was the only language course offered at Magee High School, I phoned the School Board, as the principal had suggested, and was told I could take a language course by correspondence in a 'study class,' which was basically to sit in the school cafeteria and teach myself the language of my choice using material sent to me by the School Board office.

I thought, *What should be my criteria for making this decision? What will I be doing for the rest of my life, and where in the world will I possibly need to speak another language?* The only thing I could think of was that our church had several missionaries in the Dominican Republic and maybe God would call me to go there, too. I decided to study Spanish.

In my second year of high school, I was again failing my English Literature class, so I was demoted to a 'General Program English Class', which therefore took me out of the 'University Program,' meaning that I would not be allowed to go to university after high school. I thought, *Why bother with Spanish, then? I don't need to pass two years of a foreign language class in order to graduate in the General Program.* So I dropped my Spanish course (not knowing that one day I really would want to speak Spanish).

Looking back now, I believe that God wanted me to start learning Spanish way back then so I would be prepared for what He had in mind for my future. But I did not recognize His guidance at the time—and I suffered because of that later in life.

In my first and second years at Magee, I was again elected president of the Christian Club. But in my third year, the principal called me to his office to tell me he would no longer allow our club to meet in the school. He said, *"If I let you Christians have your club, then I will have to offer clubs for all the religions in the world—and I don't have enough teachers to sponsor all such clubs."*

I knew this was not a ruling from the school board, but chose not to argue with the rationalization he used to advance his personal opinions. I started going to the school cafeteria instead of going home for lunch, arriving every day as quickly as I could to reserve a table for my Christian friends. So we no longer met as one of the school's official clubs, but just as a group of Christian students, and we continued to have fellowship this way. (I now see that God was teaching me that there is always a way to serve Him, and for like-minded Christians to meet together despite opposition. This was an important lesson to learn, because God was preparing me for what would come later: serving with a missionary organization involved in communist countries.)

In 1965, during my third year at Magee, Billy Graham came to Vancouver. I wanted to make it another opportunity for Christians to do something at our school, despite what I presumed would be the principal's personal objections. I decided to organize a parade of cars that would begin at Magee High School and drive across Vancouver, stopping at other high schools to have more cars join our parade, which would end at Empire Stadium where Billy Graham was holding his Crusade. The core group of cars from each school would be driven by students from the Christian clubs, with the intention of drawing some of the non-Christians from these schools to join us.

But I would need to do some advertising at school, and would need permission from the principal's office to do so. I prayed, and it happened that the day I went to seek approval, the principal was not well and would likely be out for a week. *Good!* I thought, and asked if the vice principal was available. The secretary ushered me into Mr. Donaldson's office, and he asked how he could help me.

I said, *"I know you're a Christian, and I'm going to ask for your approval to do something I already believe the principal will not allow."* He started to interrupt me, but I asked if I could tell him my whole idea before he responded, and he agreed. I continued, *"I understand you're going to retire after this school year, so I'm not sure what the principal could do that would create a big problem for you. So will you step out on a limb for me? I really want some of the students to come to the Billy Graham Crusade. Can I put up some posters around the school inviting them to the Crusade and informing them of our parade?"*

He said, *"Why not. Go ahead."*

So I got some posters from the Billy Graham Crusade office and enlisted my Christian friends to put them up all around the school. Some of us also had a large banner made that we hung across the school's main hallway, right in front of the administrative offices. We had invitations everywhere, even in the bathrooms. It was outrageous! But I knew they all needed to be up for that one Friday.

Of course, I was called into the principal's office when he returned the following week. He chewed me out as I expected, but then concluded, *"But what has been done is done. Just don't ever do anything like that again."*

I got off easy, and thought, *That little bit of persecution was worth it,* because many of my friends were encouraged to stand up for Christ, and many others who joined us heard the gospel. It reminded me of what Jesus said in John 15 (my own abbreviated paraphrase): "If the world hates you, remember that it hated Me first. I have chosen you and I have appointed you, so go and bear fruit. Testify about Me. This is my command." *We had done well,* I thought, even though some more mature Christians at our church said that I went a little overboard—and I guess I had.

That same spring, I was asked by Terry Winter if I would like to join The BC Outreach Team and travel to a few places in British Columbia over the summer to hold evangelistic meetings, going particularly to some of the smaller churches. Terry would be the main preacher, while others on the Team would visit homes surrounding these churches, inviting people to the meetings.

I thought that since I had no real direction in my life, maybe this would be an opportunity to expand what I might be able to do for Jesus in the future. Oh, I knew I was going to go to Bible school that fall, but I did not know what I would do after that. I had no set goal to be a plumber, an electrician, a carpenter, an architect, a fireman, a salesman, an accountant, a lawyer, a teacher, or even to be a missionary. (But I have done all these things and more in my life since then.)

At the beginning of that summer in 1965, I was nearly killed—or so I thought. I had been delivering invitations to the meetings in Penticton when I came to one home a couple of blocks from the church. A man came to his door holding a shotgun, and yelled, *"You had better get off of my property! I don't want to have anything to do with you Christians!"* He then raised his gun, and I immediately left, thinking, *Now that was a reaction I didn't expect. I guess we can be persecuted in different ways, even here in Canada.* But I reminded myself that God was looking after me, so I had no reason to be afraid.

That summer, a new phase in my life began, as I came to really understand that God was calling me into full-time Christian service. And I thought, *I can do anything and go anywhere God calls me. He will provide all I will need, and He will protect me in every situation.*

PHASE THREE

Bible School in Chicago

Before leaving high school, I considered going to a Bible school after graduation because I wanted a good understanding of all that the Bible teaches, in order to be able to do what God was calling me to do. I thought, *That's where I'll get an education that will not only benefit me for whatever God wants me to do throughout my life, but it will also be beneficial for all eternity as well. 2 Timothy 2:15 says that I should study so that I can be approved by God as an unashamed workman.*

I requested and received information from several Bible schools in Canada and in the United States, and chose to go to Emmaus Bible School in Chicago (actually Oak Park, Illinois, about twenty-five miles west of downtown Chicago). Afterward I felt a little like Abraham, sensing God's leading in my life and desiring to obey Him. I would be stepping out in faith, leaving my home behind to go to a foreign land so many miles away, not knowing what life might entail. Still, I was sure that God was directing and the result would be that many people would be blessed (see Genesis 12:1–4; Hebrews 11:8–10). So at age eighteen, I left home and ventured to a city over two thousand miles away.

So much happened during that first year at Bible School. I learned how to manage life on my own and to become a responsible young man. I worked as the Dining Hall Steward, which gave me just a little more money than my schooling costs. I had to be wise in how I spent the balance—which taught me how to be frugal, and not spend money impulsively. My other responsibilities of managing, organizing and overseeing each evening's dinner and the various special banquets the school held throughout the year, laid that basic foundation that I would need for the many activities and events that I would initiate and manage later in my life. So in addition to the vital Bible knowledge I was getting at Emmaus, I was learning many other very helpful skills.

I also volunteered as a Young Life leader at one of the high schools not too many miles from Emmaus. This was not my first experience with Young Life; however it proved to be quite challenging because this Club was in Cicero, a city near Chicago where there was a lot of gang activity. My involvement was of course helpful to the program, but also helped me to reach outside of my comfort zone to those with a more worldly background than mine.

I had attended a Young Life club while I was in high school. It was more upbeat than the Christian club I led on campus, doing crazy things to attract students—like dividing the group into two teams with each team choosing one of the popular students in the school as their team leader. Then there would be a contest with the losing team making their leader swallow a live, wiggling gold fish in front of the whole group.

These contests were drawn out over several weeks, and they certainly attracted a lot of students, both in Vancouver and in Cicero, and each week a gospel message was given to the large crowds that came. For example, at the Young Life club I attended at Magee (a school of just over nine hundred students), almost three hundred students showed up on the final night of one of their contests.

So my experiences with Young Life, both in Vancouver and in Cicero, helped me to think more broadly about how to reach young people for Christ.

After my first year, I returned to Vancouver for the summer to live at home and work to save enough money to return to Bible school in the fall. But when I returned to the community called Kerrisdale in Vancouver—to the house I had lived in from grade four until my graduation—I found that my family no longer lived there. My parents had sold the house and moved to the rural community of Tsawwassen, about a forty-five-minute drive away. All my fond memories of growing up in Kerrisdale started to erode—it was a bit of a sad shock.

So I went to Tsawwassen and lived in my family's new house that summer, commuting to Vancouver each day to work in one of my father's hardware stores.

About a week or so after I returned home, I told my parents that it was likely I would return home from Chicago the following summer engaged to a girl I had met at Emmaus. They asked more about her, and when they learned that she was of Asian descent, it was like a bomb had gone off. "How can you even think of an interracial marriage?" they asked. "This is certainly *not* what God would have you do!" And then they paraphrased part of 2 Corinthians 6:14: "Don't be unequally yoked."

Well, to say the least, I was very upset. They were taking this passage out of context, and I then realized that I had another decision to make. So I went to my room, packed my bags, and proceeded to walk out the front door with my suitcases in hand.

I did not get far down the driveway before I was accosted and forcibly brought back into the house. Within a couple of days, everything seemed to calm down, but I still knew I had an important decision to make. I felt so conflicted and thought, "*How can this be? This will be devastating for my girlfriend! Am I to follow an out-of-context interpretation of the Bible? Absolutely not!*" But I knew I must obey my parents, and as a result, I spent most of that summer in mental anguish.

What I did not see then was that God had a different plan for my life – a plan that involved Lorraine Roberts.

From the moment I met Lorraine during my first year at Emmaus, I saw her as a really beautiful girl that I'd probably never get to have a relationship with. And throughout my first year at Emmaus, even though I was in love with my Asian girlfriend, I was captivated by Lorraine's smile and her personality. Lorraine was not conceited or flamboyant. She was *down to earth*. And, as I got to know her better, her desire to overcome the many obstacles she believed were in her life also attracted me to her.

After that turbulent summer of 1966, I decided to return to Emmaus by train—from Vancouver to Seattle, and then from Seattle to Chicago. Low and behold, when I boarded the train in Seattle, bound for Chicago, Lorraine was there—on the same train. That was the opportunity I needed and I was bold enough to take the seat beside her. Then we started talking—in fact we spent most of our time over the following three days on that train talking and getting to know each other. Little did we know that this was the start of a relationship that would last over fifty years.

Shortly after the semester started, my girlfriend asked me what had changed—she knew something was bothering me, and something was upsetting our relationship. I said, *"I'm not sure what you mean"*—trying to avoid the conversation that I knew must take place. So I explained how my parents had reacted when I told them about our relationship. She was very hurt. And we were both upset, knowing that because of their feelings we must discontinue our relationship.

One good thing came of it, however. Through all of this, I developed a love for non-Caucasian people, despite my parent's prejudice, not knowing at that time I would spend many years of my life as a missionary among Mexicans.

A few weeks later, I got up the nerve to start talking with Lorraine again. Then over the following few months we spent more and more time together and became good friends. As our relationship grew stronger, so did our ideas for spending the rest of our lives together.

In April 1967, I gave Lorraine an engagement ring—actually it was a *promise ring* I had made from some bread-bag twist-ties. Emmaus Bible School prohibited students from getting married or engaged during the school year (September through early May), so she did not receive her real engagement ring until later that summer.

Throughout my second year at Emmaus, I could feel the foundation of my life becoming more solid with all that I was being taught, and through the many activities I was involved in.

During Easter break that year, I was privileged to be involved in a Campus Crusade for Christ outreach in Daytona Beach, Florida. Each day during that week, we went out to the waterfront and struck up conversations with other students who were really only there for their spring break parties. This experience helped me to lose some of the inhibitions I had about sharing the message of salvation with perfect strangers, and to learn how to start conversations about Christ with others.

During these two years, living near Chicago and going to Emmaus, I did and saw many other things as well—much of which helped me learn about and understand the real world we live in. I learned not be so naïve, and not to take everything for granted. For many people life is difficult, and many disasters are unavoidable, while others seem to be cared for in unusual ways. My eyes and my heart were continually being opened.

It shocked me one day to see a man shot and killed in downtown Chicago. I was also surprised when being driven through one suburb to see men working in gardens in front of some of the homes, holding what looked like machine guns—then I was told we were in an area where it was believed some of the leaders of 'the mob' lived.

Then we had a tornado come through the areas around Chicago. The sky turned the color of pea soup as the heavy rains poured down and the winds howled. We opened all the windows in the school dormitory so the building would not explode as the tornado went through, then waited out the storm in the basement.

Afterward, some of the students shared their varying experiences. A couple of them talked about how they were in their car as it was lifted up and then miraculously put down right side up some distance away. Then we saw on TV how many homes and neighborhoods had been totally destroyed only a few miles away from us.

Chicago also introduced me to what winter can really be like—with its bitter-cold temperatures and seemingly constant winds. Life for many people in our world brings with it various difficulties to deal with—some seem normal, while others seem unfair. But I could see that God was there in every place. This was a great truth to not only believe, but also to experience.

My relationship with Lorraine continued to grow and deepen that year. In fact we were both planning on not returning to Emmaus for a third year, but rather I would return to Vancouver and Lorraine to New Westminster, BC (cities close to each other), and then getting married a few months afterward. I knew that this was the woman I wanted to spend the rest of my life with.

Lorraine was born in 1946. Her mom was from Yakima, Washington and her dad was from Harriman, Tennessee. They met and were married in Bremerton while her dad was stationed there. He was in the Navy and when deployed, her mom went to live with her parents, who were living near Bonneville, Alberta—and it was there that Lorraine was born.

After her dad finished his active duty with the Navy they moved to Tennessee near where he had been born and had relatives, but only lived there for a year before returning to the West Coast. A few years later Lorraine's parents divorced and life became difficult for everyone. But her mom did the best she could to raise her children on her own while also working at Boeing. When work was unavailable, they sometimes had to receive welfare, which they found humiliating. Lorraine, being the oldest of three children, did her best to carry out many of the responsibilities at home because her mother was not able to do everything.

I believed Lorraine was a very capable homemaker, and looking forward to making her life count for something. She too wanted to do whatever God would call her to, and I believed we could be a great help to each other. So I believed we were a good match, and we were falling in love with each other.

In His Hands

PHASE FOUR

Life in Vancouver

When I returned home from Bible School after my second year—the summer of 1967—I told my parents that Lorraine and I had embarked on a serious relationship. At first I did not want to say too much, fearing that their reaction might for some reason be negative, as it had been when I told them about my previous girlfriend. So I did not tell them right away that we were already informally engaged; rather, I chose to tell them more about Lorraine over the following weeks, and slowly break this news to them.

My parents were both Christian and came from Christian homes. My mom was raised in Vancouver, British Columbia, by parents who had immigrated to Canada from England. My dad was born in Moosejaw, Saskatchewan, but raised mostly in Vancouver by parents who had immigrated to Canada from Denmark and Sweden. My parents were married shortly after World War II, and lived in Vancouver, where I was born in 1947. We moved to North Vancouver after my brother was born, and it was there that my first sister was born. When I was in grade four, we moved back to Vancouver to live in the Kerrisdale neighborhood, and that was where my other two sisters were born. So I had one brother (Bob, later known as Colin), and three sisters (Marilyn, Nancy, and Yvonne) all younger than me.

My parents weren't ultra-conservative as some religious people can be – rather they were conservative in doctrine and somewhat legalistic in practice. My father was the dominant leader in our family – we all did what he decided and said. I don't mean to imply that he was unreasonable or that he was always loud and demanding or physically abusive, because he wasn't. Dad just expected us to respect him as the head of our family, and to never question his instructions.

My mother was a quiet and submissive person. She always obeyed my father, though that appeared to be difficult for her at times, especially when my father did raise his voice. She was very careful about spending money, so we almost always had very basic meals. We had a lot of canned soups, spaghetti, and pork and beans. However Mom sometimes tried to dress it up a little and add a few chopped wieners or meat balls to it. Sometimes Mom made meat loaf, or Shepherd's Pie – which was a casserole of mashed potatoes with a little ground beef at the bottom. We ate a lot of hot dogs too, but to be creative she sometimes would cut the wieners along the side, and put a piece of cheese in the slice she'd made, and then she'd bake them in the oven – that was good! She'd occasionally make her own macaroni and cheese – and that was really good! We had spam too – but she'd dress that up by putting a little brown sugar or maybe a ring of pineapple on top, and then bake that in the oven. Mom made her own bread (by hand, without a bread machine), because that was cheaper than buying ready-made bread. She also canned a lot of fruit in the summer, because that was cheaper than buying canned fruit. Sunday's however were different – Mom splurged and made roast beef with Yorkshire pudding – we always looked forward to that! But that was the only exception to our very frugal life.

My father was a hard-working man who was faithful to his word, his wife, and his family. He owned his own hardware business and worked in his stores every day of the week, except Sundays – Sundays were reserved for church and for rest. He and I did not spend time in the evenings or on the weekends playing ball or some other sport, or working together on a hobby like many fathers would do with their sons. He was just too tired when he got home from work. He hardly ever took time away from work to take us on a family vacation – I can remember only three times we went away as a family during my childhood.

My parents always seemed to be penny-pinching, only having enough money to meet expenses and nothing more. This was why they sold our house in Vancouver and moved to Tsawwassen, where houses were cheaper. Dad often said, "Save the pennies so that we can spend the dollars." I remember many times when Mom made dinner, she would divide up the peas among everyone else at the table, but not take any for herself – instead she'd drink the water the peas were cooked in. One time, when my feet grew and my slippers became too small, I was told we didn't have money for new ones, so Dad cut the front of the slippers I had, and my toes hung over the fronts of them. When I needed new shoes, they sometimes bought ones a size larger than needed and stuffed newspaper inside them. I remember one time when I had a bad cold and had used a lot of Kleenexes. Dad told me, "...lay the used ones out on the bed and let them dry out – that way you can use them again. Don't just throw them in the waste can after one use!"

Mom and Dad never seemed to have any friends when I was growing up – I thought they were probably too busy: Mom raising five children, and Dad working all the time. Later in life however, after I had left home and Dad was no longer tied to his hardware stores, they did have a few friends. But these friendships didn't last more than a few years. Dad made people feel that he was always right. He tended to jump to conclusions quickly, and had a hard time controlling his anger at times. He held grudges, too, and it seemed he never forgave anyone. But don't misunderstand me: Dad had a good heart – he always wanted to do what was right. He was a giving person, but just not socially adept.

I had two uncles who lived with their families in Vancouver, but we rarely got together with them. Dad seemed to have some distaste for them – I have never fully understood why. We did however sometimes go to my grandparent's home for a Sunday dinner.

When I left home my brother was fourteen years old, my oldest sister was nine, my middle sister was seven, and my youngest sister was only two. So I never really got to know my sisters very well, and my brother always had different interests than me. So throughout my life I've felt somewhat distant from my brother and sisters.

Through it all, it became evident that my father was a very proud man who wanted people to appreciate him for his abilities, and for what he had been able to make of himself. He would sometimes help people financially, but there were always strings attached – nobody appreciated that. Later in life, when he had become more financially successful, he set up a Foundation so he could give money to some very worthy causes – but he also let people know about his giving. He was not what you would call a humble man.

I believe both Mom and Dad loved me, because I believed they were always doing the best they could, no matter what the circumstances were. They certainly did not treat me badly – there was never any physical abuse. Oh, I got a spanking now and again; but not too often – I was almost always what you would call a good kid.

When I was young, my mother would kiss me when she put me into bed, but I don't remember ever being hugged. In any case, after my attempt at suicide, I started to look at many things differently, and came to believe that my mother has always loved me. I also believed that my father loved me too, but that love was never expressed with a hug or a kiss as I can remember – not until much later in life, when on a few occasions Dad and I did hug each other.

I don't think my parents ever thought they neglected me, because there was never any intentional neglect. It's just that the younger ones always needed more attention – just because they were young. I always felt like there was a baby in the family that needed to be looked after – and so that's who always got the most attention. As a result I often felt left out.

I believe it was this feeling of being neglected or less important that caused me to always struggle to feel loved or accepted by people, and was what led me to consider suicide when I was a young teenager.

In June after my second year at Emmaus, a couple of weeks after I moved home, my brother graduated from high school and then had a heated argument with our parents. This was not the first time, because Bob was living in a way our parents did not approve of. He was popular at school, and often went to parties where there was a lot of drinking.

Dad made all this a greater issue when my brother graduated, telling him that he needed to change his lifestyle and not come home drunk anymore. He explained to Bob that he had our three sisters to raise yet, and did not want them influenced by the way he had been carrying on. So Dad gave my brother the ultimatum to either clean up his life or move out. Bob chose to move out, which hurt my mother tremendously. In fact, everyone was surprised. Bob never came back to visit that summer, and a short time later he even changed his name—and has basically had nothing to do with our family ever since.

Other significant changes were happening at home while I was away at Bible school. My father started closing his five hardware stores one by one and bringing the stock from one store to another, until he was left with only one store, Kerrisdale Hardware, the most profitable one.

It may sound like Dad had a successful chain of stores, but in reality that was not the case. He told us that the only store that really made any money was Kerrisdale Hardware. The history goes something like this: My grandfather, Dad's dad, was a successful carpenter/builder in Moosejaw, Saskatchewan. But when my grandmother developed allergies and then severe asthma, they agreed that she should move to Vancouver with their three boys. This was when my dad was very young. Then sometime after the Depression, my grandfather moved to Vancouver to rejoin his family, and sometime thereafter opened a hardware store.

My grandfather died in 1954 without life insurance, so basically my grandmother was left with only his hardware store. But she was unable to operate the business, so my father bought it and made payments to her so she would have funds to live on. But he found out within a short time that there was not enough profit for us all (our family and my grandmother, who had her own house at that time) to live on. So Dad went to the bank and got a loan to start a second hardware store, and used some of the money for us to live on for a short time. After this, Dad did the same thing again and again, until he had five hardware stores. He tried to make the other stores profitable, but eventually had to admit defeat and close all but the one.

I had several decisions to make when I returned home that summer, in 1967. The first three were, "What should I do next? What kind of work should I do? And where shall I work?"

Considering what had been happening over the years, I went to work for my father. It was not that I did not feel drawn to any other particular line of work, but because I wanted to relieve my father of some of his responsibilities at the store so he could spend more time with the family.

He had been working six days a week for as long as I could remember, and dad came home exhausted every night.

We rarely took vacations as a family since Dad had to work all the time. However we did have breakfast and dinner as a family most days. Sunday mornings we all went to Sunday school and the Worship Service following. But then the afternoons were usually spent at home doing something quiet as Dad rested, before we went back to church for an evening service. Dad rarely did anything with us otherwise, and Mom was almost always busy with chores around the house and with the rearing of my younger sisters. This was the way we spent our lives as a family when I was growing up, living on what some would say were only the basic necessities, and without our parents giving much personal attention to my brother and me. It was this that had likely led my brother to live as he did, and that caused me to consider suicide when I was fourteen years old. So I wanted to do what I thought I could to help remedy the problems I was aware of, so my three sisters would have a better upbringing.

During that summer, Lorraine left Emmaus and went with some of her friends to visit Washington, DC, before becoming involved in an evangelistic campaign in Utah. She then returned to Seattle and spent some time volunteering at a Christian summer camp on Whidbey Island—and it was there that I presented Lorraine with her engagement ring. The informal engagement that we had made earlier that spring with twist-ties from a bread bag was now formalized.

In late August, Lorraine left Seattle and went to live with her grandmother in Coquitlam (close to Vancouver, B.C.) and soon after she started working for Henry Electric.

In early September I told my parents that Lorraine and I wanted to get married the following April, after my twenty-first birthday on April fifth, but they told us that would not work. They said we had to either get married by the end of October or wait until the following summer, because my mother was pregnant and did not want to be seen in public from November through June. (Many women in those days, especially those from conservative backgrounds like ours, did not want to show themselves to be pregnant in public.)

Not wanting to wait until the following summer, we immediately started to make our wedding plans. We were married on October 28, 1967, and had a weekend honeymoon in Vancouver before returning to work. I went back to Kerrisdale Hardware and Lorraine went back to Henry Electric, where she worked until we were expecting our first child. (Lorraine did not work again until the children were older, because we felt it would be best for our children if mom were at home looking after them during their younger years).

Jason was born on April 8, 1970.

About a year after we were married, our landlord wanted to raise our monthly rent from $110 to $120 per month. We began looking at alternatives to apartment living, and found we could have a small home built for us not too far from Vancouver in Beach Grove, one of the suburbs of South Delta, which was also close to my parents' home in Tsawwassen. So we bought our first house for $19,500, with a small down payment and a mortgage payment of $114.92 per month. We lived in that home for almost five years.

Two years after we moved into our home, I started to build a three-hundred-square-foot addition onto it, learning as I went all that was necessary to do most of the work myself. For the work I could not do myself, I hired people, then watched them carefully, learning the skills that would be helpful to me in the following years.

During this time, since I was working full-time for my father, he started working in another business. When Dad no longer needed to take a salary from Kerrisdale Hardware, he asked if I would like to buy the family business. He said it should go to me, the oldest in the family, and offered it to me on very reasonable terms: he would allow me to immediately double my take-home pay and pay him installments over ten years.

Despite how attractive this offer was, I knew I could not accept it because God had called me into some kind of full-time Christian service. Working at the store had been a wonderful opportunity to learn how to operate and manage a business, and understand how to deal with people, but it was time for me to move on to another phase in my life.

In His Hands

PHASE FIVE

Beginning 'Full-Time' Ministry in Vancouver

While growing up, I went to Bible camps every summer—to Pioneer Bible Camp on Thetis Island when I was eight and nine years old, then to Daybreak Point Bible Camp on Anvil Island every year thereafter. I was there for at least one week every summer, first as a camper and then as a cabin leader and water-ski instructor.

I was in my mid-twenties when the Lord spoke to me, saying, "I need someone to follow up with those campers who don't go to any church." So I spoke to the elders in my church and asked them what they thought about the idea of my visiting each of these kids' homes.

They agreed this was a need, and so I approached the Board of Daybreak Point Bible Camp and shared the idea with them. They agreed that it would be a worthwhile endeavor, but determined that I could only do it on a volunteer basis; they would not be able to provide me with a salary. Their belief was if the Lord was indeed calling me into this ministry and I needed financial support, then the Lord would supply. I should not advertise my needs or ask people for financial support, but quietly trust that He would supply everything we would need. I knew other missionaries who had lived this way, and believed their testimony that God had never failed them.

However, believing other missionaries' testimonies was not enough. I had to have my own personal beliefs and convictions in order to live without any guaranteed income. So I started my introspection. Personally, I had learned by then that I could trust what God said in His

Word. I had proven some of it to be true in my own life, as I had never been disappointed by God when obeying His Word. I was also certain that I had been called by God into full-time service for Him. This is why I had gone to Bible school—to prepare myself for serving Him. I had stood up for Christ in junior and senior high school, and had taken other opportunities to tell others about Christ from a young age. I had preached in some churches, at summer camps, and at the City Mission, and people had responded well.

So I concluded that I had been chosen by Jesus Christ Himself and appointed by Him to testify about Him, and I believed that because He had called me, He would look after me, just like Matthew 6 says. So I was ready to step out in faith, and again approached the elders at my church and shared my convictions with them. After praying with me, they agreed unanimously that I should follow the Lord's leading and then shared my calling with some other churches in our denomination. Four of them joined with my home church in sending me out into this mission field—albeit the 'home mission field'.

During the following summer, I attended all the summer camps at Daybreak Bible Camp. Some weeks I was a camp counselor, while other weeks I was the water-ski instructor or guest speaker. I had a great time getting to know the kids and spending time with them. At the end of each week, I would tell the group that I would be visiting some of their homes to help their parents realize the importance of going to church.

That fall, I started visiting the homes of the children who did not go to any church. I had some wonderful conversations with many parents, and discovered that most of these families had gone to a church in the past, but for various reasons they had stopped—many because they had been offended in some way.

I told them that their experience was indeed unfortunate, but that not all churches are the same. I told them of the churches that were nearby, and encouraged them to go to the church of their choice. I explained the importance of attending a church that believed the Bible was God's Word, and encouraged them to enter into a relationship with God through Jesus Christ if they had not already done so. Then before I left their homes, I prayed with those who would allow me to.

During the couple of years I did this, I also led the young people's ministry at my church and on occasion would preach in other churches. I enjoyed studying the Bible and teaching it. My focus was always on the practical side of things, and because of that I was invited to one church to teach a course on how to do door-to-door evangelism. Within a short time this church entered a building project due to increased attendance. It was an encouraging time.

Our daughter Deborah was born on January 25, 1972. What an exciting experience. A bad snow storm blew in, and we had to drive an hour to get to the hospital in Richmond for the delivery because there was no hospital closer to us.

We enjoyed living in Beach Grove, only a couple of blocks from the beach, and walking that area. While there, we commuted about thirty minutes to our church in Vancouver, because that was where we had been married and had our connections for ministry.

During those years, we tried to reach out to our neighbors, especially the young couple across the street from us. Then one day, my neighbor George said to me, "If you want me to believe what you've been telling me, you need to be doing something for the community. I need to see more evidence of all this in the way you live."

I replied, "Well, you're a volunteer fireman, so if there's a need or an opening for someone else at the fire department, please let me know. I'd be happy to join."

About six weeks later, George came to me and said, "Come on down to the fire hall next week. We have an opening."

So I became a volunteer fireman.

We had weekly training meetings at the fire hall, and following the first meeting I attended, during the practice time following the teaching session, the men started challenging me. It began with an 'initiation' of sorts—with hard physical challenges like running a hose line, and climbing a ladder carrying a hose, and to do this as fast as I could. I had a lot to learn.

At the end of every training meeting, the men hung around for about an hour or so drinking beer, playing cards, and talking about sports. I asked if I could have a Pepsi or Coke, explaining that I did not drink beer, and that started things rolling.

They liked to tease me because they saw I was different from them. During the following weeks we had a good time together, and so when I thought I had established a good enough rapport with them, I started a Bible study in our home for the volunteer firemen of Beach Grove and Tsawwassen, which ultimately led to two families accepting Jesus Christ.

In the spring of 1972 Lorraine and I decided to sell our home in Beach Grove and move to Vancouver to be closer to the families I was visiting for Daybreak Point Bible Camp. We had bought the house for $19,500 and sold it for $28,000, although considering the work I had done to it to add the family room and office, we really did not make much of a profit. However we were pleased with the sale price, even though the home in

Vancouver cost us $39,000 and we had a bigger mortgage expense each month.

The following summer we were invited to go to Rosebud Lake Bible Camp where I would be the featured speaker, and it was there that we met and came to appreciate Will Dawes, a missionary pastor from Trail, British Columbia. He explained that he had been there for over twenty years and was needing someone like me to come and lead the young people's ministry in the Trail church that he was pastoring, and also to help pastor the church in Rossland and lead the young people's ministry in that church as well. After Lorraine and I prayed about this and talked with the elders at my church in Vancouver, we decided that we should move to Rossland, British Columbia to fulfill this need.

We had only lived in our Vancouver home a few months, and we had signed a mortgage agreement that had a non-assumable clause and a no-cancellation clause, meaning that a buyer could not take over our mortgage payments. In fact, we could not sell our home without incurring a huge penalty. When we had purchased this home, we had no idea that we might want to move so quickly, so entering such a mortgage seemed like no problem.

So we prayed and then went to see the bank manager about our desire to sell the house. He asked why it was necessary for us to sell and get out of the mortgage contract, and not knowing if he was a Christian or not, I wondered if he would truly understand. In any case, I explained how we felt led to move to Rossland and that we had the backing of our home church, to which he replied, "We cannot have the buyer assume your mortgage, but in your case we'll be glad to cancel the mortgage when you sell. And because of your circumstances, we won't require you to pay any penalty."

Wow. Lorraine and I were shocked and pleased. We knew God had to have His hand in this, and accepted this as an added confirmation that we were moving according to God's directions.

So we made a trip to Rossland and found an older house that had been built before 1900. It needed some work, but we believed it would be a good home for our family. It was only $11,500 and just a couple of blocks from the only evangelical church in that small city— the church where I would be working.

The next phase of our lives was about to begin.

PHASE SIX

Serving the Lord in Rossland and Trail

Rossland, British Columbia, is located in the Kootenay Mountains, close to the United States border and approximately four hundred miles east of Vancouver. It was a small city of about three thousand people when we were living there, and Trail, a city of about twenty thousand people, was just six miles downhill.

Trail is located on the Columbia River. Its main industry was smelting—mostly lead from ore taken out of the neighboring mountains, including from the mines in Rossland. Although Rossland was one of the busiest centers of the famous Gold Rush years earlier, its main attraction had changed to skiing. Red Mountain was becoming more and more popular, and Rossland was starting to become what today we would call "trendy." The sleepy bedroom community for workers at Trail's COMINCO Smelter was starting to come alive again.

The only evangelical church in Rossland had bought one of the old hotels from the Gold Rush days, located on the only corner of town that had a flashing street light. It was called Rossland Gospel Chapel, and was the church where I learned how to be a pastor. During the five years we lived there, I preached in this church almost every Sunday, except for when I was leading local Summer Bible Camps. About thirty people attended the church when we arrived, but more and more people came, and within a few short years we had almost a hundred and twenty people in church each Sunday.

Being in the mountains, we were used to getting thirty feet of snow each year. Sometimes we had to shovel as much as eighteen inches when we got up in the morning. Almost without fail, the snow would start falling on October 31, and we would have snow on the ground until sometime the following May.

Our neighbors across the street were avid skiers, so one day Kim took me to Red Mountain to teach me to ski. I rented some skis, he gave me a few pointers, and then we got on the chairlift. Kim said, "Learning to ski is like learning to swim. The best way to learn how to swim is to be thrown into the water—you may thrash around a bit, but then you will just start swimming." So that day he was going to have me ski the face of Red Mountain, which was very steep; but Kim said instead of facing myself straight down toward the lodge, all I had to do to make my way down the hill was to go from one side to the other.

To say the least, I was scared. We got off the chairlift on the backside of the mountain and started to ski around toward the face. But I could not slow down, so being afraid, I put my right shoulder against the cliff, and of course I went into a tumble. When Kim found me, he asked, "What happened?" He had been ahead of me and could not see me as I tried to follow him.

"I was going too fast and couldn't slow down," I explained.

He shook his head, then told me to remember all that he explained before we got on the chairlift and I would be fine.

We got to the face, and if I had thought I was scared a few minutes before, I was really scared now. It was a very steep slope for my first time on skis, but I gradually started going from side to side, turning as I had been taught. When I reached the lodge at the bottom, I was still shaking but had done it.

Isn't this just the way it is in the Christian life? I thought.
*It's a totally different way of living and can be scary at times.
But we can all live it successfully. All we have to do is be willing
and then put aside whatever is holding us back and go for it.
That's what living by faith is all about.*

In Rossland, I led the young people's activities every
week at Rossland Gospel Chapel and at Bethany Chapel in
Trail, as well as a monthly interchurch young people's
group that I had started.

At that time we only had a mid-size car, and I wanted
a larger car so I could drive more young people to our
activities. Not telling anyone of my desire, I prayed that
the Lord would provide a station wagon for us—and not
just any station wagon, but one with the extra rear seat so
I could get as many kids in it as possible.

Then one night I had a dream or vision of a station
wagon—the one with the extra rear seat—and this car in
my dream also had some luxury items: a roof rack, wood
paneling on its sides, electric windows, and even electric
leather seats. I awoke saying to the Lord, *"Really, we don't
need all the luxury items, but yes, this would be wonderful!"* So
I began thanking the Lord for this car, even though we had
not yet received it.

A few days later the phone rang and a man asked if I
could use a station wagon, and if so would I come to
Vancouver and pick it up. Of course I agreed. When I got
to Vancouver, there it was: a dark blue Dodge nine-
passenger station wagon, with all the things that I had
seen in my dream. God was showing us that not only
would He continue supplying our basic needs, but He
would also give us the desires of our hearts and provide
some extras as well.

The verses near the beginning of Psalm 37 came to
mind—verses that were written on a plaque that my
grandparents had given me some time before, and words

that I had memorized many years before that: *"Delight yourself in the Lord and His ways, and He will give you even the desires of your heart. Commit your ways to Him and trust Him, and He shall bring it all to pass."* (My own abbreviated paraphrase.)

Although I knew these words and was putting them into action, life was still stressful. It was like we were always brought to the edge of a canyon but (thankfully) never pushed off. Each month it seemed we had only enough money to meet our needs. That did not stop me from doing things in faith, though, like arranging to rent a projector and a Christian movie to show at a young people's meeting on Friday, when there was nothing in my wallet or our bank account. We simply acted as though the money was there—and the money we needed arrived just in time the following Monday.

This is just one example of how the Lord provided financially for us. We always received enough for our daily living expenses and our ministry expenses, but usually not much more. These funds mainly came through the mail from various people at different times, never from the same ones each month, but always from people who had been praying for us.

We learned from personal experience that the Lord would always provide whatever we needed, be it food, clothing, a mortgage payment, or a ministry expense. We could always step out in faith trusting the Lord, because the Lord was truly faithful. We had also proven Matthew 6:25–33 to be true. I knew God had called me, saying, *"I have chosen you. I have appointed you. So go, testify about Me, and bear fruit. This is My command for you."* (My own abbreviated paraphrase of John 15:16.)

Always being aware of His calling upon our lives and experiencing His constant provisions, I knew we must always do His bidding and should never be discouraged. Life for us was a mix of faith and trust, living in the darkness but always having His light, sensing God's leading and following in obedience, living on the edge but never pushed over, and always having needs yet always experiencing His provision. As I embraced this vital life lesson, the Lord began teaching me another.

One afternoon during the winter after we received our station wagon, I was driving down a slight hill in Rossland with a car full of young people. At the bottom, there was a bit of a curve in the road, after which the road continued up another slight hill. The road was a little icy, when suddenly another car came over the second hill and started sliding toward us.

Just as his Jeep reached this curve, so did my car. Our vehicles slid into each other, with my car hitting his just behind the driver's door. The door flew open, and the driver fell out onto the snow-covered road. I was astonished. I had not hit his car hard. In fact, there was no damage done to either vehicle.

When I jumped out to check on the man, I realized that he was my dentist, and because of the strong smell of alcohol, I knew he had been drinking. He got up, brushed himself off, and just drove away without saying anything. *What now?* I thought. *What kind of accident report should be filed? Should any report be filed at all? There are no injuries, and no damage was done to either vehicle.*

So we thanked God that no one was hurt—experiencing not only His provision for everything, but also now His protection. Yet for several days, I pondered how the accident had affected the young people who were with me that afternoon. I kept thinking, *What had they told their parents? How might this affect my testimony in Rossland?* I must admit I was a little worried.

The following week, I happened to have an appointment with this dentist. I clearly remember what took place that afternoon, although I do not remember our words exactly. In any case, as soon as we saw each other, we began to talk about the accident. He said, "Don't worry about it. Neither car was damaged." I was relieved, and as he looked in my mouth, he commented, "I see a small cavity, but it's not that bad. We can take care of it."

"Thank you," I said.

"My assistant will do the prep work. She knows how to make people relax." And with a smirk on his face, he left the room.

His assistant, having seen the look (or instruction) on his face, approached the chair I was seated in. And in a seductive manner she said, "You really don't need any Novocain. Let me help you relax," and she started unbuttoning her white uniform shirt.

"Oh no, you don't," I said and quickly got out of the chair. And without another word I left the office, and never went back.

I wonder if I might have a problem, not having filed an accident report, I thought. *But he said not to worry. I wonder what people might say around town, if they hear what happened in the dental office. How could both of these incidents affect my testimony in this small town?*

But nothing was ever said around town to my knowledge, and no problems resulted. I was relieved. I knew by experience now that God would not only provide everything for us as we serve Him, but that He would also protect us in ways we might not even recognize. There was no need to worry.

When we are serving the Lord, Satan will engineer events and cause people to say and do things to thwart the gospel from being received by people. I also knew the Lord had called me to serve Him there, and because I was being obedient to His call, He was looking after every need and concern I had. He was providing for us and protecting us, and He would not allow His plans to be thwarted!

For three years while living in Rossland, I drove a school bus for the Trail and Rossland School District. I did this not so much for the money (they paid very little); but to show my support for the community. In Beach Grove, I had learned that for people to listen to me, I had to show that I cared for them in a tangible way—and because I was in a public ministry as a pastor, I felt the need to show my community support in a public way.

I had many experiences as a school bus driver, some of which showed people not only that I supported the community but also that I was somehow different, and somehow protected. I wanted people to see that having God in my life was what made this difference—and have them desire to also have Christ in their lives.

When I was driving one route, I picked up most of my load of students at one location before going to the other bus stops on the route. This first gathering point was about ten miles from the high school where I delivered my load, and every day for the first week on this route, the students would push and shove to be near the front of the line (they wanted certain seats on the bus).

I didn't want this unsafe crowding at the door to continue, and I had told them so. "This kind of behavior is unacceptable. Next time when I come, please line up in an orderly manner." However, one particular Friday I added, "If you continue to push and shove, I won't allow you to get on the bus. I'll just drive away, and you can walk to school."

That next Monday morning, they again pushed and shoved, crowding around the door to the bus before I could even open it. So I did not open the door. I just drove away, leaving them to walk. I then picked up the students at the other stops and delivered them to the high school.

The next day when I went to the garage to get my bus, the dispatcher asked me what had happened the day before. None of the students from that first stop had shown up for their classes. I gave him a full explanation, and he told me that I was wrong and that I should have driven them to school anyway. After I left the garage, the dispatcher called the principal of the high school to explain what had happened and let him know he had instructed me to never do it again.

That Monday, and every day thereafter, all the students going to the high school were well behaved and respectful toward me—and this continued throughout the year. In fact, a couple of weeks after the incident, the dispatcher told me not to worry about what had happened, because the school board would not be taking any action against me. They even wanted me to know that they appreciated my boldness and willingness to teach these students a lesson—and that it had worked—because they were now better behaved in their classes as well.

The following year, I was asked to drive a different route—one on which previous drivers had problems with the students they picked up. I was told that it was the route that picked up the autistic children throughout the Trail area (there was an abnormally large number of children with autism in Trail, probably because of the smelter that was there). The dispatcher said the reason I was being asked to take this route was because of how respectful the students I had driven to school the previous year had become. He thought maybe things for these children would be different if I drove them to school.

I agreed to take on the new route, and I treated the kids with kindness. I talked to them, never shouting and always explaining things. After a week or so, all the problematic behavior stopped and I never again had a disturbance. Again the school board was surprised and pleased, and they instructed the dispatcher to encourage the other bus drivers to follow my example.

The third year that I drove a bus, I was given a route in Rossland. One winter morning, after it had snowed all night, I was on a stretch about a half a block long where the snow had been piled high on both sides of the road, but the sides were sloped toward the middle, leaving only enough room for one large vehicle to go through at a time.

I entered this short stretch of road, and an oncoming truck driver judged that we could both make it through at the same time. I moved closer to the right side of the road, which tilted the bus even more, and then heard a popping sound. I felt nothing, and the truck carried on down the road. *That was odd*, I thought. After stopping the bus, I looked and saw that all the clearance lights on the left side of the bus had been broken. Each light's housing was still in place; only the plastic covers and light bulbs had been broken. I explained to the dispatcher what had happened, and he told me not to worry. I would still receive my three-year safe-driving certificate.

Through these experiences, several things stood out in my mind. The Lord can and will give us wisdom, kindness and boldness when serving Him, in addition to providing for us and protecting us.

On July 6, 1975, our second son Nathan was born.

That summer, I planted a vegetable garden beside our house—a piece of land that was about thirty feet wide by one hundred feet long. I cleared away the brush and weeds and piled them up. It became a fairly large pile that would have required a large truck to take it all to the dump, so I decided to burn the pile. Then I thought the best way to get the fire started would be to use a little gasoline.

I got the gas can that I used for the lawnmower and poured a little on the pile. But it was not easy to start, so I poured more gasoline on and then threw a match at the pile. *Kaboom!*

Wow, I thought, *I'll never do that again.* The next day, I spread the ashes across my new vegetable garden plot, rented a rototiller, and started preparing the soil. It was a lot of hard work, but I got it done—the whole three thousand square feet! We planted all kinds of vegetables and, filled with optimism and excitement, we watered the new garden every day, and kept pulling out new weeds as they came up.

It was a real chore, but we were pleased with our wonderful harvest. So much of everything! Then I began to wonder if it was really worth all the work we had put into it, and concluded that it was good to have all the fresh vegetables. But we never did plant such a large garden again.

The house we lived in was built in the 1880s or early 1890s and then added on to several times over the years, so it really needed some updating. I started by installing a wall in one of the bedrooms, creating two small bedrooms and making our home a three-bedroom house. I removed the wall between the dining room and the living room, installed new carpets, and painted or wallpapered all the rooms in the house. The attic became a playroom for Jason and Deborah, and I built an office for myself in the basement.

The house sat on the side of one of the mountain's hills, so it had a half basement—one side of it was one large rock that the house was set on, and the other portion had a cement floor. Mice and other critters easily got in, especially when it was cold outside. In any case, we set mousetraps and did our best to keep the population of these varmints at a minimum.

One day, Lorraine went to the pantry, got a box of cereal out, and shook it to determine how much cereal was in the box. As she did, something *thump-thump-thumped* in the box, and she shrieked. As I came running, a mouse jumped out of the box, and there was cereal all over the floor. So we got two young white Siamese cats to keep up with the challenge of trying to rid ourselves of the mice.

I decided that our next remodeling job would be in the kitchen. Part of the ceiling was made of thin plywood held in place with overlapping straps, and I thought it would look better to have a fully dry-walled ceiling. But when I bent the end of the first piece of plywood down, trying to remove it, a rush of mice excrement came rolling down into my face. I quickly pushed the plywood back into place, and that ceiling never did get updated.

Another time, when I was in my office, I heard Lorraine scream (maybe I should say *shriek*). I came running and found her in our bedroom on her knees. She reached for the belt on my pants, and grabbing it, pulled me to the floor. I thought, *She's gone crazy.*

"There's a bat in the room," she said as she tried to catch her breath.

Sure enough, there was. It had come in through the small window in our closet. I got a shirt from the closet, waved it around, and the bat left through that same window. That was not the first time there was a bat in the house either. We even had birds fly into the living room through the front door one time.

With all our challenges, we decided to sell this old house and rent a house for a short time while working on plans to build a new house nearby. Our old house sold rather quickly, and because we were about to go to Grand Forks, to the Pines Bible Camp, we moved all our things into some available space in the Rossland Gospel Chapel. I was to be the director of this Bible Camp that summer, just a few miles west of Rossland.

Our construction plans were then quickly finalized so the building of our new home could start immediately while we left for Grand Forks.

Reverend Willie Murray was our featured speaker for the Family Camp that summer at the Pines Bible Camp. When I was not busy with some responsibility, I got to spend time with him, and before the week was out he had extended an invitation to us to join him in serving with Mission to Europe's Millions, a part of the larger European Christian Mission, which was a conservative inter-denominational missionary organization operating in Western and Eastern Europe.

He explained that he was looking for an administrator to manage their mission office in Calgary, Alberta, and someone to help with their expansion and development work. As the week progressed, and as Willie watched and talked with me, he thought I could possibly fill both of these positions—and my heart was moved. I do not know how else to explain it. It seemed that from that moment on, the Lord was speaking to me and drawing me toward accepting these responsibilities. So knowing a decision was before us, I began to pray.

Upon our return, we rented a townhouse in Trail and moved most of our things from temporary storage at Rossland Gospel Chapel, leaving a few things behind that we really would not need in a small townhouse. Construction was set to be completed a couple of months later.

While we were praying about the idea of moving to Calgary to work with Mission to Europe's Millions, several thoughts entered our minds. *Would a move to Calgary be easy? We were currently living in a rented townhouse, so we didn't need to sell a home to move, which was good. But we were in the process of building a new house in Rossland. Wouldn't this complicate things?* And then we wondered, *Why had our home sold so quickly? Why had we started to build a new house, if the Lord was moving us to Calgary? Could all of this have been set in motion by God to just start us thinking about moving?*

We continued to pray and think about all of this. Then one day I spoke to Will Dawes, our missionary pastor friend from Trail, sharing with him the needs and opportunities that Willie had shared with me. I also explained our openness to making such a move, if that was what the Lord would want us to do. A few days later, Mr. Dawes said that he too felt the Lord was leading us to make this move. He went on to say that he would be going to Vancouver a few days later, and while there he would contact the five churches that were supporting us in our ministries in Rossland and Trail, to let them know that this was the Lord's leading, and do whatever he could to have these five churches continue supporting us as missionaries with Mission to Europe's Millions.

We were delighted that Mr. Dawes would make these personal presentations for us to our supporting churches. Personal presentations were best, and we did not have the money to make a trip to Vancouver at that time. Mr. Dawes was a man respected by these churches, so I agreed that he should make these important contacts for us while he was there.

The Lord appeared to be clearing the path ahead of us, and confirming that He was definitely leading us to make this move. Mr. Dawes seemed to be convinced of this as well, and now we just had to wait for his return from Vancouver, believing all the while that our supporting churches would understand and continue supporting us.

While Mr. Dawes was in Vancouver, we had a lengthy discussion with our builder because he was not building our new house in Rossland according to some of the written specifications in our contract. We also told him of the possibility that we would be moving to Calgary, and would therefore be selling our new house rather than moving into it. He told us that his construction costs had been higher than expected, and that he would be glad to cancel the contract we had with him. Then he would sell the house when it was completed, with the idea that he could make the profit he had originally expected when making the construction contract with us.

That went very well, I thought. *The problems we were having with him are actually helping us make the move to Calgary. Wow, who would have thought?*

And then these words came to me: "*God causes all things, whether we think they are good or might be bad, to work together for the good of those who love God and who are called by Him and working according to His purpose.*" (My own abbreviated paraphrase of Romans 8:28)

That's us, I thought. *We've been called by God and we are serving Him.* I looked up the reference and continued reading the verses in the rest of that chapter and was further encouraged. Words from another verse stuck in my mind: "*If God is for us, who can be against us?*" *(Romans 8:31b)* And I thought, *He will graciously go before us, moving every concern out of the way, and give us everything we need.*"

I continued reading: "Who will bring any charge against those whom God has chosen? It is God who justifies. Who then is the one who condemns? No one. ... Who shall separate us from the love of Christ? Shall trouble or hardship or persecution or famine or nakedness or danger or sword? ... No, in all these things we are more than conquerors through him who loved us. For I am convinced that neither death nor life, neither angels nor demons, neither the present nor the future, nor any powers, neither height nor depth, nor anything else in all creation, will be able to separate us from the love of God that is in Christ Jesus our Lord." (Romans 8:33–34a; 35, 37–39)

With a start, I asked myself, *What troubles could we be facing if we will be following God's directions? Well, whatever they might be, God will take care of us.*

Lorraine and I both believed that the Lord appeared to be clearing the path ahead of us because everything was falling into place. So another phase of our lives was about to begin.

In His Hands

PHASE SEVEN

Serving the Lord in Calgary and in Europe

We purchased a home in Calgary, Alberta, and then planned our move. We would rent a U-Haul truck, pack it first with all the things we had in the townhouse in Trail, and then drive to Rossland to pack what we had in storage at Rossland Gospel Chapel. It was our plan to drive to Calgary that same day, but that did not happen.

Our younger children, Nathan and Deborah, were playing in an upstairs room at the Gospel Chapel while we were loading the truck. Both were familiar with the room because it was where they had their Sunday school classes each week. Suddenly, we heard a loud crash that sounded like wood on wood, then some other sounds.

We rushed upstairs to find Nathan unconscious on the floor. Deborah, while not physically hurt, was quite shaken up. Nathan had apparently climbed up the front of a bookcase and it had fallen over, landing on top of him. When Nathan started to move, we rushed him to the Rossland Hospital to have him checked out. Thankfully, the hospital was only a few blocks away.

After examining Nathan, the doctor wanted to keep him there overnight to watch him. At the same time, he also reassured us that he believed that Nathan was fine and would be released the following morning.

We had deadlines to meet, so I left that afternoon, driving the truck to Calgary as planned. My parents drove their car, taking Jason and Deborah with them, while

Lorraine stayed at the hospital with Nathan. She would then follow the next day in our car.

As we all went our separate ways, we kept praying for Nathan, and God gave us the peace that surpasses understanding (see Philippians 4:6–7). We were all sure he would be fine, and the doctor confirmed this the next morning, saying again that he just wanted Nathan in the hospital overnight to be sure.

We were seeing that life was not necessarily going to be without any problems when following the Lord's directions, but also understanding that God would not forsake us or leave us; rather, He would protect us and provide for us, giving everything we needed. According to Ephesians 2, God had given us faith to trust Him, and He was proving to us that He is faithful and trustable. I knew God had given me love in a special way in order to minister to the men at the City Mission years earlier, and now he had given us peace in the same way.

God had taken care of everything. Life was difficult at times, but He always came through. We were ready to embark upon this next phase of our lives.

Soon after we moved to Calgary, I realized we had made one serious mistake: we had moved without making any direct and personal contact with our supporting churches. I had trusted Mr. Dawes to speak to them for us because he had offered to do so, and because he had said that he believed this was indeed the Lord's leading in our lives. While he returned from his trip to Vancouver without clearly saying so, he led us to believe that he had spoken to the leaders of these five churches and that they would continue to financially support us in our new endeavors with Mission to Europe's Millions.

Then to our astonishment, we learned after our move that Mr. Dawes had not actually spoken to anyone at these churches. He had apparently changed his mind. At some point he had found out that these five churches, which had also been supporting him for over twenty years, did not believe they should financially support interdenominational missionary organizations; they wanted all their financial support to stay within their own denomination. Therefore feeling that his own financial support could be at risk, he chose not to speak on our behalf.

I sent a letter to our home church to convey everything that had happened and to explain how bad we now felt having just learned that they knew nothing about our move. I apologized and requested a meeting with them, to which they agreed.

I went to Vancouver and explained everything in detail. The chairman at that meeting quickly reacted saying that he did not believe that Mr. Dawes would ever have agreed that this was the Lord's leading, and said that he could not believe that someone would leave their denominational mission to join an interdenominational mission organization. The others present at that meeting agreed. They could not believe that Mr. Dawes would have promised to speak to them on our behalf, and to encourage them and these other churches to continue supporting us with an interdenominational missionary organization. "He would have known better than that," they said.

The elders of our home church would not accept anything that I explained, because they were set solidly in their ultra-conservative views. They simply stated that they were withdrawing their "Commendation", and that we could expect the other four churches to do the same. (In this denomination a *"Commendation"* was equal in other denominations to a formal letter of recognition or appointment, in this case as a Pastoral Missionary). This meant we were effectively being excommunicated and defrocked. They cut off all communication with us, they no longer sent any financial support to us, and we were no longer asked to speak in their churches. In fact, we were no longer welcome to attend any of these five churches.

I was devastated. *How can this happen?* I thought. *We were following the Lord's leading. This had been confirmed to us in so many ways.* But as I talked all of this over with the Lord, I was assured in my heart that somehow this was part of His plan—and I wondered how all of it might be a benefit to us, or to those churches. I thought, *Maybe through all of this the Lord is using us to open their hearts to other missionary organizations and opportunities.*

After that meeting, on my way back to Calgary, I felt led to stop in Trail to visit Mr. Dawes. At his home, I explained that I was on my way home after meeting with the Elders of my home church, and shared with him what I had told them and their response. He had little to say that would help us. I could tell he felt like I had backed him into a corner, so to speak. He knew he had done us wrong, and there was nothing he could do about it.

In any case, I said something to him that I will never forget: "You know you have done wrong to us, and you've done this in the sight of God. You must speak to these five churches and tell them clearly all that has transpired, regardless of what it may mean to your financial support. If you don't do this, you will see Bethany Chapel in Trail— the church you've been working in for over twenty-five years—close within two years. So do what is right, or God will judge you for what you have done to us." I really do not know what possessed me to speak to him like that, but I did.

I felt a little like David had when he tore a little off of King Saul's robe, but left it all in God's hands and did him no harm... (I Samuel 24)

Almost three years later, we heard Bethany Chapel had closed its doors. It was no longer functioning. I was dumbfounded. All I could think was, *I don't know why I said what I did on that day—it just came out from my mouth. And now it's happened. Yes, he wronged me, but now I've possibly caused the destruction of his ministry.*

I was reading Matthew 16:19 and 18:18 a few days later, and I saw these words: "whatever you bind on earth will be bound in heaven." This indeed had likely happened a result of what I said, and I felt humbled.

I learned three important lessons through all of this:

1. The words we speak are powerful, so we all need to be extremely careful what we say to people.

2. It is possible that even the best of men (I had been working alongside Mr. Dawes for several years and thought very highly of him) will sometimes fail us.

3. I believe the Lord was testing me through all of this, to see whether I would remain faithful to His leading in my life. I also believe He keeps testing us throughout our lives, to keep us strong and dependent on Him alone.

I had spoken to Willie Murray, the director of Mission to Europe's Millions, on several occasions about all this before taking my trip. When I returned, I shared with him all that had taken place in Vancouver and in Trail. Then I asked what he thought about it, because the question we believed was now before us was, "Should we continue with Mission to Europe's Millions without the covering or sending from our home church?"

He replied by telling me three things. First, he believed I had done the right thing by going to Vancouver and meeting with the Elders. Second, he believed I had done the right thing by going to Trail and approaching Mr. Dawes, giving him the opportunity to explain himself and apologize. Finally, he believed the Lord had been leading us to join Mission to Europe's Millions and that the Lord would prove this by supporting us financially through other means.

A few days after we spoke, I was reading 2 Corinthians 3, particularly verses 1–6, and it felt as though the Lord was speaking clearly to me: "The apostle Paul did not always need letters of commendation, so neither do you. If people question you on this matter, simply share with them why and how you felt called by God and point them to the fruit that has resulted from what you have done previously in Vancouver, and more recently in Rossland and in Trail."

After reading the verses and receiving this word from the Lord, my heart and mind were at peace and I felt confident that the Lord was completely in control. I believed we had nothing to worry about.

People have asked, "How did you survive financially without the support of those five churches? Did you receive sufficient financial support to carry on serving the Lord in Calgary?" To answer these questions, let me say this: We made no great appeals to people. We did not send out letters trying to justify ourselves. But remarkably, some of our friends and family members decided, at the Lord's urging, to send us gifts now and again. Sometimes it was difficult, but when we added all the gifts together each month, it was always sufficient to meet our needs. This fact continued to strengthen us, because the Lord showed Himself to be faithful to those who trust Him.

We enjoyed living in Calgary very much. The summers were warm and wonderful, and the winter skies were usually clear and sunny. One winter we even flooded the backyard of our house and made a skating rink. And I was glad I did not have to shovel so much snow – like I had to do in Rossland.

We were in South Calgary one evening during our first winter there, when I noticed that one of the car tires was low in air pressure. It was a Sunday night, making it difficult to find a place that could fix the tire, so I drove to a nearby gas station and just pumped it up. I then drove a few more miles, stopped, and pumped up the tire again. I did this several times before we arrived home.

After dropping off Lorraine and the children, I drove to a place that could fix the tire the next morning and left a note on the windshield. I then started to walk home, but what I did not realize was how cold it really was. I had not taken into consideration the winds either. I was not dressed warmly enough for the short walk home, but I walked quickly. Then I heard a cracking noise coming from within my chest. I started to run a little, but my chest started to hurt and soon I became very short of breath.

I realized then that the sound I was hearing was the air in my lungs turning to ice and then the ice breaking up. I slowed to a walk but I knew I could not stop. I got home a few minutes later and collapsed on the sofa, realizing that I had almost killed myself. Lorraine calmed me down (the good mother that she was), got me a blanket and made some hot chocolate. In a few minutes I was back to my normal activities, and we both thanked God for His care in this situation.

We spent five years with Mission to Europe's Millions, which was a great time in so many ways. As their Business Administrator, I organized and managed the day-to-day functions of the North American headquarters office in Calgary, and received financial reports, etc. from our sub-office in Pennsylvania. I was responsible for all the financial aspects of the organization, both in Canada and in the United States. This was before we had computer systems, so everything was done on paper. Using skills I had learned in high school, I set up a double-entry bookkeeping system to better manage all the funds.

All these responsibilities were really quite easy for me because I have always been an organized, detailed person—in fact, someone recently said that I appear to have 'O.C.D.' (Obsessive-Compulsive Disorder). (Oh well, a little of that may have been a good thing!)

After a few months, I also took on the responsibilities of the Director of Development. At first, I went to a few Bible schools in Western Canada with Reverend Willie Murray to set up a display and talk to students about Mission to Europe's Millions and European Christian Mission. Later that year we began thinking about what we might be able to do to increase the involvement of people in our missionary organization. I came up with the idea that some of the financial supporters of the organization might like to take a holiday trip to Europe to visit some of our missionaries, as well as to see some historical sites— if such a European Tour could be organized. So I started to collect information and put together a bus tour for May, 1980. Lorraine and I both got interested in going on this Tour—because it would help us with representation of our missionaries and their needs in North America, and it would also give us an opportunity to go and see various parts of Europe.

In my second year as Director of Development, Willie said, "Let's you and I put together a formal summer-internship-type program so that Bible school students and other young people can go and assist our missionaries in Europe."

This 'Short Term Missionary Service Program', as we called it, would consist of a training week before the students would leave for either Western or Eastern Europe, and then a few days at the end of their time in Europe when we would bring everyone together to share with each other what they had done during the summer.

We would then give these students some important guidance on how to re-enter the American/Canadian culture after their summer in Europe, and how to share their experiences with their families, friends, and supporting churches.

About thirty students joined us the first summer. Some were sent to assist our missionaries with their church-planting in countries in Western Europe, while others went to Vienna, Austria—where they would then travel into several Eastern European countries, smuggling in Bibles, clothing, food, and other things that the Christians in these countries were having a hard time obtaining.

The following year, I visited more Bible schools, and did more to promote our Short-Term Missionary Service Program. More than sixty students from Canada and the United States joined the program that year. By our third year, we had over eighty students. Both our orientation week and debriefing days were held at Albright College in Reading, Pennsylvania. At that time, it was closed for the summer, so we were able to use their dormitories and one of their classrooms at no cost. (This was where Mission to Europe's Millions had an office to do the financial receipting for gifts from American donors.) The location was good because it was closer to Europe than Calgary was for students joining the program from all over the United States and Canada.

In early 1980 we were gearing up for a busy year which would include going to various Bible schools in the first few months and recruiting students for our Short-Term Missionary Service Program. The last few seats on the European Bus Tour for later in May needed to be sold. There were preparations that would need to be made for our summer programs. And, in early May there would also be the E.C.M. Missionary Conference.

Each year in May, many of the missionaries associated with the European Christian Mission got together at the

Black Forest Academy in Kandern, West Germany. (The
Black Forest Academy is a Christian boarding school; and
Kandern is also where the European Christian Mission had
its international headquarters). The missionaries
attending this conference served in Western and Eastern
Europe; others attending were from the offices of
European Christian Mission in Australia, New Zealand,
and South Africa, as well as representatives from the
offices of Mission to Europe's Millions in Canada and the
USA. Each year that I was with Mission to Europe's
Millions, I attended this conference to get to know and
network with the missionaries, and learn more about their
ministries. This helped me properly represent everything
in Canada. It was a good time to talk to missionaries about
our Short Term Missionary Service Program and how their
participation could benefit them and their ministries.

In May 1980, I was at the Missionary Conference, and
heard that Sali (the European Christian Mission
missionary who produced the only Christian radio
programs being beamed into Albania at that time) was
under house arrest. He had gone to the Yugoslavia/Albania
border to visit with some of those who had accepted Jesus
Christ as Savior as a result of his radio programs. He was
just outside of Skopje, Macedonia (which was part of
Yugoslavia at the time).

Sali needed someone to bring documents to him that
he'd purposefully left in England before traveling to the
Albanian border, but many of the missionaries attending
the conference had passports that had been stamped when
entering other communist countries—and if they were to
take him the documents he needed, and this was found
out as they entered or were in Yugoslavia, they too would
be exposed as Christian missionaries and quite possibly be
arrested.

So I volunteered to go because my passport was
basically clean: it had never been stamped as having

visited a communist country, or even stamped to show that I was a seasoned traveler. Tom Lewis, another European Christian Mission missionary, agreed to go with me because he knew Sali personally, and because he had been throughout Eastern Europe and was familiar with all the border crossings. However, when crossing the borders or being approached by the military, we agreed that we would appear not to be together.

I was so glad Tom went with me, because while I trusted the Lord that nothing would happen to me, I still appreciated all Tom's insights and guidance. In fact, it was really me going along with Tom; I was just the one smuggling in the documents.

Tom and I flew on Aeroflot Airlines from Vienna to Zagreb, Croatia (then part of Yugoslavia), and from Zagreb to Skopje, Macedonia. As we were landing in Skopje, I looked out the window and saw trenches dug perpendicular to the runway that we would be landing on. We got closer, and I saw there were men in those trenches with large cannon-like guns pointed at our airplane as we were landing. It could have been frightening, but I knew I was doing what I believed the Lord had led me to do, and was under His protection. I again had the peace that surpasses all understanding (Philippians 4:6)—this peace kept me calm as the Lord protected me from all that was to follow.

We disembarked the plane on the runway, and were kept in a line by army guards and as we walked toward the airport building. Then just after we entered the building, the line became single file. As we approached the Immigration personnel, with military men both to the left and right of the line, I noticed that they were randomly taking people from the line and frisking them. One of the people just ahead of me was pulled out of line and they had him against the wall. They ripped his clothes off and we could all see his bare backside.

Tom was in the line a few people behind me, praying—
I was sure—just as I was. I thought, *I hope they don't search
me. I have those papers tucked inside my shirt and under my
belt.* Then all of a sudden, I felt a kind of warm peace run
from my head to my feet, and then it was my turn to be
checked by these serious Immigration personnel.

They took my Canadian passport and thumbed through
it. Then without asking me anything, I was told to
proceed. So I walked as any tourist would—as though I
had not noticed what had taken place against the far wall
and had not a care in the world. I picked up my suitcase
from the baggage handlers and left the building. Outside
the building, I waited as Tom went to rent a car, then we
were off to find some place to eat before going to our hotel.
Tom said it was too early to check in.

It was already dark outside, and most of the restaurants
we came to were closed. But we found one, maybe the only
one that was open. They were starting to close for the
night, so they were only serving their soup special. I don't
remember what it was called, but it was pork rind—boiled
pig's fat.

I thought, *how am I going to digest this?* But I was hungry
and there were no other choices, so I asked Tom if I could
have a glass of wine with my soup—to help with what I
believed could become a stomach problem. I remembered
the apostle Paul telling Timothy, "'Take a little wine for
your stomach's sake'" (I Timothy 5:23), and Tom
encouraged me to do so, saying that a glass of wine would
probably be necessary. He had a glass of it too. I had not
traveled in Europe much at this time, but I came to
understand that it was common throughout Europe for
Christians to have wine with their meals.

Around 10:00 p.m., we left the restaurant to go to the
hotel Tom had chosen. I don't remember its name, but
Tom said it was our best option and that he had chosen
this particular hotel because it was the one most tourists

would go to. That way, we would not likely raise any undue suspicion as to why we were in Skopje. As we entered the hotel, again there were military personnel seemingly everywhere—outside the entrance and in the hotel lobby as well. I thought nothing of it, believing they were there for the safety of the tourists who were staying in the hotel.

As we registered, the man at the front desk took our passports, saying we would get them back in the morning when we checked out. (This I found to be a common practice at that time in many European countries, particularly the communist ones. This was so that the local Immigration office could be informed about every person traveling in the area, and so they could detain anyone they thought should be interrogated).

Tom later told me that we would be leaving early the next morning before the Immigration office would open, so the hotel would not be able to call or take our passports to the office to have us checked out. He said that my passport probably would not alert them to anything because I had never been in an Eastern European country before, but because he had visited most of these countries many times, his passport could give them cause for some suspicion. He went on to say that if it did, we would both be detained and interrogated, because we shared the same hotel room.

So we got to our room late, slept well, and got up early, just before sunrise.

As we were checking out of the hotel, I asked the desk clerk why all the military personnel were still in the lobby.

He said, "You don't know what's going on here in Skopje these days?"

"No, is something special happening?" I asked, and he replied, "There are meetings happening in this hotel with the leaders of all the Eastern European countries present, including the highest leaders of the Soviet Union."

"Wow. I didn't know that" I said, and was careful to not ask any more questions, but left thinking, *We've just been in the lion's den, and the lion's mouths have been kept shut. Thank you, Lord, for protecting us once more.*

We left the hotel and did not stop for breakfast before traveling to see Sali. The restaurants were all closed anyway since it was so early. When we arrived at the house where Sali was under arrest, the person who greeted us asked us if we would like something to drink. We said yes, and I saw a woman go to a tree in front of the house and break a small branch off. She then broke it into pieces and put them in a pot on their stove. A few minutes later we were served a hot drink. It was the bitterest drink I have ever tasted. Then the woman brought out the sugar, and I thankfully put a little in my cup.

Sali joined us as we were drinking this awful tea, and I gave him the documents I had been carrying. He thanked us, and continued to talk to Tom in German, of which I understood little. Then we prayed, and as we got up to leave, Tom reached into his bag and gave him a pound of coffee.

He and the woman expressed their tremendous appreciation and we left, returned the rental car, and proceeded to the airport in Skopje to fly on to Vienna, where I spent a few days before returning home.

At around 9:30 p.m., I arrived at the airport in Calgary. My neighbor picked me up because Lorraine was looking after our kids and they would be in bed (at least this is what I thought would be the case). But after Ken made a couple of turns with the car, I asked, "Where are we going?"

Trying to be casual and not alarm me, he replied, "Well ... I thought you'd like to see Lorraine before I take you home."

"What? Where is she?" I asked. "Why isn't she at home with the kids?"

He then explained that she had been riding a horse a few days earlier and fallen off. "She's been in the hospital now for a couple of days," he said.

When we got to the hospital, Lorraine told me how it had happened. She had been visiting some friends up in Innisfail, about an hour north of Calgary, and had been wearing the wrong kind of slacks (polyester) and slid off the horse when it suddenly stopped while approaching a fence. Actually, she was thrown head-over-heels forward off the horse and landed on her back, breaking her pelvis and sacrum.

The next day, I again visited Lorraine in the hospital, and asked her how she was feeling. She explained the pain she was in, and how disappointed she was in not being able to go on the European Bus Tour that we both were looking forward to.

So I spoke to her specialist and asked him how serious the situation was. "Is there any way that Lorraine can travel to Europe with me in a few days?" I wanted to know.

He thought about it, then replied, "Well, I wouldn't advise it, but if she takes special care of herself, and you can assure me that others will help her, then I could give her some powerful pain medication ... and then yes, she could go. But why is this so important to her or to you? Can't you put your trip off to another time?"

I explained to him that for several months I'd been putting together a twenty-three-day tour of Europe for a busload of thirty-nine people, and on this tour we would be visiting missionaries in several countries as well as going to various tourist sites along the way, including going to the Oberammergau Passion Play.

I explained further that the tour bus was fully booked, and Lorraine and I had agreed to be the hosts, with a knowledgeable guide to accompany us.

He agreed to give Lorraine the medications, and also put together a list of things we would need to take with us—crutches, a wheelchair, a sponge donut for Lorraine to sit on, etc.

So less than two weeks after Lorraine's accident, we were on our way to Europe. The whole trip, while being a wonderful time in so many ways for everyone (including Lorraine and me), was at times a painful experience for Lorraine. Being pushed in a wheelchair over the cobblestones at the Palace of Versailles was especially difficult, and at times some of the men had to carry the wheelchair with Lorraine in it. As days passed she started feeling better so she used the crutches instead.

The tour participants were so understanding and helpful. Lorraine also got some special favors because of being in a wheelchair, like being taken up a special elevator in the Bell Tower at St. Mark's Square in Venice, Italy. To avoid stairs at the Vatican, she was taken up a private elevator and then her wheelchair was pushed through a room where a lot of paintings were in the process of restoration—something visitors generally do not get to see.

The trip was a great time for everyone—visiting many countries, seeing historical sites, and visiting with missionaries along the way—learning from them directly how their ministries were going while sitting with them in their home towns and cities.

Lorraine often teases me that in Venice I pushed her (in her wheelchair) up to a wall so she could see the view down one of the canals, and then proceeded to tell her how beautiful a site it was, not realizing that she could not see over the wall. But she was glad to have been able to go on the tour and did see many things; and I, too, was glad she was on the tour despite some of the inconveniences. In fact I think her condition helped open the hearts of the other tour participants—not only to help Lorraine with her special needs on the tour, but also to see the local people's needs around them as they travelled. What could have been just a fact-finding mission for the tour participants became a soul-moving experience.

It was sometime after all this that Lorraine explained why she had not phoned me while I was in Europe to tell me about her accident. Then I shared with her why I had not told her in advance that I would be going into Yugoslavia, close to the Albanian border. We had both trusted God to take care of everything and did not want to give out information that would only cause unnecessary worry.

We both knew the Lord had supplied everything we had needed to that point, and how He had cared for us in all kinds of situations. So for us, these times were not as stressful as they might have been had we not had such experiences in the past, and such resulting faith to carry us through. It was evident that God strengthens us through difficult times so we will be able to handle more difficult situations ahead.

In the fall of that year, Willie started talking about the possibility of moving Mission to Europe's Millions' North American headquarters from Calgary to somewhere in the area of Vancouver, British Columbia. Because our Short Term Missionary Service Program was becoming so well received, he believed that this was indicative of other potentially great things in the future, if we were in an area like Vancouver. He encouraged us to pray about whatever these related things might be and how they might all come together, explaining that flights to Europe were easier and less expensive from Vancouver than from Calgary. It just felt like the right thing to do, so we started praying.

Not long afterward, Willie and I started talking about developing another program, this one for new missionaries. The program would be an "Internship Program for Missionary Candidates" to help them become oriented to the culture and the people they felt called to serve, and to learn how to adapt their church-planting ideas to the countries they felt called to.

The idea would be to have English-speaking Canadian and American missionary candidates come and live in the Vancouver area and work for maybe two years under pastors in ethnic churches (of which Vancouver had many). A missionary candidate who felt called to Italy would work in an Italian-speaking church, a missionary candidate who felt called to Spain would work under a pastor in a Spanish-speaking church, and a missionary candidate who felt called to Eastern Europe would likely work in a German-speaking church.

Our ideas were starting to come together. We believed that our Short Term Missionary Service Program was the first step for people interested in becoming missionaries somewhere in Europe, and that this new program would be the next logical step. In the following months, we made several trips to the Vancouver area, then settled on renting space in an office complex in Tsawwassen.

Before we actually moved the office, Willie, trying to encourage me one day, said that he believed this move would make our new program a great success, because our office would be in an area where many ethnic churches were located. He concluded, "We can do this. It's God's plan."

Not long after this, Willie started talking about Vincent and Sandra Price from Ireland, who were missionaries in

Austria, saying that they would like to move to Vancouver to help us with the expansion of Mission to Europe's Millions. This was encouraging news, because I had met them while on my trips to Europe, and I knew Vincent to be a strong individual and a powerful speaker. We felt that their possibly coming to Vancouver was a confirmation from the Lord that we were indeed moving in the right direction. Then I was given the responsibility to work with Canadian Immigration to make the move possible for Vincent, Sandra and their children.

We were all looking forward to Vincent visiting the Bible schools, preaching in churches, and promoting our two programs: the Short Term Missionary Service Program and our upcoming Internship Program for Missionary Candidates. It seemed like these programs would really take off with him helping us.

Then one day Willie surprised us all when he told everyone in the office that he and his family would not be moving to Vancouver with the staff; rather, he would be staying in Calgary to become one of the pastors at the First Alliance Church. Trying to encourage everyone, he assured us he would still be directing us and be active in overseeing the affairs of Mission to Europe's Millions, albeit from Calgary.

So we moved the office as planned. Willie kept in contact with us, and Vincent and Sandra Price arrived with their children, all within a few months.

Then another surprise came: Vincent told me that he was now going to oversee and manage everything in the office, taking over my position.

As if that was not enough of a shock, he said that I was also no longer to be involved in the Short Term Missionary Service Program that I'd help develop, or with the development of our Internship Program for Missionary Candidates. He was going to do it all.

How is he expecting to be able to do all this by himself? I thought. *He obviously doesn't know all about what we've been doing, and he really doesn't have any idea how to develop and manage our new program.* Then I wondered, *What does this leave me to do?*

I was dumbfounded. I asked Vincent if he or Willie thought that I was not doing a good enough job in these areas, and he replied, "No, that's not it at all. We believe that you've been doing a great job. It's just that the European Christian Mission headquarters apparently has some concerns." He went on to explain that they had asked him to come to Canada and manage everything under their direction.

I questioned what Willie's role was going to be, because it sounded like Vincent was taking over his position as well. Vincent replied, "No, Willie is remaining as one of the leaders of the organization for the time being." So I asked what he had in mind for me, since it sounded like he was taking over all my responsibilities. He responded, "I really don't know. I'm not sure there's anything left here for you to do any longer."

Wow. I could not believe what was happening, and I did not want to believe it either. *What's going to happen with our Short Term Missionary Service Program and the plans we have for the development of our new program?* I thought. *And what's going to happen with Mission to Europe's Millions as we know it?* He said he was not firing me. But I'd been effectively replaced and told there is nothing left for me to do. *So what am I going to do?* Then I wondered, *What can I do about this?*

I knew I had carried out my responsibilities well. I knew our Short Term Missionary Service Program was also going well. I believed, as I knew Willie did, that our new Internship Program for Missionary Candidates was the right thing to do next, and we had been assured that Vincent was being brought on board to help us get more missionaries to Europe through these programs.

But what had happened to change all this? I could not comprehend it. One thing was for sure, though: I knew that I had not done anything wrong, and I was told so by both Vincent and Willie. Still, a question lingered in my mind: *What do I do now?*

So I went home and shared all that had happened with Lorraine.

We were both devastated. At this time, our children were all under ten years old, and I knew they would feel the repercussions from the struggles I was facing and would face over the following months.

After praying about it, I phoned Willie in Calgary and explained what had happened. Willie said he was sorry that Vincent was doing things this way, but said that, unfortunately, he could do nothing about it. He then explained that Vincent was under the direction of European Christian Mission and that he (Willie) was now only in an advisory capacity. He had not understood that European Christian Mission wanted Vincent to come to Canada for this reason, and had thought Vincent would be a great asset to the development of Mission to Europe's Millions in Canada and the United States, and for that reason he had agreed to his coming.

I asked Willie what I should do, and he just said, "I'm sorry. I can't help you. You'll have to do whatever Vincent tells you. He's in charge now."

I felt my words had fallen on deaf ears. I asked if I could have a letter of explanation to give to the people who had been supporting us, with the hope that they would understand, and would continue financially and prayerfully supporting us while I looked for another ministry to connect with. Willie said Vincent would have to write the letter, and Vincent claimed he could not do it. (I believe he realized at that moment that he had gone about this whole thing the wrong way, and to save embarrassment and potential loss of Mission to Europe's Millions supporters, he decided to just let me suffer it out).

I was worried that our friends and supporters would have difficulty accepting any explanation I could give them. I wondered if they might even go so far as to question my integrity, even though there was no just cause to do so. I was so distraught that I just did not know what to do about anything.

I prayed, and Lorraine and I prayed together, and the next thing that came to mind was to contact the pastor of the church we were members of. I told him what had happened, and he said, "Well, you must forgive Vincent, and you'll just have to move on."

That was not what I wanted to hear. It just did not seem right at all. And what did he mean by "you'll just have to move on"? I had no vision as to what I should do next. I felt he really had not given me any direction at all.

So I wrote a letter to all of our supporters explaining what had taken place, and asked for their prayers as we sought direction from the Lord.

The next phase of our lives was about to begin.

PHASE EIGHT

Life as a Realtor in Vancouver

Before the letters went in the mail, I decided that I should speak to my parents and explain everything to them. In response, my dad offered me a job working with him for a while if I wanted to. He and my Uncle Ken had an office building that suffered a big fire and had been torn down, but they were working to rebuild it. The plans had been drawn up by the architect and approved by the City of Vancouver, and reconstruction was set to begin.

We prayed about this opportunity, as well as what other opportunities there might be to serve the Lord with another missionary organization. Nothing seemed to be surfacing for our immediate future, so I accepted my father's offer and rewrote the letter to all the people who had been supporting us. I briefly explained what had happened, thanked them for their support, and asked them to continue praying for us, but not to send any further financial support to us, as I was now starting a job with my father and uncle.

Everything, from what had happened to how we were trying to accept it all, was very difficult for us to deal with. But as Pastor Jerry had told us, we tried to move on, while people kept asking what had really happened. Many of them thought that I must have done something wrong, and some said this would not have happened otherwise. My integrity was indeed put into question.

I had been teaching an Adult Bible Class at our church, and was looking forward to taking on more responsibilities, but instead the pastor chided me for not having quickly accepted everything that had taken place and immediately forgiven Vincent. I explained how difficult the situation was, but because I had not forgiven Vincent (or Willie for that matter), Pastor Jerry believed that I must have done something wrong and was hiding it. So now my own pastor was questioning my integrity, and I was no longer allowed to take on responsibilities at church.

What a difficult time in our lives. We were totally crushed. But at the same time I knew I had not done anything wrong and that we had not been forsaken by the Lord. He was our only solace, our Comforter, and He strengthened us and renewed us over the following years.

Months after all this happened, I came to realize what had likely taken place. Someone told me that another missionary organization in the United States was at one time part of European Christian Mission and the two separated. Apparently, this other organization in the United States had been sending more missionaries to Europe than European Christian Mission was receiving from Australia, New Zealand, South Africa, or even from countries within Europe. As a result, the leaders of European Christian Mission believed that the U.S. organization was starting to take over the control and direction of European Christian Mission.

This person went on to say that they believed the reason the two organizations separated back then was over this control issue, and because our Short Term Missionary Service Program had sent over eighty students to Europe the previous summer, and because we were now talking about a new Internship Program for Missionary Candidates and had recently moved the Mission to Europe's Millions office to Vancouver, they believed European Christian Mission was afraid once again that they were losing control of their organization. So to prevent the Canadian/U.S. organization from taking control, Vincent had been sent to Vancouver by European Christian Mission to take over the management of everything.

This made some sense to us and helped us begin to deal with everything. But it did not change the things that had happened. I was sure everything could have been handled in a much better way; but at least now we had some understanding, and that gave us some peace of mind.

In any case, the next phase of our lives had started.

I was now the liaison between the architect and the construction manager of an office building, and I began going to the construction site almost every day to ensure that everything was being built according to the plans and to approve any changes that were needed. This went on for several months. As the building neared completion, I was asked if I would like to approach all of the former tenants to see if they would like to move into the new building—and some did. This introduced me to at least one aspect of the Real Estate business.

In the course of promoting the smaller businesses to return and lease space in our building, I found out that there were other options for them. Some of these small businesses had moved into what were called Business Centers or Packaged Offices. These facilities were comprised of a number of individual offices that shared a common reception area and boardroom, and some even shared secretarial staff. So I began thinking about starting such a business with Lorraine in my father and uncle's building. After sharing the idea with her, I put together a business plan and told my ideas to my dad. He suggested we go to his bank to get their opinion and possibly apply for a loan to get started.

The Loans Manager asked if I had a business plan to submit, and I gave him the twenty-page document I had prepared. He asked who had prepared it, and I explained that I had. He was impressed (I told him I had never created such a document before), and a few days later we were asked to return to the bank to sign some papers—because our loan for Progressive Business Centers had been approved, provided Lorraine and I would put up our home as security for the loan (which we did). We then signed a lease with my father and uncle for just over eight thousand square feet of office space—a full floor of their newly reconstructed office building—so the space could start being built out for our needs.

Through all of this work—overseeing the construction work, liaising with the architect and the owners, trying to lease the office building, as well as now doing the tenant improvement for our own Packaged Offices/Business Center—I developed a strong interest in the Real Estate business (not knowing where such interest might take me). Lorraine was working for one of the Vice-Presidents of Columbia Trust at the time, in the international mortgage finance business, and she was being encouraged to take the Mortgage Brokers Course at the University of British Columbia (UBC). So I enrolled in the course along with her, as it was something for us to do together and because it was one aspect of the Real Estate business that might open doors for me in the future. To my surprise, I did well, achieving a 92 percent on my final exam.

Someone then encouraged me to take the Real Estate Salesman's Course at UBC, since this was the way that most people got into the Real Estate business. I enrolled even though I had not taken the required high school courses to enter UBC, and I was able to take this course under the classification of Adult Student—the same as I had done for the Mortgage Brokers Course.

Again, I did well—achieving over 90 percent on my final exam. I told a few people that I attributed my good grades to having a large chocolate fudge sundae and a couple of cups of strong coffee right before my exams. Really, I was sure that was not the reason for my scores on these exams—the Lord had a hand in it—but I had never done so well on any exams in my life.

When all the tenant improvements had been completed for our Progressive Business Centers, Lorraine left her job at Columbia Trust to work at our new business, and I started leasing out office spaces to small businesses. Signing up new tenants was not going very fast, so I started to sell residential real estate with Delta Realty in Tsawwassen.

I enjoyed listing and selling residential properties, but knew that if I was ever going to manage a Real Estate office, I would also have to take and pass the Real Estate Agent's Course at UBC. So I did, and although many people had to take it several times before passing it, I scored a 92 percent on my first try.

Lorraine left for work by 7:00 a.m. each day, and did not get home until between 6:30 and 7:30 p.m. I would help the children get ready for school in the mornings, then go to work but be home by 3:00 p.m. whenever I could, and then go out again by 8:00 p.m. to list or close the sale on homes. At the same time, I was taking this Real Estate Agent's Course one night a week for several months. I usually had someone to show properties to on Saturdays, and most Sunday afternoons I held Open Houses.

It was a busy time in our lives, with both of us working full-time jobs and raising three children, and while it might seem like we had all our bases covered, we had financial pressures to contend with. Residential sales were not going as well as we had hoped, and we were not leasing enough offices at Progressive Business Centers to make ends meet.

During all of this, as in times past, our children did not know the struggles we were having, and I know they sometimes thought they were not high on our list of priorities—and that bothered us and hurt them. I had a heavy load on my shoulders that I just could not get free from, and all this affected my work and unfortunately my family too.

I was not sure that I wanted to sell residential real estate for the rest of my life. The hours were long and on Sundays I usually had an Open House, so I did not have the time to be the kind of father and husband I wanted to be. I was not selling as many homes as I would have liked, either. Even though I knew it would complicate my schedule further, I decided to take more Real Estate classes. In the long run it would be beneficial in many ways—and it was, as I obtained the designation R.I.B.C. and then became a member of The Real Estate Institute of British Columbia. I started attending their meetings and met some wonderful people who assured me that doors would now open for me in other areas of the Real Estate business.

I left Delta Realty and began working for Park Georgia Realty because the commission arrangement was better—hoping that I really would do better financially. I enjoyed helping people find the homes they wanted, so much so that the purchasers did not want to move every few years—but this meant repeat business for me was slow.

The whole method of selling homes to people that I had learned in my classes did not sit well with me. If a client wanted a three-bedroom house, I was to find him something smaller and convince him to buy it while looking for the ideal home. Then I was to spend some months taking him out to dinner and developing a strong relationship with him so that I could sell him a bigger home within a couple of years. I never felt right about selling something to someone that was not what they really wanted. I spent more time looking for the ideal home for my clients the first time around, so it took more time and resulted in fewer repeat sales. Of course, I needed more clients than other realtors did and had to advertise more to get them; but I felt like I was serving my clients better, and was much more settled in my soul about the whole process even though it meant that I didn't make as much money.

One day I received a phone call from a person living in the Yukon who was being transferred to Vancouver. He told me he wanted to buy a three-bedroom home on his own private lake and he would like to spend no more than $100,000. That sounded quite impossible, but I was up for the challenge. So I asked him where he would be working (he said in downtown Vancouver), and I asked how long of a commute was he willing to make each day. He said one to two hours. I asked him what his work hours would be, and he said he would need to be at his place of business by 4:00 a.m. and that he would finish work by 2:00 p.m.

With this information, I took a lot of time and found him the home of his dreams just east of Vancouver—for $85,000. He was excited, and I too was pleased, but the commission really did not cover all that it took to put this deal together. So in many people's eyes, I was a very successful realtor, and from one perspective they were right. But at the same time I knew I was not a financially successful realtor.

Then one day the Lord led me to believe that the housing market was going to slow down, and I was seeing signs of this already taking place. So I made an appointment to see a friend of mine and asked him what the requirements were to become one of their Commercial Property Managers. He explained that they were only hiring people who have RIBC and RPA (Real Property

Administrator) designations. I already had my RIBC designation, but not my RPA, so I thanked Wayne for his time and the information, and said I would keep him informed with my progress in obtaining my RPA.

I contacted the Building Owners Management Association, who put on classes for people wanting their RPA designation, and was told that they offered evening classes each year in various cities in Canada and the United States, and that a person taking one or two classes each fall and spring should receive their RPA in three to four years. However, in some cities they also offered a full semester class in one week of all-day classes.

I enrolled in a fall course in Vancouver that year, and at the same time started flying to cities around the United States to take the other courses required. Then early the following year, I phoned Wayne again and explained that I now had my RPA designation and how I was able to obtain it so quickly.

Wayne was impressed, but went on to explain that his company did not have an opening for another Commercial Property Manager at the time. However, he said he would be talking with the vice-president of another large property management company—one that managed properties all across Canada—and he would tell him what I had done.

About a week later and after several interviews, I was asked if I would accept a Commercial Property Manager position with their company and I accepted the position.

A couple of months after I joined REM(WEST), I was served notice that I was being sued. It all started just after I had completed the Property Management courses. I had listed a builder-friend's new house, and shortly afterward I held an Open House for Realtors. It was raining that day, and one of these realtors—a woman of about sixty years of age—fell on the wood planking that led up to the house from the street. I called for an ambulance, and she was taken to the hospital, where she was treated for a broken foot, a broken arm, and a couple of broken ribs.

How she could have suffered all these injuries was a mystery to me. The plank was not raised but lying flat on the ground, and she had only slipped. In any case I felt bad for her, so I visited her in the hospital and took flowers with me, which I gave to her in an effort to help cheer her up.

This realtor, after she got out of the hospital and was off work recovering, decided to sue the homeowner and his insurance company. So this insurance company was suing me to mitigate any damages they might suffer in this lawsuit.

I was being sued for a huge amount of money on the basis that I was negligent because I had not put up a sign to warn people. They believed that I should have posted a sign at the street stating, *Slippery Plank. Use at your own risk.* I could not believe it! They were suing me for over a million dollars. She had apparently calculated this amount to be her loss based on the physical damages she had suffered, her loss of work during her recovery period, and (for unknown reasons) her potential estimated loss of income for the rest of her life. Was I ever shocked!

As a result, I did not sleep very well for many months. The stress I was under affected my business and my family life. It seemed that all day long my thoughts turned toward the damages this realtor suffered, and yet how extreme her lawsuit was. I found it difficult to concentrate on business activities and on my family responsibilities. The stress seemed overwhelming at times, and it was easy to get angry at the littlest things. And, also as a result, Lorraine and our children did not get the kind of attention they deserved during those months, and the feelings that created in me sapped a lot of my energy at that time. I knew that the Lord would handle everything according to His good will, but I still felt as though I was carrying a heavy burden, not knowing how the Lord would work things out or what the outcome would be.

I wondered, *Will my insurance cover all of this?* Then I found out that Park Georgia Realty's insurance coverage only applied to their salesmen while working in the office, and not when showing homes or holding open houses outside of the office.

At that point, I became really depressed, so much so that I considered suicide for the second time in my life. A part of me was saying: *At least my personal life insurance will help my family. That might be better than declaring bankruptcy and maybe going to jail.* But each time I felt this way, I reassured myself that it was the devil trying to trick me and tempt me.

I knew I needed a good lawyer, but I did not know any. Then I thought of a very prestigious legal firm in Vancouver that was a tenant in one of the buildings REM(WEST) managed, and I wondered what it would cost to have them defend me. I went to their office and enquired, explaining my situation. Thankfully, the lawyer agreed to take my case with a minimal retainer of only $2,000, which still seemed like a lot of money to me at that time.

A couple of weeks later, the lawyer suggested, "To mitigate any damages you might suffer in this case, we should file a lawsuit against Park Georgia Realty for not supplying the insurance coverage you thought you had, based on your contract with them." He went on, "We should also file a lawsuit against the Real Estate Board of Greater Vancouver because they have allowed a real estate company (in this case, Park Georgia Realty), to not only be a member of their Real Estate Association, but also to be known as (in their printed materials), "a company in good standing", because now in our opinion they have not acted as a good company."

So here we were, with a total of five people or companies being sued (all with the buck stopping at me) for potentially over a million dollars—and likely more should I lose the case and have to also pay the legal costs for these five people and companies. (The five being: the homeowner, the homeowner's insurance company, me, Park Georgia Realty, and the Real Estate Board of Greater Vancouver.)

Several months went by without anything taking place, until my lawyer called me one day. He wanted me to come into the office so he could explain the defense he had planned. While saying that he had a good defense strategy, he explained that he was concerned that we would not be successful—because I had visited this injured woman when she was in the hospital and given her flowers. He said that the lawyers on the other side could say that I did this as an admission of guilt, and that would be a very strong argument.

"How can it be argued successfully that it was wrong for me to show love and concern for her, especially when she was hurt so badly?" I asked. "No matter who is at fault, surely giving someone flowers can't be viewed that way. And I was not at fault! I didn't place the planks there. The owner did that. And it was her choice to use the planks. She could have walked up to the house on the driveway. I guess I probably should have been more firm with the owner when I told him those boards should have been taken away after he put down the gravel in the driveway."

My lawyer reminded me that I was the agent for the owner at that time, and therefore I was responsible.

I had originally thought he was going to tell me that his defense strategy would be so strong that I had nothing to worry about, so as I left, the fog of depression set in again.

Before we went to court, a meeting (called a Discovery) was held with all parties present, and each one briefly explained their position in the case. The first day of Discovery was convened by the lawyer who represented the injured woman (she was not present). The meeting was held in a meeting room of a mediocre hotel in Vancouver, and it felt crowded since there were more people present than her lawyer had anticipated. There was the injured lady's lawyer, the homeowner's lawyer, two lawyers for the homeowner's insurance company, two lawyers for Park Georgia Realty, two lawyers for the Real Estate Board of Greater Vancouver, my lawyer and his partner, and me – a total of eleven people sitting behind six tables. The injured woman's lawyer was at his table in front of the other five tables.

The room was full of ten professional, proud, and well-paid lawyers and me, who had never been in such a situation before. I felt uncomfortable as the case was presented, and each of the other defendants stated their positions and how the buck would stop at me since I was the agent for the homeowner at the time of the accident.

I was present during all of Discovery, Day One, listening to the opposing lawyers. First the facts of the case were laid out, followed by their arguments. Each one stated their point of view with supporting evidence, all of which would again be given later in the courtroom. The value of Discovery was to give both sides the opportunity to research for the evidence and precedence that would best justify their positions, leaving the judge or jury to make the best judgment call based on the facts of the case, the evidence of what happened, and the decisions made in previous courtrooms for similar cases.

After the introductions were made, the instructions of order were given, followed by the facts of the case: during construction, the owner had placed wooden planks on the dirt from the street to near the front door of the house for people to walk on. Also a few days before the Open House the owner placed gravel as a base for the concrete that was soon to be poured for the driveway up to the house. And, on the day of the Open House it had been raining slightly. However there was no signage posted at the street advising people to walk on the gravel driveway. The woman who suffered the injuries chose to walk on the wet wooden planks, and she subsequently fell.

After the facts were presented, the argument was laid out by one of the lawyers: while it was the general practice for construction crews to have such planking in place leading up to the house until the concrete driveway was laid so that people would not walk on the dirt and track the dirt into the house, it still would have been reasonable for there to have been signage posted at the street to warn everyone—and possibly advising people to walk on the driveway – and there was no such signage posted.

Another lawyer stated that the injured woman had a clear choice as to whether she would walk on the gravel or the planking, and she chose the planking. And, while it might seem like she made the wrong choice, she had been wearing high-heeled shoes and thought she might get her heel stuck between some of the gravel stones and twist her ankle. He went on to state that from her perspective, it was more rational to walk on the planking. This was all the more reason why signage should have been posted at the street: to leave the planking there was providing an invitation for the general public to use it. Therefore, the homeowner and his agent were liable for all costs related to this woman's injuries.

Another lawyer stated that it might have been a better choice for this woman not to view this house on that day, but she did not want to miss the opportunity of a sale. She had clients who would potentially buy this home, as did other realtors. He stated, "It would have been prudent of Mr. Karsgaard, the owner's agent, to cancel his Open House on that day and to reschedule it, or for him to have removed the planking before his Open House. But he did neither, therefore leaving himself and the homeowner open to the liabilities that this case is all about."

At the conclusion of this first day, my lawyer gave everyone an invitation to have the following day's session held in the Boardroom at his office because it was larger and would be more comfortable for everyone.

At 9:00 a.m. the following day, the second day of Discovery, everyone arrived at my lawyer's office, high up in one of Vancouver's most prestigious office buildings called Park Place. As each person arrived, they were ushered into the Boardroom, told where to sit, and invited to enjoy the donuts, Danish rolls and coffee provided by my lawyer. Each of the opposing lawyers seemed awestruck as they entered the luxurious room, and commented on the fantastic view of Vancouver and the Northshore Mountains.

We all sat around one very large oval mahogany conference table. All the opposing lawyers faced the fabulous view, while my lawyer and his assistant were sitting with me on the other side – with our backs to the view.

On this second day, the focus was on me, giving me an opportunity to answer questions. So each of the opposing lawyers took their turn presenting their list of questions, which I responded to as I had been instructed by my lawyer the week before these Discovery meetings. After each question, I asked the quizzing lawyer to repeat or rephrase his question. Then I would ask if he could provide more detail to his question so I could understand what exactly it was that he was asking.

It seemed like I was going above and beyond when handling each question this way, but my lawyer encouraged me to carry on exactly as I had been doing. He believed I was handling everything very well from his vantage point. But the opposing lawyers were becoming very frustrated with me, which was my lawyer's intent.

As we neared the end of the morning, it appeared that almost everyone had had a good time. It certainly had not been a dry, fact-finding Discovery. At times, the lawyers had even burst out laughing because they could see what my lawyers were having me do—question every question, even when it was not necessary to do so. (After all, it was my right to obtain clarity on all questions before answering them.)

My lawyer had told me that the strategy of the other lawyers would be to put me off guard by asking me many questions that were unnecessary, and ask questions in such a way that I might say something that could be misinterpreted and used to their advantage.

My lawyer did not want the opposing lawyers to trip me up or for me to say anything that would unfairly jeopardize our defense, so he had explained how I should reply to every question with a request for clarification. This was not a simple case for just a few thousand dollars—it was a simple case of negligence with the hopes of over a million-dollar reward for the plaintiff, as well as sufficient funds to cover the fees of ten hungry lawyers. "A simple case," they called it, because just one slipup could bring the guilty verdict they were trying to obtain.

It was now 11:45 a.m., the end of the morning of the second day of Discovery. I had answered all the questions the opposing lawyers cared to put before me. My lawyer rose to speak, and he had two points to make before we broke for lunch. First, to reduce the amount I would need to pay should we receive a guilty verdict, he brought up the indisputable fact that the injured woman suffered from osteoporosis and her bones could break easily. Everyone was in agreement.

He then stated, "We are all in agreement that it was the homeowner's responsibility, and therefore the agent's responsibility, to do all that was necessary to help and protect the general public." Everyone nodded in agreement. "However not everyone in the general public has osteoporosis. In fact, only a small percentage have this condition, and had this fall happened to anyone else, the injuries would not have been nearly so bad. Therefore, if my client is considered guilty, as you allege, he ought only to be responsible for the injuries that would have occurred had this lady not had osteoporosis. However, I do not believe my client is guilty."

He then went on to explain that several days before the Open House, I had asked the owner to remove the planking after the gravel had been laid out, but that had not been done before the day in question.

Finally, just before everyone left for lunch, he asked if anyone would have more questions for me. No one did, so I was dismissed from the rest of the proceedings of the Discovery.

A couple of days later, my lawyer called to inform me that the Discovery had ended without the need to go to court—a settlement had been agreed to. I would never know how much the injured woman was to receive because it was not made public. That was between her lawyer and the homeowner's insurance company. I was let off the hook because I had asked the owner to remove the planking prior to the Open House; therefore, the responsibility rested solely upon the homeowner.

Because I was no longer responsible, my lawyer recommended that we drop our cases against Park Georgia Realty and the Real Estate Board of Greater Vancouver, which I agreed to.

The injured woman, not being satisfied with the outcome of this Discovery, did not drop her lawsuit against the homeowner's insurance company, claiming the appropriate signage should have been in place. The insurance company, realizing the costs that would be involved in proceeding with a court hearing, decided to negotiate a financial settlement with her, which she agreed to.

However, each of the lawyers still sent bills to their clients to cover their expenses up to this point. My lawyer's bill was $10,000, which might not seem like a big bill today for a lawsuit of initially over a million dollars, but in the 1980s it was a lot of money for me. But I was extremely thankful that I did not have to pay more, and especially thankful that I was not found guilty. Deep in my heart, I had known the Lord would take care of everything; but all of this had affected my work, and my family as well.

One positive outcome resulted from this case: The Real Estate Board of Greater Vancouver, together with Park Georgia Realty, recommended to the insurance industry that a new addendum to their Commercial Liability insurance policies be made available to all Real Estate companies in the future to cover their "Off-premises Temporary Offices," referring to Open Houses, to their kiosks in shopping malls, etc. And as a result of this case, this type of insurance coverage is available to everyone today.

So the Lord had His good purposes in all of this. One was to make positive changes in the insurance industry, and He had chosen me to be part of that. I learned through all of this that even when I do not understand or appreciate what the Lord is taking me through in my life, I can and should never doubt or question Him. For no reason should I allow stress to take control when I have given Him control of my life.

I really enjoyed the many and varied aspects of the Commercial Property Management business while working with REM(WEST). I managed five large downtown office buildings, as well as the largest piece of vacant land in Vancouver—the forty-acre old and unoccupied Burlington Northern Railway site.

My responsibilities were to carry out everything that was in the Property Management contract that the vice president had signed with a client concerning their property, except for the leasing of office spaces. That was done by the leasing office of Royal LePage Real Estate. So my responsibilities included hiring various architects and engineers, and to create, bid, award and manage construction contracts with various companies to do the tenant improvements required and/or remodel or update these office buildings.

It was also my responsibility to hire and oversee the maintenance personnel in each building, and to create and manage contracts with cleaning companies, security companies, etc. Each day I had to make sure that each of the people and companies I hired did their job well, and if they did not, to fire them and hire replacements. And, since it was important to have every contract bid on, I did not have the same engineers, companies, or contractors working in every building I managed.

I was also responsible for setting some of the rental charges for these buildings, following up with each tenant for their rental payments, and policing every other performance issue stated in each company's lease.

The job was time-consuming and challenging. At one point, I had twenty construction projects (not all in the same building) going on at the same time, on top of all of my other responsibilities.

As you might expect, everything did not always go well in the buildings I managed. Problems arose, and I had frustrated people to deal with. Let me give you some examples:

The removal of asbestos from one of these office buildings was not being done well, requiring me to confront the contracted company as well as the engineers responsible for overseeing the project, and then requiring some of the work to be redone. This created issues with some of the tenants who had been moved out of their premises while the work was being done. It was not a happy time for anyone, and I was looked on as the bad guy for having created time delays and overtime costs.

There seemed to be a possible electrical issue in the same office building, which could prevent a whole floor of office space from being rentable, so I contracted with an engineering company to have an electrical study done. This caused both the owners and the leasing agents to be upset with me because in their minds I was holding things up, and quite possibly just trying to overstate my abilities as a new property manager. They became even more upset when the analysis came back showing that they could not lease the remaining floor because there was insufficient electrical capability in the building with its current wiring and transformers. The result was that the building needed a whole new electrical system installed and the entire building needed to be rewired—all at tremendous cost—and this had to be done before they could move ahead with leasing the vacant floor. Again my diligence caused people to be very unhappy with me, even though they were benefiting from what I was doing.

One day I received a phone call from one of the tenants in another building, a large legal firm that occupied three floors in this eighteen-story office building. The firm requested the use of the elevators the following Saturday, as they had decided to move out that weekend, break their lease, and stop paying their rent. I studied their lease and saw that they really could do this because their lease had been poorly written before I took over the management, so I allowed them use of the elevators as requested. The landlord was extremely unhappy, and even though everything was out of my control, I received the brunt of the landlord's initial negative reaction.

I had to confront moral issues as well as physical and legal issues during my management tenure. One night, my security guard discovered one of our tenants partying with prostitutes. The guard tried to get the ladies to leave, but a fight broke out and I was called in. The tenant insisted that I was interfering with his right to use the premises 'according to his desires', which was the language in one part of the lease. I explained to him that his personal desires did not override other clauses in the lease, nor did he have the right to disobey the provincial and federal laws against prostitution; and it was wrong for him to have picked a fight with my security guard over this issue. It was a tense situation, but the tenant slowly backed down.

Crime was another issue I had to deal with. On one property in particular there was an old building that would never be repaired or occupied because it was in extremely poor condition. This made it particularly attractive to illegal activity. There were break-ins and murders and a very active prostitution ring—all things I had to deal with. So I decided that the only way to stop this permanently was to tear down the building. I hired a demolition company that came and removed all traces of the building over a weekend. But on Monday I had my knuckles rapped by the City of Vancouver and the Vice President of REM(WEST), because the building had been designated an 'historical building'. No charges were brought against me because of the crime problem and the extreme dilapidation of the building, but I was still told not to do anything like I had done ever again.

During all of this, as in times past, our children did not know much about the things I was dealing with, nor did Lorraine know everything. They just could not understand my frustrations, and why I did not treat them as I should have at times, and that bothered me a great deal. In the middle of all the stress, I felt compromised for not being able to spend quality time with them, and I was ashamed of how I reacted to them on many occasions.

During the time I was working at REM(WEST), Lorraine and I also dealt with some interesting people and companies at Progressive Business Centers.

One couple, a man and his wife, specialized in handwriting analysis and served as consultants to companies during their hiring process. They were wonderful people, although we were skeptical of their 'expertise'. Another man was selling and printing advertising on the back of cash register receipts, and he said that he was the first in the industry to do this. He also developed printed advertising for vehicle windows, where drivers can see out, but people on the outside only see the advertisement. He was a young and very ambitious man. Another tenant was a woman who started and developed a popular and successful women's magazine. We also had a tenant who sold fax machines—a remarkable invention at a time when most businesses were still using telex machines—and another section of our offices were rented by a division of the Canadian General Electric Company.

In late 1985, we rented space to the division of the United States government that was preparing for the 1986 World Expo in Vancouver—and this brought us close to an international tragedy. On that fateful January day in 1986, as Lorraine was driving to work, she heard the news that the Space Shuttle *Challenger* had exploded. As soon as she arrived at Progressive Business Centers, she went to their office and explained what she had heard on the news, because they had not yet learned of the tragedy. Lorraine was sure that they and her secretarial staff, who answered their phones, would be inundated with inquiries from the press, and her early visit to their office that morning allowed them time to determine how to respond before they even received their first phone call. So in the midst of everyone's shock and grief, Lorraine was able to support them in a very practical, loving way.

The experience we had with another tenant, though, was very stressful personally. Two men had come in and rented office space from us, paying their rent in cash, when early the next morning we heard on the news that these men had been indicted for illegal programmed stock trading—we found out some time later that these men were the ones who had been the primary cause of the stock market crash on October 19, 1987 which became known as Black Monday. So we were dismayed to have rented an office to them! They were certainly not the sort of tenant we wanted at Progressive Business Centers, and had we known of their indictment, we would not have leased an office to them.

But the Lord intervened for us over the next few months, as the men stopped paying their rent. We did everything we could to help them get caught up, but eventually I felt that all I could do was change the locks and prevent them from entering their offices until their back-rent was paid. The next several days saw repeated phone calls from their lawyer advising me that what I was doing was illegal, but I held firm. Finally, I informed their lawyer on a Friday that if they did not pay what they owed by the following Monday morning, I would turn whatever files were in their office over to Canada Revenue (similar to the Unites States' IRS). I had no idea what was in their office, but I imagined they had some files they would not want Canada Revenue to see! Within an hour, their lawyer had arranged a meeting for the next morning, advising me that they would pay their rent and move out. As it turned out, they had no intention of paying us what they owed. They offered us a little money and offered to leave some of their equipment to cover the rest of what they owed. It was not an ideal situation, but the stress was over and we were very happy to see them leave.

We were able to identify another potentially illegal situation, this time before any lease was signed. A prospective tenant told us that he specialized in 'introduction services' and that his staff would be using the offices in the evenings. It did not take me long to realize that he was a pimp, so I explained that our packaged office company was not open for business twenty-four hours per day. He left, and I breathed a sigh of relief.

While I was dealing with these interesting and sometimes difficult situations at Progressive, I was also struggling with all of my responsibilities at REM(WEST). Then one day my dad and my uncle told me they had sold the office building where Progressive was located. But they said the new owner of the building seemed happy with our company being one of his tenants since we occupied one full floor of the building. However, when it came time to renew our lease with him the following year, the new owner told us that he had other plans for the space we occupied.

We now had to make other plans. As we thought about it, we realized that even though our Business Center was the largest by square footage in the City of Vancouver, we were not financially successful. We offered all of the services that our tenants wanted at very good prices, but the building was not in the best location. In fact, when considering what most prospective tenants desired, Progressive Business Centers was in a poor location. (This was why we never had full occupancy.) We considered moving the business to a more desirable location in the city, but then decided that in the process we would lose most of our tenants and have to start all over again—and to build a new Business Center, we would have to borrow more money from the bank, and we had not yet repaid the loan from seven years previously.

Instead, we decided to close Progressive Business Centers and sell our home, as well as to borrow money on our credit cards to pay off the loans we had with both my father and the bank. This was a hard decision to make— to become house-renters instead of homeowners and to carry large balances on our credit cards. But we did what we thought we had to do under the circumstances.

We gave notice to all of our tenants regarding the situation, and in due course we closed Progressive Business Centers. We then brought in professional auctioneers to sell off the furniture, equipment, etc. It was a very stressful time – not only due to closing Progressive, but also because my responsibilities at REM(WEST) were numerous, and now Lorraine was out of work and we had credit card debt we couldn't pay off.

So Lorraine started working part time with a secretarial temp agency, and this meant our children were sometimes alone after school. Not something we wanted, but we had to do it.

Because of all this, I began to drink—not alcohol, but more and more coffee, sometimes as many as eighteen to twenty cups a day. It seemed necessary at the time, just to manage everything.

I did not understand what this addiction was doing to me. Living on mostly caffeine and adrenaline, my mind seemed to always be focused, and I was able to carry out my many responsibilities. What I did not realize is that I began to neglect our children and to treat people poorly— especially Lorraine. She managed to live through it all, but many times I have wished I could have made the necessary changes earlier—especially because of the toll it was taking on Lorraine and our children.

I went to my doctor for my annual check-up, and he asked how everything was going and if I was under a lot of stress (he could see something in my eyes that was not normal). I admitted that I was under a lot of stress, and that I was drinking probably too much coffee to keep me attentive to all I was doing. I told him that I did not have time for exercise and was working six days and up to ninety hours each week. He then gave me a referral to see another doctor, suggesting that he may be able to help me manage things.

I went to see this other doctor, hoping that maybe he would prescribe some medication that would help me handle everything without having to drink so much coffee. Instead, he told me, "You don't need medication. You just need to discipline yourself, lower your stress level, and stop drinking so much coffee. And if you don't, you will likely die within two years."

I left that doctor's office more stressed than when I had gone in, not knowing how I could reduce my responsibilities or adjust my lifestyle to accommodate at least some time for exercise. I knew I had problems, but could not see how I could make any changes, and it was becoming more and more difficult to keep up with even the minimum payments on our credit cards. I thought nobody understood my situation, and wondered, *What choices do I really have?*

I was referred to a third doctor, and went, hoping he would provide an acceptable solution. But he told me the very same thing, "If you do not lower your stress level and stop drinking so much coffee, you will not likely live for more than two more years..." To his credit, he did suggest, "The most effective way—in fact, the easiest way and yet a difficult way—to make the necessary changes is for you to move your family to another city and start over. A city not too close to where you live now. Move far enough away that your friends, parents, and other family members aren't close by. It won't be enough of a change for you to just take on the same work with another employer here in Vancouver, or even in another city. You need to move somewhere you haven't lived before and do something new—possibly something that you have enjoyed doing in your past. You also need to make this move as soon as you can."

I appreciated this plan even though it was drastic. So I went home and explained it to Lorraine. Then we prayed about it.

I had some vacation time coming from REM(WEST), so I took it, and for a couple of weeks we went on a family vacation. We traveled through North Cascades National Park and enjoyed visiting Leavenworth, then we went as far as Sandpoint, Idaho, and stayed there for a week. Lorraine and I enjoyed the time away, the change from our regular responsibilities, and the much-needed physical rest, although our children found some days to be somewhat boring. On the way back to Vancouver, we traveled north to Bonners Ferry and then on to Creston, British Columbia, before heading west.

We stopped in Kelowna, British Columbia, and decided to stay there for a few days. Since we liked Kelowna so much, we thought maybe we ought to move there. So we prayed about it and then visited Trinity Baptist Church, where we interviewed the Youth Pastor (we would not move to Kelowna if we could not find a good church for our children). We were impressed with what Pastor Alan Mertes had to say, so we started to look for a home to rent.

One of the first homes we saw in the newspaper sounded like it could fit our needs, so we went to look at it and found out that it was owned by an acquaintance. We thought, *This is interesting. Maybe the Lord is trying to tell us something.* When I was a young boy, I took piano lessons from a man by the name of Jim Cochrane. He also played the organ at our wedding. Mr. Cochrane had passed away and his wife, Daphne, had married Frank Radelja, and they owned the house we were looking at. *What a small world,* we thought, while believing in our hearts that the Lord was in it all. We prayed again, and as we considered the possibility of moving to Kelowna, the Lord gave us the peace that surpasses understanding.

Upon returning home, we told my parents that we would be moving to Kelowna, and why the move was necessary according to the doctors. They could not understand the need for us to move away. I tried to explain further, but they did not seem to want to listen—and unfortunately took it personally.

Next, we wondered how we would be able to afford our moving expenses.

For a few months, I'd been growing a mustache, and by now it had become quite a good-sized handlebar mustache, and a couple of the other property managers at REM(WEST) had asked how large I was going to grow it. I had replied, "I'll take my mustache off when I get a raise, or when I give my notice to leave the company."

One Monday after we returned from our trip, I approached the vice-president at REM(WEST) and reminded him that I believed I was owed a raise because of all the extra work I had been putting in with all of the construction projects, etc. that I was having to manage. I also said, "Tomorrow I'm going to give you my notice in writing that I will be leaving the company."

He asked me to take a couple more days to reconsider before turning in my letter of resignation.

As soon as I arrived at the office the next day, I was told the vice-president wanted to see me. I made my way to his office, carrying my letter of resignation, and before I could say anything, he said that at the end of the day I would be receiving a bonus check for $10,000 "for working so hard." I thanked him but also gave him my letter. He responded that he was sorry I was leaving, but said I would still receive the bonus.

Two weeks later, I shaved off my mustache before going to work, and at the end of that day I left the company.

So we had our moving expenses covered and money left over. Praise the Lord! Within two months of my last doctor's visit, we were on our way to Kelowna.

It was not at all an easy move for our family. Nathan was fifteen years old, and about to enter his last year of high school, so he of course moved with us. Jason, our oldest, was twenty, and he also moved with us. But Deborah, who was eighteen and in her own apartment while attending college, decided she was not moving to Kelowna. It was difficult for all of us to leave her behind, as the next phase of our lives was beginning.

PHASE NINE

Life as a Realtor in Kelowna

What would I do for work in a new city? I knew I wasn't going to go into Commercial Property Management again but I didn't have any idea of what else I could do, and didn't have a lot of time to decide. So I thought it was reasonable to go back into selling homes, and because we needed an income quickly, I thought it best to be with a well-recognized company. Therefore I joined the REMAX Company and did a lot of advertising—and my name quickly became known.

My first year in Kelowna, I was inducted into the REMAX President's Club, having earned over $100,000 (a lot of money in 1990–1991). But after deducting all of my advertising costs and other related expenses, we were actually trying to live on only about $20,000. So it was hard, especially because we were still carrying some credit card debt after the closure of Progressive.

Within a couple of years, I was given the opportunity to become the Agent-Broker/Real Estate Sales Manager for Gallagher's Canyon, one of Kelowna's prestigious golf courses. They were building and selling luxury homes around their golf course. While I enjoyed the work, I found it difficult working for them because my supervisor was unreasonably demanding and rude. Unlike others, who also did not appreciate this man's demeanor but put up with it, I left and became the sole sales agent for another developer who was building a gated community of new homes in Kelowna.

What I did enjoy about working for these companies was that I did not have to spend any money on advertising—the companies did all of that. I also did not have to spend any time listing homes for sale. In the past, that had taken up a lot of my evenings, as did negotiating sales agreements and presenting offers. Working for the developers was mostly day work, which allowed me to have my evenings free to spend more time with my family.

While working at Gallagher's Canyon, I had been approached by Okanagan University-College to teach their evening Real Estate Property Management courses, and I taught there for two years while keeping my day jobs. I really enjoyed teaching, and being a teacher at a university was a real 'feather in my cap,' so to speak; I had not gone to a university after high school, so I did not even have a Bachelor's degree. Yet I had become what they called a university professor, so this was a real honor for me.

After my first year of teaching, I was complimented highly during my yearly review, so I thought it would not hurt to ask for a raise. The university told me a raise was not possible because I was already their highest-paid professor, going by my salary and the amount of hours I worked. *Wow. Another feather in my cap*, I thought.

In 1995, it appeared to me that the Real Estate market was entering another difficult period when sales would be slow, so I decided to make a change and took the Life Insurance and Investment Brokers course. I did very well, and became a licensed life insurance salesman with one of the prominent life insurance companies. But it was a struggle.

What I did not know going in was that good life insurance salesmen start earlier in life when their clients are making decisions about what percentage of their incomes would be spent on insurance and investments, before they lock themselves into mortgages, etc. when they would have less disposable income. So most of my potential clients would be in their twenties and early thirties. While most people in this age group prefer to deal with salesmen who are experienced in the business, they do not really want to do business with those who are older than them by ten to fifteen years.

In 1997 I would be fifty years old, and this reality was bouncing around in my head. I started to reflect on what I had been doing for the past fifteen years. I had been involved in various aspects of the Real Estate industry, and Lorraine and I had had some wonderful experiences. We had been used of the Lord to influence the lives of others for Christ. However, not everything had gone well—we had encountered problems, struggles, and business failures. Life had not been easy in many ways. As I began this evaluation, one thing stood out: there had been a certain lack of joy and peace in my life. Yet at the same time I knew the Lord had been with me in everything I had done.

As I continued thinking about all of this, a quiet voice within me reminded me that throughout my life, starting from when I had been just a young boy, the Lord had told me that I was to be involved in full-time Christian ministry—this was His 'Plan A' for my life—and I had been a pastor and a missionary for fifteen years. But things had changed—through no fault of my own, I believed. So I had become involved in the real estate business for fifteen years. And, while I believed the Lord had been involved in our lives during these years also, I had this feeling that for the past fifteen years I had been living 'Plan B'. I felt as though I had been like a train, sidetracked to let another one pass me by; and as a result my life had become less fruitful for God.

As this evaluation continued, I began to wonder, *'Had I not decided to start working for my father and uncle on the reconstruction of their office building, would I have been led by the Lord into another ministry? Had I just taken the first easy option that was put in front of me at that time? If I had waited on the Lord longer, would things have turned out differently?'*

I could never know the answers to those questions and nothing can change the past, but decisions could be made at any time that could change my future forever.

As I thought more about this, I believed it was time to get back with God on His 'Plan A'. I believed deep in my spirit that I could be influencing many more people for Christ if I were doing something different. This brought out the critical questions in my evaluation. Was what I was doing now the best use of my time and talents? Were the gifts and abilities the Lord had given to me being used to glorify Him? Were people being brought into the Kingdom of God through my career choices? Could I be doing more to honor Christ in my life? All of this, in a quiet way, kept snatching my focus away from everything I was trying to do in business and at home—it became in my mind like a merry-go-round, and I knew the only thing that was going to stop it was to make the right decision.

However, I did not know what the options were, or the decision that needed to be made. All that I knew was that soon I should leave the employed and begin living by faith—to become involved once again in full-time Christian ministry. Then it struck me—the decision was simply to decide to do what I knew I should do, despite not having the complete picture of what would lie ahead.

I knew the Lord was speaking to me! I knew I needed to agree with what He was telling me! I knew that all I needed to do was to decide that I would just 'trust and obey' Him—like the song that I had sung so many times in my life says.

But into what specific ministry, or with what Christian agency or missionary organization, I did not know. So I did two things. First, I spoke to the Pastor of our church in Kelowna and explained to him what I thought the Lord was urging me to do. I asked him to pray with us, and to advise us on what steps we ought to take next. He had me talk with the board member who was in charge of Missions for the church, and it was agreed that we should follow up on any leads the Lord might put in our path.

Then I remembered a Christian organization called Intercristo that I had heard about when we were in Bible school. They helped Christians find their fit into full-time Christian service opportunities. I found the organization's website and sent off some basic information about my education and my experiences.

Intercristo sent me information on approximately twenty Christian organizations with offices in Canada and the United States that might be interested in having me work with them, so I wrote to ten of them, asking for more information, and we continued praying. One of these missionary organizations struck a chord with us—they were helping people physically as well as spiritually and I believed the two were somehow inseparable. I believed that to be effective in sharing the message of salvation with people, you had to at the same time show them physically that you loved them—something I had learned during my fireman and bus driver days. So we were impressed with Mexican Medical, Inc., and within a couple of days, they phoned asking us if we would come to San Diego for an interview. That was in February 1998.

My parents had a winter home in Palm Desert and, not knowing anything about what we were contemplating, asked if we would like to come to Palm Desert in March for a one-week vacation with them—and they would pay all the expenses. We accepted, and shortly after we arrived, I told my parents what we were considering and that we had been asked to come to San Diego for an interview. I had figured Lorraine and I would rent a car and just be gone for a day, but they offered to drive us.

The Lord has been arranging everything, we thought. *He's even been looking after all of our expenses.*

When we met with the president, vice-president and treasurer of Mexican Medical we were told more about what they did in Mexico as a missionary organization. They had been building and staffing hospitals on the Baja Peninsula and in other parts of Mexico since 1963. Then to help with these construction projects and the maintenance of the hospitals, they had groups of volunteers come from churches throughout the US. These teams would be led by the Mexican Medical missionaries, and in addition to working at the hospital site they would help with evangelistic outreaches at nearby churches. This would involve the showing of evangelistic films in the evenings and also conducting children's programs similar to our Vacation Bible Schools during the afternoons.

Mexican Medical was looking for people who had previous experience recruiting missionaries and who also had experience developing short-term missionary endeavors because they wanted to increase the number of teams that were coming to help them from churches across the United States and Canada. They were looking for someone to join their office staff to help promote and coordinate it all.

As we talked, we all realized how my time as a Youth Pastor and my involvement with Mission to Europe's Millions would make it easy for us to fit into their organization and what they were doing.

Four other reasons made us believe that joining Mexican Medical was the direction the Lord was calling us to go:

1.   We were impressed that this organization was helping people both physically and spiritually, not just being involved in what we would typically call "spiritual" activities.

2.   While we were prepared to go anywhere the Lord would call us to go, Mexican Medical would not require us to move away from our home in Kelowna (Nathan had not finished his university education, and we wanted to provide a home for him during that time). Mexican Medical was delighted with us staying in Canada to develop and promote the organization there, and to bring or host teams from Canada to Mexico.

3.   We did not need full financial support to get started, and Lorraine could continue working at her job while we started to raise our support.

4.   We could start almost immediately, as soon as we could have a letter of reference sent from our home church stating that they believed this was, from their perspective, the Lord's leading.

The next step would be for me to understand what my responsibilities would be with Mexican Medical, and they outlined the following:

1.   I would visit churches and Bible schools in Canada, and go to conferences each year to promote the short-term missionary opportunities that Mexican Medical offered.

2.   I would need to get firm commitments from evangelical churches to send teams—both youth groups and adults—to Mexico for one-week stints, to help with necessary maintenance and the construction of hospitals in the mornings, to conduct children's evangelistic programs in the afternoons, and to help with the showing of evangelistic movies in the evenings.

3. I would organize, accompany, and lead some of these teams.

While I was comfortable with each of these responsibilities, there was one problem, and that was in the area of obtaining the personal financial support we would need. We understood that all our financial support would have to be raised from our friends and family in Canada, and from the churches we had most recently been a part of in Tsawwassen and Kelowna. The problem was that Mexican Medical was not a registered charity in Canada. We had been told that they had tried to create a sister organization in Canada, but that it was impossible for them to do so from the United States.

So while we left San Diego believing that the Lord was leading us to join Mexican Medical, we also knew there was what seemed to be this final hurdle to get over: Mexican Medical needed to be a registered charity in Canada before we could move ahead.

When we returned to Kelowna, I remembered a lawyer who could probably help us. I had been a board member of a Christian organization called Christian Info while we lived in Calgary, and it was led by a woman whose brother, Blake Bromley, was a well-known and respected lawyer in the field of Christian charities in Canada. I phoned him, and he explained that the reason Mexican Medical was having difficulty getting a sister organization in Canada was because they were trying to create a charity that would be led and controlled from the United States. He went on to say that it would be relatively easy for us to create a new charity in Canada, which could coordinate its activities with Mexican Medical as long as the majority of this new charity's board members were Canadian citizens living in Canada, and the decisions of this new charity were not dictated by Mexican Medical in the United States.

As we continued praying about all this, I felt more and more that we were moving in the right direction; and through what I was reading in the Bible, I believed we ought to move ahead and join Mexican Medical. The Lord had certainly gone before us, clearing the way and providing for us through each step. There was this one last obstacle, but by faith I knew that it too would be overcome. Some excitement, and the peace that surpasses all understanding, flooded my soul.

I went back to our pastor and gave him an update, and he offered to send a letter to Mexican Medical stating that the church was behind us in making this decision.

Near the end of March 1998, I phoned Reverend Mel Peabody, the president of Mexican Medical, and told him that our applications were on their way along with a letter from our pastor. He said there would be no hesitation in us being accepted into the organization. Then he asked if I could spend the summer in Mexico, going to each of their hospitals to familiarize myself with the operations and needs, and to spend some time with all their missionaries at each location.

My next phone call was to Blake Bromley, who started our application to start a new charity in Canada which we would call Help Heal a Child.

In early April, I approached the manager of the life insurance company I was working for, explained some of what had been taking place, and gave him my written resignation. Even though he was a Christian, he said, "I understand. But I won't send your letter to our head office right away. Why don't you go to Mexico this summer and get all of this out of your system, then come back rejuvenated and get back to serious employment." I thanked him for his offer, but stated that my commitment to the Lord was firm.

Then we told our family and friends what we were doing, asking them for their prayers and financial support.

In July, we received our incorporation documents, approved by Canada Revenue, and then a couple of weeks later I left Kelowna to visit all of the Mexican Medical hospitals and missionaries in Mexico, so that starting in the fall I could appropriately represent their locations and ministries in my efforts to support them with short-term workers and teams from churches in British Columbia and Alberta.

To our joy, we received a confirmation letter from the Canadian government accepting and approving our application to change the name of our Canadian charitable organization from Help Heal a Child to Mexican Medical Ministries before I began visiting churches to raise support. We had wanted to do this so people would realize we were aligned with Mexican Medical, Inc.—which later become known also as Mexican Medical Ministries.

From September of that year through the following spring, I visited all the churches in Canada that had previously sent teams to Mexico with Mexican Medical, informing them of our new Canadian organization that was cooperating and coordinating its activities with the U.S. organization. I encouraged each church to consider sending another team to Mexico and to share their experiences with Mexican Medical with other churches, so that they, too, would become interested in sending teams to Mexico.

In January 1999, I set up a booth at Missions Fest in Vancouver, which at the time was the largest missionary conference in the world. Over four thousand people attended this conference that year, and almost all of them took time to walk through the area where missionary organizations had booths set up.

In February, I went to Missions Fest in Edmonton, Alberta, to again set up a display and inform people of the opportunities to become missionaries and be part of one of our Missions teams.

Going to these conferences was something I did while we were living in Kelowna, and later while living in San Diego both Lorraine and I went to them. In addition to setting up a display booth and representing Mexican Medical that way, I also became one of their many seminar speakers.

During the summer of 1999, I spent a few weeks leading teams from churches in Canada and in the United States to the Buen Pastor Hospital in San Quintin, Baja California Norte, Mexico, about a five-hour drive south of San Diego. I also enjoyed taking a couple of teams from our church in Kelowna to Cabo San Lucas. Each of these teams worked on hospital-related construction projects each morning, then put on children's programs at local churches in Cabo and in migrant worker camps in San Quintin. We also showed evangelistic movies in the evenings at a few migrant worker camps in San Quintin.

Significant things happened in both places, not just in the lives of the Mexican adults and children, but also in the lives of the team members. Almost all of our team participants went home with a better perspective on how they ought to be living their own Christian lives, and some even returned home having a better focus on what they might do later in life. I believe each one also returned with a better understanding of how fortunate they were to be living in Canada or in the US, and of the poverty in our world—even though Mexico is not nearly as bad as some other much poorer countries.

After the summer, I returned to Kelowna energized by all that had happened and excited to tell Lorraine all about it.

In September, I again started making plans, appointments, and reservations to visit several churches and explain the opportunities Mexican Medical Ministries offered young people and adults to serve the Lord in Mexico. I pointed out that Missions should be an important part of every church, and that sending their people to work with established missionaries in a foreign country is the best way to provide their people with a good short term missions experience.

Among the many things I did that summer in Mexico, two things proved to be quite significant years later. One of those happened in San Quintin, and the other in Cabo San Lucas.

There was a missionary couple living at the hospital in San Quintin who had their own small airplane, and they would often fly doctors into rural areas to provide medical services. Joe would also fly patients to other hospitals if the hospital in San Quintin was not equipped to provide the services they needed.

One day such an emergency flight was needed, and I was able to help load a patient into Joe's plane; but before we did, he prayed for the passenger and all others involved. The man had been in a car accident, and the young woman with him, named Ode, who had not been badly injured, had questions: "Why did this happen? Why would you fly my friend out to another hospital—and do this at no cost to the patient?"

Joe explained God's love for both of them, and told her how Jesus Christ had done the same: He came from heaven and died on a cross, paying for our salvation, thereby providing the only way to heaven for each of us— and did it at no cost to us. But we must accept His gift or we will die in our sins and not go to heaven, just as her friend must accept this flight or he would die.

Ode thanked Joe for the explanation, said she understood, and prayed right there to thank Jesus Christ and to accept Him as her Lord and Savior.

Why was the flight that day so special? All this was quite routine for the hospital and Joe always prayed for each patient (and whoever else was involved) before every flight, and sometimes the patient or another person involved would pray to accept Jesus Christ as their Savior.

But several years later, Ode came into my life once again, making the events of that day especially memorable for her and for me. We were in a church in Insurgentes, Baja California Sur—only one and a half hours from Loreto—holding one of our evangelistic Health Fairs and Ode was translating for me as I preached in her church.

We were all enjoying coffee at the church after the meeting, and I asked Ode how she had come to accept Jesus Christ as her Savior. She recounted what had happened several years previously in San Quintin. I asked her, "When exactly did that happen?" and after she told me, I explained that I was there praying for her that day. We both had tears of joy in our eyes.

That same summer, in Cabo San Lucas I did something I have done only a few times in my life: I picked up a hitchhiker. I was driving on the highway into town and saw an old truck stopped beside the road. A woman was getting out of the truck, and a man stood at the back of his truck wearing black pants, a white shirt, and a tie. He was trying to get someone to stop, so I did. His truck was out of gas.

As I was driving him into town, he (Juan) asked many questions about what I was doing in Cabo, and I told him about the team I had working on a hospital. We got to the gas station and I provided a can for the gas he needed, then drove him back to his truck. On the return drive, I asked what he did for a living, and he told me that he was the chief of police and an instructor at the Police Academy in Cabo San Lucas.

I was wonderfully surprised to have been able to help such a man, and somewhat relieved that I did not get in trouble for picking up a stranger. When we parted, he gave me his name and said, "I will remember you. If you ever need anything or have a problem with anyone, just call me and I will help you."

Five years later, just after we had moved to Loreto, we had our first team arrive and I was meeting with them in a church explaining the week's program of work projects, Health Fairs and the children's outreach program that would be done. But a couple of Immigration officers interrupted the meeting to tell me that I could not speak to or lead any group of people in Mexico. "You are also not to promote anything religious," they said, "because you only have a tourist visa."

"How should I go about doing all of this then?" I asked. "What do I need to do that will make what we want to do acceptable to the Mexican authorities?"

They did not have an answer for me, so they said they would get back to me. The two young Immigration officers left, and a couple of hours later they returned, saying, "Our Loreto office has checked with our office in Cabo San Lucas, and we don't know why, but we have been told that we are not to stop you from doing anything you want to do." So we continued with our planned events.

I immediately thought about what I had done in Cabo San Lucas five years earlier. But I had not made a phone call to the police chief who was hitchhiking, and that I had picked up that day. Even so, it seemed obvious to me that the Immigration Office had checked to see if I had a police record—and I guess I had, *a good one*—because to me there was no other explanation for the response given to me by those Immigration officers that day.

PHASE TEN

Moving to San Diego

In October 1999, I received two urgent phone calls from Mexican Medical.

Reverend Ed Whitford, the vice-president, called first to inform me that Mel Peabody, the president, had just been diagnosed with an aggressive form of prostate cancer. Ed said that he remembered well the interview I had with them in March of the previous year, and went on to explain, "We now have a need for someone with your experience to come and help us out here in San Diego, and I believe you are the Lord's man for the job."

A few hours later, Mel called saying that he and Ed, as well as Treasurer Fred Neumeister, believed that I was qualified to help lead the organization. They wanted to know if I would consider moving to San Diego, because, as he put it, "I will likely not be able to carry on with all my many responsibilities for much longer."

He went on to explain that the organization had just been given an office building, and that they needed to find tenants to occupy its second floor. The appropriate leases would need to be drawn and tenant improvements done and then the building would need to be managed.

He then said that they believed I was the right person to fill the position, because of my previous activities and responsibilities as a youth worker and pastor as well as my responsibilities and experience with Mission to Europe's Millions. I had already done a lot to promote Mexican Medical in Canada, and they valued my extensive real estate education and experience.

Wow, I thought, *The Lord has all of my past contributing to what He has led us to be involved in with Mexican Medical.* When I had started my personal evaluation a couple of months prior, I was dismayed that possibly I should not have been doing all that I had done for the past fifteen years. I wondered if I had been completely side-tracked during those years. But now I could see that what had happened—even leaving Mission to Europe's Millions— was all in God's hands. This huge revelation brought excitement, hope, and joy back into my life.

But then like a fiery dart from the evil one, the thought came to mind, *'You can't work in the United States. You are a Canadian...'*

But peace overwhelmed me with the realization that it would not be impossible for me to work in the U.S. because Lorraine was both a Canadian citizen and a U.S. citizen (she was born in Canada of American parents). And, with this calming peace came the thought, *'The Lord has been directing my life and our path ever since I was young when I put my life in His hands."*

That next month, in November 1999, I flew to San Diego to start helping out with the administrative details at the Mexican Medical office. I did not want to rent an apartment on my limited budget, so I made my home in a six-by-ten-foot storage room in the new building (which was fine, because I worked most evenings and six days a week during my time there).

After five weeks, I returned to Kelowna for one week, then went back to San Diego for another five weeks. This schedule continued for the following eight months, and the travelling, living in such tight quarters, and working sometimes for twelve to sixteen hours a day was difficult for me. But it was more difficult for Lorraine to be on her own for such long periods. However, during this time the Lord was preparing her heart for all that was to lie ahead. And we used a computer 'chat program' frequently to communicate back and forth with each other—that way we didn't have to pay long distance telephone charges.

Our son Nathan would be graduating from university in the spring of 2000, and we believed that by that summer we would have sufficient financial support coming in that Lorraine could quit her job, (which she was by then wanting to do). So we started to plan our permanent move to San Diego. The first thing we had to do was get Lorraine a U.S. passport—but there was a problem.

Initially we thought that because Lorraine was an American citizen, it would not be difficult for her to get a US passport, and then I could get a Green Card piggy-backing on her passport. But early that year we learned that we first had to prove that her parents were both American citizens. For her mom that would be easy, because she had a birth certificate showing that she was born in Washington State. But her dad was no longer living, and never had a birth certificate. He was born in the hills of Tennessee and delivered by a midwife, and his birth had never been registered.

So we had a formal search of school records done, but no one with the name Alvin J. Roberts was to be found. The search did however show that there were two boys named Junior enrolled at the time her dad was, so we were sure he had to be one of them because everyone called him Junior.

We had a search done of the U.S. Navy records, and found out that when he enlisted, the Navy told him that he could not be called Junior, so they gave him. the name Alvin Jack Roberts. But all of this did not provide sufficient proof for the U.S. Government to believe that this man was in fact her father.

However we were told, because of the difficulties we were having, that the government would be satisfied if we could provide them with written, notarized testimonies concerning her father's identity, from two members of her dad's immediate family who were alive when he was born.

Fortunately, her father had an older brother and an older sister still living. They were both in nursing homes in Tennessee, and when Lorraine explained the situation to her Aunt Lucille, the youngest living sibling, she said she would have her brother and sister sign the required documents.

Lucille got in touch with a notary right away and together they had the required testimonies written down and notarized. Thankfully, this was done without any delay, because neither her dad's brother nor his sister lived very long after this.

Soon after these documents were submitted to the U.S. Government, we received confirmation of Lorraine's U.S. citizenship, and in March she received her U.S. Passport.

In April, when I was in San Diego, a man came to the office with a large truckload of donated medical supplies in what appeared to be a new U-Haul truck. A couple of weeks later, he returned with a second load, again with what appeared to be a new U-Haul truck. At that point, I found out that he worked for U-Haul Truck Rentals. So I told him about our pending move from Kelowna to San Diego, and that we did not have the money to hire a commercial moving company, so we would likely be renting a U-Haul truck.

He said that he could help us so our move would not cost us as much as we were expecting. I thanked him, and he told me he would check with his company about how we could go about doing this and then give me a call.

A couple of weeks later, he called and explained that he would be able to provide us with a new twenty-six-foot moving truck for just $75.00—not $75.00 per day, but $75.00 total. What a tremendous savings! However, there was a condition: I could not pick up the truck in Kelowna as I had planned, but rather I would have to pick up the truck in Portland, Oregon. But we could have the truck for twenty-one days.

Well, that was not going to be a problem. We made our plans to pick up the truck sometime after the middle of July, drive it to Kelowna, pack the truck and drive it to San Diego—but not in a rush since we had twenty-one days. So we took our tent with us and camped along the way down the Oregon-California coast. Our move was going to be a wonderful trip—not a difficult, rushed, or expensive move—and we were delighted.

The Lord was looking after us, providing in so many ways and proving His guidance in the process. Our move was now only going to cost us $75.00 plus gas—WOW!

When I got to Kelowna with the truck, we packed it with all the personal things we needed, and then had a garage sale to sell what could not go in the truck. From that sale, we had just over $2,000 to set ourselves up in the townhouse I had rented when I was previously in San Diego.

On August 1, 2000 we left Kelowna and started driving south, tenting along the way.

I applied for my Green Card immediately after arriving in San Diego, which would allow me to work in the United States. (Previously I was "volunteering" at the Mexican Medical office, but now that we had moved to San Diego, I needed to update my status.)

I chose not to use a lawyer to make the application, because that would have cost money. Even though people told us that it was an involved process and that I could be denied, I believed that I was capable of completing the application without help.

I went to the U.S. Immigration office early one morning, submitted my application along with the required fee, and sat down to wait.

After an hour or so they called me to the wicket and told me what documents I needed to submit next, believing I would return another day to do this. But to their surprise I had brought these additional required forms with me. They asked me again to take a seat, and said that they would call me up to the window a little later. At about 2:00 p.m., I walked out of that office with my Green Card in my hand, praising the Lord.

In the spring of the following year, I again searched the internet for all the forms I would need to apply for U. S. citizenship. I completed them and again without the use of a lawyer, went down to the U.S. Immigration office in San Diego.

At 5:00 a.m., I stood in the long line that made its way to the door. The office opened at 8:00, but it was about 10:30 before I actually got through the doors. Then when it was finally my turn to approach the wicket, I submitted the forms I had completed, along with the required fee. I was told to take a seat and wait until they had reviewed the forms.

About an hour later, I was called back to the wicket and told what additional documents I would need to submit. Again they were surprised that I already had these forms with me. I gave them to the woman across the counter and was again told to take a seat. This happened three times, until I was finally called to the counter and told that now I simply had to wait until I received a written notice in the mail detailing what to do next. I again walked out of the Immigration Office praising the Lord.

A couple of weeks later, both Lorraine and I were sitting before a U.S. Immigration Officer in a different Immigration Office. He had only a couple of basic questions for Lorraine—how long had we been married, was she contemplating divorce after I received my U.S. citizenship, etc.

For me he had ten questions that would be randomly selected by his computer—questions about U.S. history, the U.S. structure of government, and people in the current political scene. After having answered all the questions correctly, I was told that in just a few weeks I would attend a swearing-in ceremony, at which time I would be given my Certificate of Naturalized Citizenship.

After I had been working in the San Diego office of Mexican Medical for only a short time, it became apparent to me that they had financial problems because many donations were not being used according to their designated purposes.

For example, when one of the hospitals in Mexico had a financial need that exceeded the money allocated to it, money would be given to that hospital from other accounts designated for other hospitals or missionaries. The intention was always to reimburse the other accounts when more money came in. But handling the finances this way meant that some missionaries were not able to receive money designated specifically for them in a timely manner.

There were many times when there were not enough donations to reimburse the accounts, which meant that monies were not being spent in the way our donors intended, and missionaries were not receiving the monies specifically designated for them

When I broached this practice with the then-president, it seemed like he was trying to hide behind a part of the law. "The laws about designating gifting state that designations given by donors are only to be thought of as a suggestion as to how any and all gifts received may be spent by a charity," he said. "The final decision on where funds are actually to be used is made by the Board of a charity—and at Mexican Medical, Inc., the Board has delegated all such decisions to me."

I researched this matter further, and found that this practice of borrowing and/or not using donations according to the designations made by their donors was actually being hidden from the Board and the missionaries. They suspected something like this was taking place, but they did not know how to approach the president about it. They could not see a solution. The board members knew the needs of the hospitals were real, and they understood that the hospitals could close if they could not meet their financial obligations.

I knew there had to be a way to correct this problematic situation, and believed in my heart that I was the one who had to do something about it. In fact, at times I even wondered if this was one of the reasons the Lord had called me to join Mexican Medical and move to San Diego.

After praying about it, I believed it would not be constructive to challenge the president about what he was doing. He knew better than anyone the needs these hospitals had, and I knew he was doing his best to raise funds to cover those needs. I could also see that the situation really bothered him.

During my discussions with the president, I learned that a lot of what he had been doing was simply kept in his notes and files as there was not a good accounting system in place. So the Lord led me to start looking at computerized accounting systems.

Then when it seemed appropriate, I asked the president if I could institute a computer software system to help him better manage the finances. He agreed that the program I wanted to use would be helpful, and said he was glad that

I had joined the San Diego office staff. He realized that I had recognized his frustrations and was working to bring about a solution.

I purchased one of QuickBooks software packages and started putting together a very detailed, tailored accounting system, implementing class entry options to manage the designations of all donors. Once everything was set up and all our records transferred to this new system, nothing would be hidden in the detailed statements that would be given to the Board. The missionaries could also be given computerized statements showing exactly when funds designated to their support and their ministries were received and the amount of these donations, and also how and when these funds were dispersed.

I realized that this could mean that the hospitals might not be able to count on us to help them with some of their financial problems, but that would be a problem that the Board would have to deal with. What I did not recognize was that installing this new accounting system would ultimately change the direction of Mexican Medical.

This transition from one accounting system and practice was not easy for everyone.

1. The woman who had been in charge of all the bookkeeping found it unreasonable to have to learn a new bookkeeping system.

2. The president realized that his borrowing practice would become evident to everyone, and, even though he had given approval to set the system up, he became defensive and tried to justify his actions to others.

3. The missionaries were delighted, knowing that they could now be sure of receiving all funds designated to them and their ministries, but they were not so happy that they now had to provide

detailed receipts for all the team funds they were
handling.

4. The people in our warehouse who were
accepting truck-loads of donated medical
equipment and supplies were unhappy that they
now had to be detailed in inventorying everything.

5. The managers of the hospitals in Mexico were
very upset that they would no longer be receiving
funds for all of their needs.

So while the benefits of the new accounting system
were appreciated greatly by our auditor, and by almost
everyone else (at least to some degree), I was not making
friends in the process.

The first change of direction for Mexican Medical was
made by the Board because they were now fully aware of
the financial status of everything. While the financial
needs of their hospitals had been known and discussed in
the past, and funds had been sent to them to meet their
needs, the Board now decided that these hospitals must
become self-supporting. This decision was not at all easy
for those in Mexico who had depended on Mexican
Medical for so long, but it was time.

Secondly, the Board decided that Mexican Medical
would no longer build hospitals in Mexico, primarily
because these hospitals would have ongoing financial
needs we really could not help them with.

It had also become a challenge for us to manage the
hospitals from San Diego. The Board believed that many
cultural differences were making things too difficult for
everyone, so, out of respect for the Mexican hospital
managers, they decided that the existing hospitals should
be turned over completely to them. The Mexican
government was getting better at meeting the medical
needs of their people as well, so we did not need or want
to be in competition with them. So instead of building and

supporting hospitals, Mexican Medical would begin to focus on conducting evangelistic Community Health Fairs.

The president and I had many conversations about this focus of the organization. He believed that the original intention of its founders had changed over the years, and it was time to get everyone back on track. He had been trying to do this for at least a couple of years. The hospitals had become almost totally focused on the physical needs of the people and were doing little in the way of presenting the gospel. Also, many of the teams that went to Mexico to help with the maintenance or construction of hospitals were not doing any evangelism either. So for a few years, Mel had been encouraging the missionaries to at least have their teams hold a Vacation Bible School for the children near the hospital where they were working.

I, too, thought this evangelistic focus was critical. This was why I had chosen the name Mexican Medical Ministries for the Canadian organization. I thought it would be a benefit for our organizations in the United States and in Canada to have the same name; and because we wanted the main focus of our activities to be on *evangelistic ministries*, we decided the organization in the United States should also become known as Mexican Medical Ministries.

We didn't want to spend money to legally change the name of Mexican Medical, Inc. and then have to make other related changes to account names, etc., so I submitted an application to the U.S. authorities for Mexican Medical, Inc. to use the DBA ('doing business as' name), Mexican Medical Ministries.

Unfortunately, one particularly patriotic American among the Mexican Medical personnel was extremely unhappy. First, because a Canadian was managing their office in the United States, and now because the American organization was becoming known by a name that had first been established in Canada. This man often berated me, and on a couple of occasions even broke out in angry outrage, so much so that I was trembling.

However, I knew we were doing what the Lord had called us to do, and I determined that I was going to remain faithful to Him and to His calling despite these struggles. The Lord gave me perseverance and enough patience to see us through. Thankfully, this problem subsided when the man realized we were not going to return to Canada anytime soon and that we had to work alongside each other.

For three and a half years, Lorraine and I worked in the office in San Diego. She was the receptionist and Secretary to the President. I was the Administrator/Office Manager, Accountant, and Building Manager, responsible for overseeing the mission's finances, all office and warehouse issues, the hiring of employees as needed, finding new missionaries to go to Mexico, and also finding tenants for the second floor of our building.

During these three and a half years, I continued to also manage the Canadian organization, and Lorraine and I made several trips to Canada to represent Mexican Medical at churches and at the conferences in Vancouver and in Edmonton, as well as making trips to Mexico to help with our ministries there.

About a year after we moved to San Diego, the Board began looking for a new president. By this time, I had taken over most of the president's daily responsibilities, and some of the Board members asked if I would consider the position. But I had come to believe that they needed three men to take on all of the responsibilities the president had. They needed an Office Manager, which I would be able and willing to do. But they also needed a Field Director, which I was not qualified to do as I did not speak Spanish and had no field experience. I also believed that they needed someone to represent Mexican Medical in the local churches, Bible schools and seminaries. This person would need a doctorate degree from a seminary in order to have credibility in the community, and I did not have that. So I told them it was my opinion that they needed three men to replace Mel. He had too many responsibilities placed on him, and that's probably one of the reasons why he had so many health issues.

A few months later, the Board finally decided on one man who should take upon himself all these responsibilities and become their new president, and then Lorraine and I spent the following year orienting him.

The new president then approached us in the spring of 2003 and explained that he believed we could better serve the ministry by either returning to Canada to promote it there and to bring and lead Short-Term Missionary teams to Mexico, or by living in Mexico as missionaries. He encouraged us to take a month to travel the Baja Peninsula, seeking the Lord's guidance.

So much had taken place in our lives during a short period of time. Lorraine and I had seen our youngest son complete his education and move out. We had transitioned from the secular workforce to becoming missionaries once again, and I had started a new charitable organization in Canada. We had moved from Kelowna, BC, to San Diego, CA, and I had become an American citizen.

We had rented and lived in two different townhouses in Chula Vista (a suburb of San Diego) during this time, and then, because rents were so high, we lived for a year and a half in a Class C motor home, moving from one RV Park to another every two weeks. We were tired of that and glad to consider living somewhere else.

While in San Diego we attended New Hope Community Church in Chula Vista, and had made many friends there;

but because we had been so busy at Mexican Medical we had not gotten involved as much in their outreach ministries as we would have liked. Our focus had been on Mexico and now we were being given the opportunity to become even more focused in that direction.

At Mexican Medical, I had helped refocus their energies in the direction of evangelism, and had brought more people into the Mexican Medical family and onto the mission field in Mexico than they had seen for years. And I had instituted a computerized accounting system so that they could become financially responsible. I had also obtained tenants for the second floor of their building, written up leases for them, and managed the construction of their office spaces.

At this particular time it seemed as though another chapter of our lives was nearing its end. We felt good about what we had accomplished, and were ready to move on. But we did not have peace in our hearts about moving back to Canada, so we were looking forward to this next month—wondering if we might soon be moving to Mexico to become more involved in ministry to the Mexican people.

Lorraine and I spent the whole month of July traveling from Tijuana to Cabo San Lucas and back, taking it slow and looking at and praying over every town and city along the way. The Lord did speak to us, confirming to both of us individually, that we should move to Loreto, Baja California Sur.

As we travelled down the Baja Peninsula, we felt there was something about Loreto that was different from all the other towns we had been through. Peace overwhelmed my soul, and we could see ourselves living there. Then we were in one of the small churches in Loreto one Sunday morning, and we were given such a warm welcome and invitation to move to Loreto.

The pastors said they felt the Lord telling them that we had a lot we could help them with—yet we had not told them anything about our past or what we were praying about as we drove down Baja. They knew nothing about Mexican Medical, but they felt the Lord had spoken to them about us.

That same Sunday evening, we returned to this little church. Without the pastor knowing that Lorraine used to sing in churches in Canada, she handed Lorraine the microphone and asked her to sing while she prayed for the people who had come forward at the end of the service. Lorraine believed the Lord was speaking, telling her that there was ministry in Loreto that He was calling her to be involved in.

We knew the next phase of our lives was about to begin, and where that would be.

In His Hands

PHASE ELEVEN

Getting Started and Established in Loreto

First thoughts

After our travels down the Baja Peninsula during the summer in 2003, we returned to San Diego and reported that we felt the Lord leading us to move to Loreto—but that we did not have any idea of what ministries we might become involved in there.

To say the least, Mexican Medical's president was pleased, believing that the Lord was expanding the organization into another area of Baja. He explained to us however that Mexican Medical would not be building another hospital or short-term missionary compound in Loreto—but we understood this before we even took our road trip. Rather, they would encourage us and help us (as they were able) to create some kind of mobile ministry.

We were delighted with this confirmation, since Lorraine and I had already been discussing such a mobile ministry as we traveled back to San Diego.

The donation of our first vehicle

That fall we were given a 1992 Ford F250 truck that we had not asked anyone for, proving to us again that the Lord would provide all that we would need for our new endeavors.

We shared our pending move with our churches: New Hope Community Church in Chula Vista, Trinity Baptist Church in Kelowna, and South Delta Baptist Church in Tsawswassen. All were in accord with what we believed the Lord was leading us into, and they gave us further encouragement.

We made our second trip to Loreto in January 2004, and arranged to rent a small house. We then traveled to Canada to inform our family, friends, and supporters that we would be moving to Loreto the following March.

In mid-February, we returned to Chula Vista from Canada, bought a small cargo trailer on the way, and started packing the things we would immediately need in Loreto, leaving behind the balance of our belongings in the Mexican Medical warehouse.

By the end of the third week of February, we were ready to start our trek to Loreto—the first of what would be many trips that year as we transferred our belongings to Mexico.

Getting the appropriate Visas

When Lorraine and I entered Mexico on February 26, 2004, we obtained our Tourist Visas at the border, knowing we would eventually need our FM3 Visas.

It then took us almost three years to build sufficient credibility to satisfactorily complete our applications for FM3 Visas.

Why so long? Because we wanted to obtain *Ministro de Culto* FM3 Visas, which would allow us to legally and freely share the gospel with people, and be able to preach, etc. What most people do not know is that it is illegal for a foreigner to proselytize in Mexico. That is, a foreigner (even one with a Tourist Visa) does not have the legal right and freedom to influence a Mexican citizen to change their allegiance from one religion or political party to another.

However, many people have come to Mexico over the years and shared the gospel with the Mexican people, not realizing that it was illegal for them to do so. They know of others who have come without getting into trouble, so they continue coming and sharing the gospel without having the appropriate visas. But we also know people who have been deported for sharing Christ with others.

We chose to obey all of the laws in Mexico and apply for these specialized visas, both out of respect to the Mexican people and to be sure we would not get into trouble with the Mexican authorities. But as we proceeded, we learned that the application process was not going to be easy. Thankfully, the Lord brought people into our lives who helped make it all possible.

Applications for the *Ministro de Culto* FM3 Visas could not just be submitted to the local or state Mexican Immigration Offices. Rather, we first had to obtain the appropriate clearances and a special Letter of Approval from the Federal Secretary General, whose offices were in Mexico City.

We had heard from others that getting this man's approval was usually not easy, but the Lord had brought into our lives a man who was at that time the Comptroller General and the Minister of Finance for the State of Baja California Sur. Roman said it would be in our favor if he included a cover letter with our paperwork. Roman also suggested that he submit our request and applications as from the Governor's office.

Our applications to the Immigration authorities also required letters from our churches in Canada and the United States, certain documents pertaining to us from the Government of Canada, letters of recommendation from respected people in Mexico, copies of our personal financial records covering the previous three years, copies of our U.S. driver's licenses, copies of our Mexican Tourist Visas, a letter of guarantee from the source of the majority of our income (which at that time was Healing & Hope International), ten special individual photos of us, and copies and the originals of our U.S. Passport Books.

After all this was obtained, we put it in a package and sent it to our friend Roman at the Governor's office, who then added his cover letter and sent it off by special courier from the Governor's office in La Paz to the Secretary General's office in Mexico City.

Only a week later, we received a phone call from the Secretary General himself, asking for a slight modification to one of the letters we had submitted—which we were able to quickly get and courier back to him within a few days. He then couriered his Letter of Approval and all our documents back to us without any delay.

What a tremendous joy it was for us to receive his Letter of Approval, and to receive it so quickly! We were now ready to go to the Immigration Office with our applications. But we found out it was still not going to be a simple application process.

We took our full application package to the local Immigration Office in Loreto, along with our Letter of Approval from the Secretary General. The man there quickly looked at everything, then asked us to return the following week because he wanted the manager to look at everything before proceeding with it.

We returned as requested, only to learn that our applications had not yet been looked at. Another week later, we did the same. Our applications still had not been looked at. This was the same story we had heard from others who had submitted applications for *Ministro de*

Culto FM3 Visas in Cabo San Lucas and in La Paz (the capital of Baja California Sur), so we were not surprised.

We continued to visit the Immigration Office in Loreto a few more times, until one day one of the newer officials took us aside. "I see that your applications are continually being put to the bottom of a pile on the manager's desk," he said. "I suggest that you ask that your applications be withdrawn and given back to you. Then take your applications to the Immigration office in La Paz and submit everything there."

So I called my friend Roman at the Governor's office and explained to him all that had happened and that we would be coming to La Paz to submit our applications to the Immigration Office there. He said he would phone the manager at the Immigration Office and make a special appointment for us.

The next week, we met Roman and went together to the Immigration Office in La Paz. The manager thanked Roman for making our appointment and then apologized for the delays we experienced in Loreto. He said that the same thing could have happened in La Paz if we had not come to him first, since few people in Baja California Sur have the special visas we were applying for and most of the people working at the Immigration Offices probably would not know how to process the *Ministro de Culto* FM3 Visa. Rather than admit it (which would be the same thing as saying they did not know how to do their job, and could get them fired), they would simply bury the application.

At the manager's request, we left our applications with him and agreed to return in a couple of weeks. We assumed that everything was now going to go through quickly, but this would not be the case at all.

We returned to the La Paz Immigration Office a few weeks later, as requested, but after a long wait to talk with anyone, we were told that we needed to come back the following day. The next day, soon after we arrived, we were simply told, "Your application papers all look to be in good order, so we'll now send your file to the Central Immigration Office in Mexico City."

We were then told that someone from their office would call to let us know when we should come back again, explaining that we should not expect to hear from them for about a month.

When over a month had passed, I called the Immigration Office in La Paz, and was again told that we must just wait for their phone call. We finally received their call about a week later, so we made our next trip to La Paz, which is about a five-hour drive from Loreto. Our appointment was for early the following morning, so this required driving to La Paz the afternoon before and staying in a hotel overnight.

When we arrived at the Immigration Office, we were asked to sign another document and told that it would be sent to the Immigration Office in Mexico City later that week, and that we would receive another phone call from their office to tell us when we should come back.

About a month later, we received their phone call and made another trip to La Paz. This time we just signed another paper for them, then made a payment at a local bank and returned to the Immigration Office to submit the receipt from the bank. We were told that our file had to be sent once again to the Central Immigration Office in Mexico City to obtain yet another approval, and that, "In another month or so, you will receive another phone call from us."

This process required us to make nine trips to La Paz— each one a ten-hour round trip—to sign papers, have our fingerprints taken, and make payments—and it all had to be done one step at a time.

We finally received our *Ministro de Culto* FM3 Visas about a year after the process began. On November 15, 2007, the final approval was given by the Immigration Office in Mexico City, then everything was returned to La Paz. Our Visa documents were then created and stamped in La Paz on November 22, but not actually given to us until December 5, 2007.

What a process! And I'll admit I got a little impatient at times, especially when people asked us, "Why are you bothering with all of this? It's not really that necessary, you know."

Well, the saga continued, because FM3 Visas had to be renewed every year. So we had to go through this same process each year, starting one month prior to the expiration of the current visa. In October, we sent our request to the Secretary General in Mexico City, and then after we had received his authorization, we went to La Paz to start again with the Immigration Office. Thankfully, this first renewal required only five or six trips to La Paz, and the second renewal required about the same.

During these first few years, we made over twenty trips to the Immigration Office in La Paz, and many times it was necessary to stay in a hotel overnight. Some people still say it was a waste of time and money, but through all of this, we met people we would not have met otherwise, connecting with churches, doctors, and others who helped make our evangelistic Community Health Fairs a success. And through it all we have built some lasting friendships.

Many people believe that if it seems like the government is getting in your way or trying to stop you, you should try to find a way around them, or just go ahead anyway with your ministry and try not to get into trouble. We have a different view, and have always tried to honor and respect those in authority over us by doing everything the legal way, even when it has been difficult or cost us a lot of time and money.

Some influential Mexican people who were well-connected politically have said, "Let us stand up for you if someone ever causes you any trouble. You don't need to worry. We'll take care of things for you. It's always who you know that counts." But I would usually respond with something like, "Thank you for your offer. We just might need to ask you to help us one day, but we still believe it is right for us to respect those in authority. Therefore, we'll do everything that's legally required to be able to do what we want to do for the Mexican people." Almost every time, people were surprised by our reply, but at the same time seemed to have more respect for us. Also as a result, we believe the Lord has blessed our ministries in a greater way.

In October 2009, we heard that one of the women we had worked with at the front counter at the Immigration Office in La Paz had been transferred to Loreto. So we went there to speak to her. She remembered us and was glad to see us, and suggested that we ask for our Immigration files to be moved to the Loreto Immigration Office. She had helped us previously and knew how to process everything for us, and this would save us all the trips to La Paz, so this was what we did. We still needed to go into the Immigration Office several times for the next renewal of our visas, but being able to do it all in Loreto sure made it easier.

The following year, when the time came to start the fourth renewal of our visas, we once again went to the Immigration Office in Loreto—but this time we were told that they only allowed three renewals for the FM3 Visa, so we needed to apply for FM2 Visas. It was the exact process that we had already become familiar with, so we sent our letter this time directly to the Secretary General in Mexico City requesting his approval for us to be able to submit applications for our FM2 Visas.

We became concerned when we did not hear back from the Secretary General as quickly as we had each time before. Then one day we learned that the Immigration laws were changing. The FM3 and FM2 Visas would no longer be issued; rather, one must apply for either a Temporary Resident Visa or a Permanent Resident Visa. Then when we went back to the Immigration Office in Loreto, we found that the woman we had been dealing with had returned to the La Paz office.

The man now in charge of the Loreto Immigration Office assured us that he knew what to do. I mentioned that we had already requested our Letter of Approval, but that we had not yet received it. He assured us that the new process was virtually the same and that the appropriate letter would likely be sent to us in due course.

A couple more days passed, and we still did not have the required Letter of Approval from the Secretary General. Knowing that our current visas were about to expire, we went to the Immigration Office in Loreto to speak to the manager again. He advised us to submit our applications to him without the required letter so that it could be shown that we tried to meet their deadlines, and said he would attach the required letter to the file when it arrived.

The next day we did exactly as we had been told, but as the manager looked at the papers, he said there must be another change made to our applications—a change we were not previously told about—and not telling us what the necessary change was, he said he would make it for us. So, trusting him, we left his office, wondering what would happen next.

Within a few days, we received a phone call asking that we return to the Immigration Office in Loreto again, which we did, not knowing if there was a problem or what was taking place. To our surprise, the manager told us that our Applications for Permanent Resident Status—

Ministro de Culto had been approved, subject only to receiving the letter of authorization from the Secretary General.

We were sure a miracle was on its way, and within the week we received the letter from the Secretary General stating we had his authorization to apply for permanent resident status.

We took this letter right to the manager of the Immigration Office in Loreto, and were issued our Permanent Resident Visa cards within just a few days. He told us that we were the first people in Loreto to receive the new Permanent Resident Visa and that we would no longer need to renew our visas every year. Praise the Lord!

Our first house in Loreto

Upon arriving in Loreto, we found that there were almost no houses for rent; but thankfully one man in the church knew of a house that had just been vacated by a tenant. We made an agreement with the landlord and rented it for just $150 per month. But there were several things I had to do to make the small, two-bedroom, cement-block house livable. The ceilings were falling down in the bedrooms and had to be propped up until I could make the necessary repairs. The kitchen had a few shelves but no cupboards. And the small bathroom needed tile repairs in its tiny shower. We had no hot water tank, no air-conditioning, and not even a refrigerator or a stove.

We were glad to have arrived, though, and I got to work immediately, making the bathroom usable, fixing the ceilings in the bedrooms, and adding some small window air conditioners. We needed to wait a short time before we could buy a refrigerator and a stove, and a while longer before I could get to installing a water heater and adding more shelving in the kitchen.

Over the next three years, we did many other things to improve the house. I fixed some of the plumbing and electrical, and painted the inside of the house (all nine hundred square feet). I then planted some trees in the front yard and several oleander plants along the rear property line and painted the outside of the house. The landlord always reimbursed us for what we had done.

Our First Team

Our first team arrived a couple of weeks after we moved to Loreto while we still had our Tourist Visas and no permanent permission to share the gospel. It was a church group of just over twenty young people from British Columbia. They stayed in one of Loreto's inexpensive hotels, the Brenda Hotel, and we had most of our meals together on the patio behind our house. As we did not have a refrigerator or a stove at the time, we used two coolers and prepared everything on our small hot plate. It was a start.

Challenged by Immigration

On the day after the team arrived, some Immigration officials appeared as I was speaking to our group in one of the churches. They asked what we were doing, how long our group would be in Loreto, and what we were planning to do during that time.

I told them that the group was from Canada, that Lorraine and I were Canadians (as well as being Americans), and that there were no Mexicans present in the church that morning.

They explained that as a foreigner having only a Tourist Visa, I could not speak to any group in public, and a church was considered to be a public place.

I told them we were planning to hold a community Health Fair offering free medical consultations and dental services, and giving away free reading glasses. They firmly told me that all of this could not be done by foreigners.

Not ready to accept what they had told me I said, "I'm sure the Mexican people here in Loreto would appreciate receiving the benefits of what we were planning to do. Could you please tell me what it is that I need to do so we can proceed with what we have planned?"

They were a little taken aback by my boldness and persistence, yet I had not made any demands, and from their perspective they were just there to shut us down.

After asking me where I lived in Loreto, they again told me to stop what we were doing and to take the group there, and that they would get back to me after they had spoken to the manager in their office.

So these two officials left to explain to their supervisor that they had stopped what we were doing and sent us home. But they also went back to their office with my question, and felt obligated to return to my home with an appropriate answer, as soon as they had spoken to their manager.

I went back in the church and explained what had happened, then we packed up, returned to our home, and prayed.

Early that afternoon, the same Immigration officers arrived at our home. "We don't know who you really are, but we have been told by our superiors in the Cabo San Lucas office that we are not to stop you from doing anything you want to do," they said. "However, we think it would be best that you submit on paper to our office what you will be doing, when and where you will be doing your programs, and the names and passport numbers of everyone who is in your group. That way, the next time someone calls our office asking about you or your programs, we can explain to them that you have the required permission to conduct the services you are offering.

I agreed and asked, "Will submitting this paperwork to you each time we have a group coming to put on these Health Fairs make what we will be doing legal?"

They answered, "It will not make your Health Fairs legal, but that way we can say we are fully aware of everyone who is part of your group and what you are doing."

So I compiled in my computer all the information they had requested, printed out the papers, and delivered it all to the Immigration Office in Loreto later that day.

And we then continued with all that we had planned.

———————————————

Why did the Immigration officials come back to me with the message they did? Could it be that my encounter with the hitchhiker five years earlier was still having a positive influence on my ministry?

In any case, we were off to a good start, having freedom to do anything we wanted to do, according to what the Immigration officers had told us.

Need and establishment of a non-profit corporation

Our Community Health Fairs were mainly done with teams from the United States and Canada at first, but it did not take us long to make connections with local Mexican doctors and dentists who would volunteer to help with these almost monthly Health Fairs.

For the first year, we submitted the names and passport numbers for everyone on our teams, as well as where we would be putting on our Health Fairs. But then an Immigration officer said we no longer needed to do this because they knew who we were and they had no problem with what we were doing. So we stopped submitting all this information.

However, after being in Loreto for a couple of years, we found out that a Mexican doctor or dentist could provide medical services legally throughout Mexico as an individual, but only as an individual health care provider. If they wanted to work or volunteer with others in a program offered to the public, they could only legally do so as an employee or volunteer under a For-Profit Corporation (such as a private medical clinic) or under a Non-Profit Corporation (such as most hospitals), called a Civil Association. And any program had to be put on by a corporation or by a Civil Association in order for the program to be a legal activity.

We then thought that if we put on our Health Fairs in churches, they would then be legal programs because churches were Religious Non-Profit Corporations. But we discovered that Corporations, Civil Associations, and Religious Associations cannot just put on any kind of a program they wish. Rather, all the programs must first be specifically described in their written bylaws. We also learned that bylaws cannot easily be changed or added to—it was an arduous legal task with necessary government approvals.

While none of the Mexican doctors and dentists or any of our other volunteers had ever gotten in trouble with the Mexican authorities for helping us; after praying about all of this, I decided that it was not right for us to continue putting on our Health Fairs in ways that were not legal, especially if it was going to put our volunteers at risk. We felt very strongly that we needed to do everything legally necessary to protect them, and not do anything that might hinder either the effectiveness or the continuance of the ministries God had called us to do.

So I continued my discussions with lawyers, notaries, accountants, and auditors, and collected information about what would be involved to establish and operate our own Civil Association. Within a couple of years, we created our own Civil Association that we appropriately named *El Curativo Y Esperanza, A.C.* (A Civil Association that proclaims "the Cure and the Hope"), which was what we were all about: proclaiming to the public the cure for their body, soul, and spirit, and proclaiming hope (the only true hope for all mankind being Jesus Christ).

Again, it could be argued that we really did not have to go to all the time and expense to set up our own Civil Association. People in Mexico and even our friends and coworkers in the United States assured us that it wasn't necessary. The Mexican authorities were very lax in enforcing many of their laws and could see the benefits we were providing to the people. And not only were there set-up costs, but there were also the monthly costs to have a Mexican accountant file all our activities with the government and pay any taxes that might be due.

We had our reasons, though, four in particular:

1. *We wanted to be obedient* to do what we believed God was calling us to do, and that meant not only putting on our Health Fairs, but also protecting our volunteers (even if most of them did not think they were putting themselves at risk).

2. *We wanted to be respectful* of the Mexican government and their laws and regulations. After all, we were in their country, and as Americans or Canadians we have no rights in their country that they do not give us, so there is no validity to being

arrogant and believing we could operate above their laws.

3. *We wanted to open doors for ministry,* not close them, so we believed that doing things legally would open doors for us to be involved in some ministries that we otherwise might not get to be a part of.

4. *We wanted to have a fruitful ministry*—the best possible—and we believed that the only way to have such results was to do everything legally. While we might not have needed it and probably never had a problem, and while we would have seen God bless what we did; we also believe that we would not have reaped all the blessings we have seen if we did not have our Civil Association. In other words, the only way to receive God's greatest blessings is to respect the government authorities God has placed us under.

Luke 10:27 says, "'Love the Lord your God with all your heart and with all your soul and with all your strength and with all your mind'; and, 'Love your neighbor as yourself.'" When we read these words, we understand that in order to love someone, we must first respect them, which requires putting aside any arrogance we might have, thinking that we are in some way better than them. It also requires trusting and believing in them, since they are just as valuable to God as anyone else.

So we have always done our best to respect the Mexican people—the people on the street, the people in the churches, and the people in the Mexican government—and also to respect the laws and regulations of their country. We were living in their country, and they were (and are) our next-door neighbors.

In practice, because we believed this was God's viewpoint that we should also have, we found it easy to truly love the wonderful Mexican people. We were not just there to put on programs.

Yes, it has cost us a lot of time and money to set up and run our Civil Association, but we believe doing everything legally under El Curativo Y Esperanza, AC is one of the reasons why our Health Fairs, and all the other things we have done, were so abundantly blessed by God.

Our second home in Loreto

After a couple of years of renting the small block house, we were given (and so glad to receive!) a large designated donation that we used to buy a larger property and start building a larger, more functional house.

The property we purchased for only $10,500 was on the outskirts of town. It was not only less expensive than in town, but it was also larger than most available lots in town—one on which we could easily park all our vehicles and trailers, and we had several by this time because of the ministries we were involved in. We had a truck, a fifteen-passenger van, and a small car. We also had a large toy-hauler trailer that I made into a two-chair Mobile Dental Office, a small 1976 travel trailer and an older 1978 RV (used for storing things and as a guest house), a small enclosed utility trailer and an even smaller open utility trailer.

We built the new house to accommodate all of our ministry supplies, and with room to hold ministry events such as pastors' meetings, Bible studies, special dinners, and the Bible school we had started.

The large donation mentioned got the construction started with several men working on it for a year, after which I slowly completed it with monies designated for it and with monthly retirement monies we received from the Canada Pension Plan and from Social Security in the

United States. We only worked on the house as time permitted, so it took over ten years to complete. I have always said, "Ministry will always take priority," so if we had an event planned, some other ministry going on, or something that I needed to prepare for, or if someone came along and needed help with something, I would stop what I was doing and focus on that.

Provisions making Health Fairs possible

When we began our free community Health Fairs, we had little equipment. Our dental ministry was conducted under a popup tent using a reclining patio lounge chair. Then a short time later, Richard Carnes and some other friends of ours in San Diego got hold of an old eighteen-passenger airport shuttle bus, took the seats out, put in a cabinet, and installed a dental chair, making it our first Mobile Dental Office. We put it into service on March 11, 2005, just one year after we began our ministries in Loreto.

We had dentists being flown in from the United States to help us with our Health Fairs in the beginning. Bill Neail, Jon Helland, and Suzi Lahitte from the San Diego area all brought many people to help us in their small four-seater planes, especially during those first few years. Landry Poole and a few other pilots also helped us occasionally, bringing dentists, doctors, or others to help. We are thankful for each one of them, as their help was absolutely critical to establishing the wonderful ministry we were involved in for almost fifteen years.

A fifteen-passenger van is donated

Dr. Jill Cottel, one of the doctors who had flown to Loreto a few times with her husband, Landry (he being a pilot), saw that we really needed a fifteen-passenger van to drive people around in Loreto, especially to help with transporting the teams. So they kept their eyes open until they found one for us, and in January 2009, they donated a fifteen-passenger 1997 Ford Van. It has been such a blessing to us in so many ways.

Special People vital to our Health Fairs

Within a couple of years, we no longer needed to rely solely on teams from the United States and Canada. We still had some people come during the following years, and we really appreciated everyone who came to help, but it did not take us long to become friends with many Mexican doctors and dentists who became vital volunteers at our Health Fairs. Let me tell you about a few of these wonderful people.

Dr. Gilberto Robles: One Sunday, a woman in the church we attended mentioned that she thought a Christian doctor was working at one of the clinics in Loreto, and she thought he spoke English as well. We went to that clinic on Monday morning and met Dr. Robles. That was in 2004. I first asked him if he was a Christian, and he said he was. Then, led by the Holy Spirit and with His boldness, I asked, "But how is it that you're not attending any of the churches in Loreto?"

He was understandably taken aback and replied, "How do you know that I'm not attending any church?" I told him that we had been to all of the churches in Loreto, and so we knew. He then told us that he had only been in Loreto for about a year, and he thought that God possibly wanted him to be a missionary someday, so he did not want to have to uproot his family from a new church and then settle into another new church in Africa or some other country.

I told him that he did not have to leave Loreto to become a missionary, because he could be a missionary right here. I told him about our Community Health Fairs, and said that if he partnered with us, he would conduct medical consultations and then pray with each patient.

He said, "I will do the medical part and then someone else can do the praying." I explained that we were not organizing our Health Fairs that way, and that it was a requirement that he pray with his patients. He argued that he was not prepared to pray with people, to which I responded that he could learn to do this within a short time of working with us—and so he agreed.

We became very good friends and soon understood that God was indeed speaking to Dr. Robles—but it was not so much to become a missionary. It was more about becoming *a real Christian*. Gilberto had read the Bible, and he of course believed all that he had read to be historically true, but he soon realized that there was more to becoming *'a real Christian'* than that. I believe that he recognized that he did not have a personal relationship with God (he had only an academic understanding), and that is why he could not pray with people. God was indeed working in his life.

About three months later, Gilberto's wife, Isis, came to me and asked, "What have you done, Don? What have you done to Gilberto? He's not the same man he used to be before he met you. He had wanted me to go to a church with him, but he was not living a good life. I just didn't want to have anything to do with his religion. But he's changed! It's like he's become a different person now."

I explained to Isis that knowing and believing the Bible to be true is not enough for anyone to be acceptable to God. I said that I thought that Gilberto had come into a personal relationship with Jesus Christ—and this is what changes a person for the better. Soon after my conversation with her, she too accepted Jesus Christ into her life, and a year later I had the privilege of baptizing her in Loreto.

During the next year, Gilberto, Isis, and their two children moved to La Paz, so there were a few years when he was not able to help us. But the Lord provided other doctors who could work with us, and I asked each of them to consult with their patients at our Health Fairs in a *body-soul-spirit* manner. I explained the connection between the body, soul, and spirit—how God created us this way, how we all need Christ's transformation in each of these areas of our lives, and how God loves all of us totally—*body, soul and spirit..., past, present and future.* This teaching then became the foundation for the way we conducted our evangelistic Community Health Fair ministry.

Dr. Maria-Elena (Malé) Gutierrez and her husband, Gabriel Cojab: In November 2007, we held our first Health Fair in Melitón Albañez (southwest of La Paz), at a small church being planted there by a church in La Paz. The pastor of this new church had invited several doctors and dentists to come and help us, and Malé and Gabriel came (Malé was a doctor, and Gabriel learned how to dispense glasses).

They came to almost every Health Fair we put on over the following seven years, and we got to know and appreciate them so much during that time. They have three children who were young when they started with us, but they became wonderful helpers. In fact, their oldest son, Jetro, began to assist the dentist and went on to take courses to become a dental technician—which he thought he might like to become.

Dr. Yxchel Clavel: In 2006, we met Yxchel. For a short time, she was a dentist at one of the hospitals that Mexican Medical built in Tijuana, but had moved away and everyone lost contact with her. Then Dr. Robles located Yxchel in La Paz. We all got together there to discuss our Health Fair ministry in detail, and from that time forward Yxchel and her assistant, Gloria Armendarez, were consistently a vital part of our Health Fair ministry for over ten years. In fact, Yxchel not only became our regular Health Fair dentist, she also translated and/or interpreted most of the messages I delivered during our Health Fair ministries in Baja California Sur.

Other Teams

Other teams of young people came to Loreto in the beginning to do construction-related activities in the mornings, hold children's ministries in the afternoons, show evangelistic Christian movies in different parts of the city at night, and hold Health Fairs on the weekends.

Teams replaced a roof on the house for one single mother, built outhouses for other single moms, put a concrete floor into another single mom's home, put indoor kitchen plumbing into a pastor's home, and more. Our requirement for the people we helped was that they be needy Christians who were active in their church. By this, we hoped to show the community that there were benefits not only to being a Christian and attending a church, but also to being active in an evangelical church. Being poor was therefore not our only requirement—we wanted the community to see the love of Jesus in action— that Christians cared for each other, and that *real Christianity* was not just something people believed with their minds.

It was wonderful. And more could have been done, but some churches in the United States and Canada told us that it was just too expensive to fly into Loreto and there were other less expensive places they could go. So we focused on our evangelical Community Health Fairs and to getting local Mexican Christians to help us.

Becoming involved with Messiah College

In 2012, Dr. Connie Ostwald contacted me. She was a professor of Economics at Messiah College, a Christian college in Pennsylvania. She explained that the college offered optional courses to its students between semesters each year, and that she would like to bring a group of students to Loreto for a course in cross-cultural studies. The students enrolling in her course would already have an interest in working cross-culturally when they graduated, although more likely in business than in missions.

It would be cost prohibitive for her students to stay in hotels and have all their meals in restaurants, so I suggested that they stay at our home. This would be an ideal opportunity to help Christian young people set their plans in motion for their future, and our involvement could possibly have an impact that might reach around the world. Now that may seem optimistic and even a bit altruistic, but I remembered the meaning of my name: *World Changer*, and how from my days in high school on, I believed that God had a plan for me to be involved in the lives of people who would have a worldwide impact.

This made me wonder if this class might be a part of God's bigger picture and plan. So with this in the back of my mind, and not sharing my thoughts with Connie or others, we proceeded with the plans to hold this Messiah College course at our home in Loreto.

For three weeks each January, from 2013 to 2016, we had twelve students sleeping in sleeping bags on cots on our patio, using our bathrooms and outdoor kitchen, and holding classes on our patio. Each morning, Connie taught her economics course on cross-cultural studies on our patio, then Lorraine and I would answer questions and give examples from our daily lives and ministry. We also took excursions throughout Loreto in the van we had been given. We enjoyed every minute of our time together—going on the excursions, sharing meals, attending local churches and working alongside them at the Health Fair.

Above all, we were very glad, over these four years, to have helped forty-eight young adults make life-changing decisions, and we have received thanks from many of them. Lorraine still enjoys keeping in touch with many of them through Facebook.

Our Mobile Dental Offices

We had to make some adjustments over the years, and the Lord guided us and supplied everything we needed in every situation. We started our Health Fairs using patio lounge chairs for our dental chairs and then moved to the Mobile Dental Office converted from the old airport shuttle bus by our friends in San Diego—what a blessing that was.

However, a couple of years later, the diesel engine on our Mobile Dental Office needed some work and we could not find a reliable diesel mechanic in Loreto. (We had assumed such a mechanic would be in Loreto if and when we needed one, but now we were being told that Loreto had no good diesel mechanics—something we should have researched earlier.) So Mexican Medical decided that it would be best to give our first Mobile Dental Office to one of their missionaries in Cabo San Lucas, and buy us a used toy-hauler trailer that I could make into a two-chair Mobile Dental Office. It was ready to be put into service in February 2009.

A replacement truck becomes necessary

The following year, our 1992 Ford truck started losing its power and having difficulty pulling our new Mobile

Dental Office up the hills around Loreto. The fastest we were able to go up hills was only twelve miles per hour. We started asking for donations to help us buy a newer truck—one that could pull the ten-thousand-pound trailer—and in January 2011 we were able to purchase a 2001 Ford F350 diesel truck. It was a wonderful truck, and could easily pull our dental trailer anywhere we wanted to take it.

An accident brings about some changes

Early one evening during the summer of 2014, we were towing a brand-new thirty-foot travel trailer on Highway 99, about seventy miles north of Bakersfield, California, when our left front tire suddenly delaminated. It lost all of its tread and left us driving on its steel belts. This should not have happened to a two-year-old tire that was properly inflated. It was later determined that it happened due to a manufacturing defect.

I could not keep the truck from swerving back and forth. It was like we were skating on ice. The force of it just got stronger as I let the truck slow down without hardly using the brakes, and before we knew it, the truck veered hard to the left from the right lane. The truck and our trailer rolled onto the passenger side, and we slid down the highway, ending up across both of the northbound lanes.

This happened around 7:00 p.m., when the highway was busy. Many cars, trucks, and semi-trailers had been constantly speeding past us, as we had been going only about fifty miles per hour. Fortunately, the semi-trailer driver behind us saw us swerving, and was able to stop just in time, avoiding running into us. If he not been able to stop, he would have hit us, or run over us—our truck and trailer had the whole highway blocked.

Thankfully, no other accidents occurred as the cars and trucks started to pile up on the freeway for many miles behind us. Later that night, one of the policemen told us that in almost every accident on this stretch of highway, some of the other vehicles lining up would hit each other as they tried to stop. He said it was *a miracle* that no other vehicle was involved in our accident, and *a miracle* that no other accident happened as a result. And because we knew God was looking after us through all this, we told him we agreed with his assessment.

So there we were, trapped in our truck on its side (actually a little more over than that, because the truck was straining in an effort to roll onto its roof, but the strong trailer hitch kept that from happening). Lorraine, in the passenger seat, lay against her door in broken glass, and I was suspended by my seatbelt above her. I had only a couple of scratches, and Lorraine had only a small bruise on her arm and some scratches. We were not seriously injured—*another miracle*.

Within about a minute (or less, it seemed), a man was above me kneeling on the driver's door, asking if I could open my window. I thought, *That's probably impossible*, but when I pressed the button, down came the window. He first helped me out of the truck, then went into the truck's cab himself to help Lorraine out.

As Lorraine was being taken to the side of the road, where she could sit on the roadside guardrail, a woman came up to me, saying, "We have been watching over you and praying for you since you first started to have problems controlling your truck, but we have to go now!"

Almost immediately after that, the police and the firemen arrived, and asked us where we were hurt. We told them we were fine, although we were shocked by what had happened. They wanted to take us to the nearby hospital to have us checked over, but we insisted that was not necessary. So one of the policemen asked us to sit on the back of the fire truck and try to relax, and after they had everything organized he said someone would take us to a hotel.

During all this, we were of course praising the Lord that we were not seriously hurt, but I was also wondering, *Who were those people who were there to help us so quickly? And why did they have to leave so suddenly, just as the emergency people were coming?* Then I recalled the woman saying, "We have been watching over you and praying for you since you first started to have problems controlling your truck." As I continued praising the Lord, I had to wonder if they could have been angels—*another miracle.*

The tow truck that came was not able to pull the truck and trailer apart to let the traffic get by. So they called in a large tow truck with a sky-hook, and this truck was able to lift our truck enough to pull it away from the trailer-hitch connection. The truck and trailer were then moved sufficiently out of the way, and the traffic started to flow again about three hours after the accident happened.

After our truck had been towed to a storage facility, the tow-truck driver returned and told us that he had ordered a flatbed trailer for our trailer, but that it would not arrive for maybe an hour. So he offered to drive us to a hotel.

He came back the next morning and took us to the storage yard so we could reclaim the personal things we would like to have. He told us that the highway wasn't cleared and back to normal until 1:00 a.m. because of all of the debris.

And again I praised the Lord that neither we nor anyone else was hurt in this serious accident.

We then rented a van, put all our belongings in it, and drove to the Mexican Medical office in San Diego, where we stayed for several days while we got things back in order. We were told that the frame of our truck was bent so badly that the truck was no longer drivable, and we were told that our trailer was so badly damaged that it was not feasible for anyone to even try to repair it. So we had some decisions to make.

A couple of years prior to this accident, we were given a small, older travel trailer that had ends (where the beds were) that folded out like a tent-trailer. We were grateful to receive this trailer, but it leaked a little when it rained, and the termites had started to work on its wood frame. We were also getting tired of setting up and making the bed every time we moved the trailer. So we started to think about selling it and getting a newer trailer.

A few years earlier than this, my parents had given us a gift that they told us was not to be used for ministry expenses but for something personal. We had not spent this money when we received it, instead putting it away until we could decide what to spend it on. While we were camping in Yuma, Arizona, just before the accident happened, we looked at a very nice larger new trailer and traded in our old one for it. But then the accident took place just six days afterward.

Our immediate question was, "Did we make a mistake buying this new trailer?" The answer was quickly understood, because this new trailer had saved our lives. If the accident had happened with the older trailer, it would have just crumbled apart, especially when the truck strained to roll over on the highway. But the new trailer, with its metal frame, stayed mostly together like one big box. The dealership where we purchased the trailer had also installed an extra-strong trailer hitch, so it did not bend much under the stress as the truck tried to roll completely over. These things prevented the trailer from smashing apart and prevented the truck from rolling onto its roof.

So rather than questioning God about whether we had misunderstood Him or made a mistake in buying this trailer, we praised Him for guiding us to buy it.

We learned later that in similar cases, due to this same manufacturing defect, some of those trucks rolled completely over when a tire delaminated, killing their passengers. So while we were disappointed that we had lost our new trailer, we were thankful to have been pulling it at that time.

When I contacted our insurance company to explain the accident, they told me that we did have full coverage on the trailer, but did not have collision insurance on our truck. I was mystified and dismayed. But a couple of days later, after they had checked their records further, they called and said that we did have full coverage on the truck as well as the trailer.

But a thought still lingered in our minds: *Was the Lord trying to tell us something through all of this?* We pursued a few ideas, and one seemed stronger than anything else, so we shared our thoughts with the president and vice-president of Mexican Medical.

I explained that one of their Board members, a truck driver, had mentioned to me previously that I should seriously consider not pulling our Mobile Dental Office/trailer, after age sixty-five. He had said, "The highways in Baja are winding and narrow, and you won't know when your diminishing capacity will start to affect you." So, I said, "Maybe the Lord was telling me to stop pulling our thirty-foot dental trailer. What are your thoughts?" I asked.

They said, "Since we have other people interested in possibly becoming full-time missionaries with Mexican Medical and moving to Loreto, we'll just ask them to bring a truck with them. Maybe this accident will help them decide to move to Loreto more quickly." So after consulting with Mexican Medical, we decided not to buy another big truck to replace the one lost in this accident.

We thought, *How wonderful! The Lord is providing for a continuation of the ministries after we leave Loreto.* We had no plans to move from Loreto at that time, but we wondered if maybe the Lord might.

The following week we received our insurance money, enough to buy another trailer and a vehicle to pull it, and have some money left over. When looking at things from a different perspective, we could see that the Lord had not only protected us during the accident, but also provided for other financial needs through the accident.

Not needing a big truck, we purchased a 2005 Chevy Tahoe and replaced the trailer with one that did not weigh as much and could be pulled by an SUV. Then in September that year, a Ford F250 (V-10) was given to Mexican Medical to replace our truck and to help with other ministry needs. But the decision had been made that I would not be pulling the dental trailer on the highways in Mexico any longer, so that meant we would need to keep our Health Fairs in Loreto for the time being. It also meant that when we needed to take the Health Fairs to another city, the Lord would provide the necessary drivers. That was how we viewed things, and, indeed, that fall, Steve Crews, the president of Mexican Medical, and his wife, Jan, started coming to Loreto to drive the truck, pull the dental trailer, and assist us with our Health Fairs.

So far, the people who had shown an interest in becoming missionaries with Mexican Medical have not made any decisions about coming to Loreto, but we are eagerly waiting to see what the Lord will do.

The Lord provided everything needed

From the small things to the large, God continued to supply each and every need, enabling us to put on the Health Fairs throughout Baja Sur. Everything we needed, whether it was reading or distance glasses, or glucose-testing machines, or test strips, was either given to us outright, or we were supplied with sufficient donations to buy them. This was true for everything else we needed too: Gospels of John for everyone who attended our Health Fairs, Bibles and New Testaments for those who wanted one, tracts and books, and hygiene gift bags for the children.

All of the equipment we needed was also given to us, including a weigh scale for babies, blood pressure cuffs, many dental instruments and supplies, an autoclave machine to sterilize the dental instruments, and the list goes on. An airport shuttle bus converted into our Mobile Dental Office, the toy-hauler trailer that I remodeled into a two-chair dental office, and the fifteen passenger van to transport people. These are just some of the major things the Lord supplied. The full list would be daunting.

The Lord provided everything we needed by urging different people at different times to help us in varying ways—and almost every time, the things we needed were given without us having specifically asked for them.

We are living proof that when a person is obedient to go where the Lord directs, and listens and follows His instructions about what they should be doing—what ministries to be involved in, and what priorities to have from day to day—the Lord will provide everything needed to carry out His plans.

Partners in Ministry

The Lord urged people in varying ways to help us in our ministries and because those people obeyed the Lord's guidance, we have seen many people blessed. It is because of this kind of cooperation by those who have supported our ministries (through prayer and/or financial support) that we refer to them as our Partners in Ministry.

Let me share a few examples of how a supporter was a partner. A couple of men living in the San Diego area prayed about how they could support our ministries. The Lord led them to the airport shuttle bus, which they had the skill to convert into our Mobile Dental Office—an unexpected and most appreciated gift.

After we had been conducting our Health Fairs for a few years, one of our supporters in Canada said, "I want to give you a donation, but it's not for your support or for supporting any of your current ministries. I would like you to develop something that would encourage people to grow in Christ."

After praying about this and receiving her donation, we decided to buy Study Bibles, large-print Bibles, a few books on apologetics, and some Bible correspondence-course materials. I then found a supplier who would give us discounted prices, and bought as much inventory as I could. We then took these books and Bibles to the churches where we held our Health Fairs, blessing people all over the State of Baja Sur. We did not just give all these books and Bibles away to people; we sold them—for less than what we had paid for them. Then the money we received from our sales was used to buy more books, so more people would be blessed than just those who got the first batch of books and Bibles.

We believed that if people paid something for a book or Bible, they would value it more. Each book or Bible was sold for about half of what it would cost in a Christian bookstore. (Most of these towns and villages had no Christian bookstores, so we were not taking business away from anyone.)

This supporter's donation, and the funds from the sales of these books and Bibles, supported and continued this ministry for several years.

Another time, a woman from La Paz helped us on one of our teams to the Santa Rosalía Prison, where she saw some men without shoes on their feet. She felt led by the Lord to buy twenty pairs of new shoes and send them to us, to give to the men she had seen.

We took these shoes to the prison, but the director explained that if we gave the new shoes to only some of the inmates, it could cause a riot, or the shoes might simply be sold so that the men could buy drugs. I then asked if there would be any problems if we gave the men used shoes, and he agreed that would be a better idea.

We went to the flea market in Loreto and exchanged the twenty pairs of new shoes for twenty-eight used pairs. This raised a lot of questions—people wanted to know why we were doing this—and this gave us opportunities to talk about our ministry in the prison. Also, because we received twenty-eight pairs of shoes in exchange for the twenty pairs we had, more men were blessed.

But when giving out these twenty-eight pairs of shoes, we found there were still eight men without any shoes. We returned to the prison the following week carrying eight more pairs of shoes. The eight men and others were impressed that we had returned so quickly. This gave more credibility to the message I had given at the prison the previous week.

So many of our supporters came up with ministry ideas, and gave us the wherewithal to carry them out. As a result, new facets of our ministry were born, and many people were blessed. We view these people not just as our supporters, but as people who have earned the right to be called Partners in Ministry.

Evangelistic Community Health Fairs

The Health Fairs, held almost every month from October to May or June for fifteen years, were the foundation of our ministry in Loreto. We held them in churches in many of the small towns, villages and cities throughout Baja Sur. We traveled as far north as Santa Rosalía, (about a three-hour drive from Loreto) and as far south as Melitón Albañez (about a six-and-a-half-hour drive from Loreto). We also took these evangelical Health Fairs into the prison in Santa Rosalía and the prison in La Paz.

Our plan at the beginning was to hold these Health Fairs in public locations, so our first one was planned in a small community south of Loreto—on their community basketball court. We first obtained all the local governmental approvals, and then did a little canvassing in the surrounding neighborhood the week before to invite people.

Many people were pleased to hear about the coming Health Fair and said they would be there. However, the following weekend, after we had set up all our stations and tables, not one person showed up. Everyone on the team wondered why.

I asked a couple of the local church members from Loreto who had joined us that day to revisit the families who had said they would come and find out why they changed their minds. It turned out that someone who had received our invitation had told one of the leaders of the local Roman Catholic Church about our Health Fairs—and that it was being sponsored by one of the evangelical churches in Loreto (the printed invitations we had given out stated this). The priest had then visited everyone in their community the day before our scheduled Health Fair and said something like, "If you go to this Health Fair, then you will be a very long time in purgatory, and most likely go to hell."

Wow. But that was the report that came back to us, and not just from one of those who went out asking what had happened, but from several.

A few months later, we planned to hold our Health Fairs in a central park in Mulegé, which is about two hours north of Loreto. We were unable to obtain the necessary approval from the local government official, however, because it was again to be sponsored by the evangelical churches. So how did we get around this?

We held a couple of our Health Fairs in the front yards of people's homes, which seemed to work well, but the ground was not always clean and level, and the yards were quite small for the crowds of people who came.

We also took our Health Fairs to the migrant worker camps near Loreto, but the attendance was always small. Those in charge of these farms wanted their workers to work six very long days every week, and it was difficult to hold our Health Fairs in the evenings because none of the buildings at these camps had electricity or street lights.

So we decided it would be better to go to other places where our efforts would yield greater results—into small evangelical churches.

In a short time, we discovered that holding the Health Fairs in churches worked much better than other public places, for several reasons:

> 1. We had between one hundred and four hundred people attending most of our Health Fairs. While no one church could accommodate four hundred people at one time, we found that people would come in a steady stream throughout the day rather than all at once. The churches offered shade, chairs for people to sit on, a friendly environment, and no

requirement to obtain government approval before each Health Fair.

2.   An evangelical Health Fair requires many Christian volunteers, and we wanted to have Mexican Christians helping us, not only because they spoke the language, but also because there would not be resistance when receiving spiritual counsel from a friend or neighbor, rather than from a foreigner.

3.   It is difficult to get people to attend the small evangelical churches, but the Health Fair made it easier, as we offered what people valued and needed: medical attention. After a Health Fair, the new people found it easier to attend a regular church service there, because a level of trust had been built with the people who regularly attended. Through attending these Health Fairs, people could also see that true Christianity was not just something in the mind, but also a way of living that helps people in practical ways.

4. Because we held the Health Fairs in churches, people subconsciously came knowing that there would likely be a spiritual element to the program we were putting on. They were therefore open to receiving the message of salvation. This same openness would not likely have been there had we held our Health Fairs in parks.

At the beginning of each day of our Health Fairs, I would speak to those who had come, explaining that we were there to treat people as whole persons—body, soul and spirit. That way, they would not only receive the physical benefits they came for, but also, if they desired, the blessings of God's health in every area of their lives.

5.   Most people do not know or understand that Mexico has laws against proselytization—in the areas of both politics and religion. But there is complete religious freedom in churches, and we had wonderful opportunities to share the love of Jesus and the message of salvation with people at every one of our Health Fair stations—because we were in churches.

6.   We quickly discovered that people in these small evangelical churches needed to be taught how to effectively share the message of salvation with people. So holding the Health Fairs in small churches gave us the opportunity to teach people how they could become involved in sharing Christ with others.

7.   When I approached a pastor about holding a Health Fair in his church, I would begin by explaining that the Health Fairs would not be an event in the park that members of his church could come to and bring their friends to. Rather, it would be at his church, not just as a benefit to his church members but also as an outreach event of the church.

I'd go on to explain to him, and afterward to his small congregation, that these Health Fairs would be *like turning the light on* in their church, and people would see this light shining out its windows and be attracted to the church, possibly in a way they had never been before.

We offered to train people prior to the event, and when they applied the teaching, the *light* would come on.

When the people in the church took hold of this idea, they took ownership of these outreach events. It became *their* outreach program, not just a program they might have given some help to in a park, and they would put all they had into it.

8. We provided churches with printed invitations to the Health Fairs, with the instruction that they were *not* to distribute them door-to-door or put piles of them in the local stores for people to pick up. They were told to give them instead to their family, friends, coworkers, and next-door neighbors—the people they already had a relationship with. It would be an invitation to their church—not to hear a preacher but to receive free medical and dental services, and to receive free glasses, etc. The church members saw this as an easy task, and they drew people into their churches in ways they had not been able to do before.

9. Because they had taken ownership of the Health Fair as being *their* outreach event, the people wanted to be trained in how to put it on. I would share with them how easy it can be to share the love of Jesus and the message of salvation with others, and gave them a simple and strategic plan to do so. Many Christians became active in sharing their faith with others and praying with others, and it became a way of life for many of them following the Health Fair. (You can read more about this easy way to share the love of Jesus and the message of salvation with others in the Appendix A.)

Our Health Fairs were not only a physical blessing to thousands of people, but they were also a spiritual blessing as well, introducing people to Jesus Christ and helping those who were already Christians by giving them instruction on sharing the love of Jesus and the message of salvation with others.

Often, at the conclusion of a Health Fair, someone from the church would ask us how soon we could have another

Health Fair there. They found it so easy to share their faith as a result of the teaching they received and the natural opportunities that these Health Fairs created. Many of these people had never shared their faith with others before, and they were excited to do it again.

In October 2007, we held a Health Fair in a church in Santa Rosalía, and the pastor there, Pastor Delmar, invited us to work with him and others who had a ministry among the inmates in the Santa Rosalía State Prison. About twenty men were meeting for Bible study and prayer almost every day, and he asked if we would consider having a Health Fair in the prison as a way of showing the love of Jesus to all the inmates there. We prayed about this, and the following year we started doing so once or twice a year for over ten years.

On one occasion, after three days of Health Fairs, I spoke to an assembly of 254 inmates. I explained that there is more evidence for God being the Creator of everything than for everything having been created by some evolutionary process. However, there is a reason why evolution is an acceptable teaching for many people, and it is this: if people can believe there is no God, then obviously there will be no Judge to face at the end of their lives, and no hell to go to for wrongs committed.

But the evidence shows that God did create everything, and everything for its own purpose, so it is easy to see that God will be there at the end of our lives to judge whether we lived out our created purpose or not. I explained that we all deserve to go to hell because of the lives we have lived and the wrongs we have done, but God offers us a way out: He will grant us a pardon, allowing us to go to heaven; but that pardon can only be obtained on His terms.

Then I said, "How do I know that this is true? Because it's all written down for us by God in this book." I pointed to the Bibles we had brought. "And you can pick one up today to read it all for yourselves."

That day, 220 Bibles were taken, and the men started to read them. A few months later, I spoke about the same thing, using a parable I had created, and another 141 Bibles were taken.

In 2016, the newly appointed director of the State Prison in La Paz asked us to come and speak with him. We did not know what to expect.

The meeting with the director and the captain of the prison began with the director saying, "We know our ways are not working, so we need to implement some changes, and we believe you can help us with this."

In March 2017, we took our first Health Fair team to the State Prison in La Paz, and over those three days, more than 250 inmates asked for New Testaments and Bibles, and over 50 inmates prayed to accept Jesus Christ as their Lord and Savior.

PHASE TWELVE

Life and Ministry In and Around Loreto

In addition to putting on evangelistic Health Fairs almost every month, we had quickly gotten busy with other ministries as well.

Pastors' Fellowship Meetings

Within days of arriving in Loreto, we learned that the pastors of the local churches did not speak to each other. One pastor even told us that if they saw another pastor walking towards them on the same side of the street, they would cross the street to walk on the other side—just so they would not have to greet each other. I thought, *How very sad! This has got to change!*

I believe the Lord blesses those who work together in unity with other believers in a greater way than He blesses people and churches individually when there is no unity. So within a couple of weeks of arriving in Loreto, we invited the evangelical pastors to our home for coffee and to share what was going on in their churches, and then to pray for each other. We only had three pastors come to that meeting, but it was a start.

We met each month in our home for several years—until one of the pastors told me privately that he could no longer come to our Pastors' Fellowship Meetings and sit across from one particular pastor. He said it disrupted his spirit so much that it often took weeks before he felt normal again. Again, how sad to think that his attendance at these meetings was negatively affecting his ministry in his church.

So we stopped what we were doing with the pastors at that time, and instead encouraged a few of the pastors who got along well with each other to continue getting together each month under the leadership of one of them. Within a few months, the second Pastors' Fellowship organization was started, and they met without giving an invitation to the "offending pastor."

However, about a year later, this particular pastor (without invitation) started attending their meetings, and soon tried to take over. So the second Pastors' Fellowship organization stopped meeting as well.

A few months later, under the leadership of another local Mexican pastor, a Pastors' Alliance was formed with our encouragement, and it continues to this day—but still with only about 60 to 80 percent of the pastors attending each month. Some of the churches represented in this Pastors' Alliance have even gotten together for some functions and outreaches.

It was a struggle getting to where they are today, but what a positive change has resulted between the pastors and between the churches since we first arrived in Loreto.

A Bible School

One example of this cooperation happened after several years of Pastors' Fellowship Meetings—three of the pastors wanted to start a Bible school in Loreto. It would be open to all members of the evangelical churches. These pastors didn't want to cause a problem between any of the churches by holding it in one of their churches, so we offered our home/ministry center as a meeting place. A Bible school was then started and held one night a week with the three pastors taking turns teaching.

The first year the enrollment was not large, but the pastors were not discouraged. After all, it was only the first year, and we all believed more students would come the second year. We were proven wrong, however. The students appreciated what was taught, but the teachers often did not arrive before the classes were to begin— sometimes they were up to an hour late. So the students lost their interest and enthusiasm, and while most of them completed the year, they did not want to enroll for a second year.

Conferences and Courses

Soon after we arrived in Loreto, the Mexican government announced that Loreto had been chosen as the next city to be turned into a mega-tourist attraction, following Cancun, Cabo San Lucas, and others. The federal government was predicting that by the year 2020, the population of Loreto would exceed two hundred and fifty thousand people. This created a local expectation and work began creating new areas where homes could be built, etc. Workers from other areas of Mexico moved to Loreto, and the population of Loreto started to grow. A movement had certainly started in preparation for this anticipated population explosion.

In 2004 when we arrived in Loreto, there were only about twelve thousand people living in the city, so this was going to bring huge changes. Therefore in 2006, I held a conference for pastors and other church leaders in one of the hotels in Loreto. The subject was, "Church Growth: What's Needed to Reach an Ever-Increasing Population."

I also helped organize another weekend conference in Loreto, this time for men only, encouraging them to grow deeper in their relationship with Christ, and to become more responsible as husbands, fathers, and men in the church. After that, some men met in our home for thirteen weeks learning how to lead Home Bible Studies.

A few years later, I organized another conference, bringing a special speaker to Loreto. This time the conference was for both men and women, and the subject was "Living the Christian Life Well Begins with Having a Firm Foundation."

However, in 2008 the world economies took a downturn and the growth of Loreto stagnated at just less than twenty thousand people. Many appreciated and benefited from our conferences and courses even though the time was not right for the City of Loreto to have its anticipated population explosion.

I continued to put on other programs in Loreto for a few years such as the "Purpose Driven Life" program, followed by "The Alpha Course".

Church programs

We assisted the church we attended in many ways, too. In our first three years in Loreto, we helped develop a Sunday school program for the children (before this, they simply provided child care).

We also showed Christian videos in the evenings, held Health Fairs, and gave Christmas gifts (books and Study Bibles) to everyone in the church, as well as doing many other things for them.

A few years later, we were asked by the pastor of a newly established church to help them start a Home Bible study program in their church, So we left the church we had been a part of and started to attend this new church.

A couple of months later the pastor of this new church said that he did not yet have mature Christians to appoint as leaders of Home Bible studies, and for several years people would attend his church for a short time and then leave. But we continued to attend and bring other English-speaking people with us.

This church offered several programs for teenagers over the years. At one point, the pastor was interested in putting on an Easter Music Concert targeting the young people in Loreto, and I was asked to help. So in 2014 we put on *"Enquentro Loreto."*

Helping churches in practical ways

We helped several pastors and churches in Loreto in a variety of practical ways, however never by just giving them money. We helped with construction, renovation, and maintenance projects, but always required the participation of their members as well. So we worked together and told them we would look forward to coming back to see the project after they had completed it.

We believed we were there to help them or partner with them in various ways, but not ever to tell them what to do, how things should be done, or to do things for them that they were capable of doing by themselves.

When people came from Canada or the United States to assist us in our ministries we made sure the same was true for them. We would all help a church build or improve their building, but only as long as there were people from the church working alongside us. Many times we provided only labor and no financial contribution.

We simply assisted these churches in what they were doing: practicing the "family of God" according to Ephesians 5, submitting ourselves to each other, not one lording over the other. We did everything this way out of respect for the nationals whom we loved, and we were respected and appreciated by all those we helped.

Helping single mothers

As I mentioned, we also helped some single mothers in Loreto, and in these cases we did pay for the necessary construction materials; but the labor was done in partnership with some of the men from their churches. Anyone who saw what we were doing would think it was the men from the church who were helping the women, with some Americans or Canadians assisting. I felt it was important for onlookers not to interpret what these women were receiving as just another gift from some Americans or Canadians.

We had four requirements for a single mother to qualify for such assistance: (1) she had to be an active member of one of the evangelical churches in Loreto (not just a frequent attender), (2) she had to have a need she was incapable of handling by herself, (3) she did not have family in the area that could help her and (4) she had to be known by Lorraine and me to be a woman of integrity.

We wanted to show people that there were practical benefits to being a believer in Christ and an active member of a church where people are loved and cared for by each other. Our hope was that other people would want to become believers and active members in these churches.

A couple of times, we helped single mothers who did not have good bathroom facilities. They were maybe using a corner of their property as an outhouse behind cardboard or a blanket attached to some kind of posts they had found. We built these young mothers good outhouses.

One of the single mothers had a son with asthma, and when we had been invited to their home for some occasion, I saw that the boy's bedroom had brick walls with dust accumulating on the cement ledges between each row of bricks. I suggested that we plaster over the bricks, filling in all the ledges that collected dust, which would make breathing easier for her son. She agreed and we had the work done.

One time, as we were unpacking some donated chairs in a church, one of the ladies helping (a single mother who was very active in that church) asked if she could have the boxes the chairs came in. I asked what she wanted to do with the boxes, and she said that she would use them to somehow make the outside walls of her house. I then asked if we could come and see her home, and she agreed. Upon seeing the structure of her home, I suggested that we buy some two-by-fours and put up at least a primitive structure for her, according to her design, to which she could hang the cardboard in a fairly secure manner. She was thrilled with the help we gave her.

Another single mother and her children lived in a house with a *palapa* roof (one made of palm fronds), and it leaked badly when it rained. We had a team help the men of her church put a new roof on her house.

Likewise, we replaced the dirt floor of a mother's home with concrete. She and her children took all their things out of the house and covered it with makeshift tarps, then the men from the church, together with a team of young people from Canada, made cement in wheelbarrows and laid a new floor for her. Once the concrete dried, she and her children moved their things back into the house.

So many people were helped in various ways—all in partnership with the local evangelical churches, and the community saw that.

Helping Churches and Pastors

The resources we received from our supporters were made available to the local churches and pastors in a variety of ways. We had a generator to operate our Mobile Dental Office, and I would set it up at times for a special outreach that one of the churches was having. We supplied many churches with cases of Bibles to be given to new Christians attending their churches. With our video projector and large outdoor portable screen, we would go with members from one of the churches into the neighborhoods and show evangelistic films.

We had six large folding tables that we used at our Health Fairs and for special events we held at our home. We also had sixty-five folding metal chairs that had been given to us for special events, and we often lent these tables and chairs to the churches so they could hold special meetings or other outreach events in the community.

We also helped pastors in personal ways by having certain things donated to them by people in the United States. We would then transport these items (such as a vehicle, an air conditioner, a TV, etc.) to Loreto for them.

On almost every trip we made to San Diego, we would return with something for someone. Many times these items were just small necessary items, but we simply wanted these people—pastors especially—to know we loved and cared about them.

Helping people after hurricanes

From mid-August through early October, the people in Baja California Sur brace themselves for the possible onslaught of one or two hurricanes or tropical storms. At times between six and fifteen inches of rain are dumped on Loreto in less that twenty-four hours. Thankfully these storms do not always come every year. Sometimes we'd go without any rain for one, two or three years; but when it does rain, there's almost always a deluge and flash flooding.

Each time a hurricane hit, trees were blown down and a general mess was made. Not every hurricane brought the same level of damage. Often, just windows were broken or roofs were torn off buildings that were not built to withstand strong winds.

But during one hurricane a few years ago, we had winds of up to 145 miles per hour, and that caused a lot of damage. During another bad hurricane, twelve homes about half a block from our house were washed out to sea.

Even if a storm did not hit Loreto hard, there was always cleanup to be done, and people helped each other. The city quickly hired people to clean up the streets and the waterfront, often getting most of the work done with hundreds of people in just a few days.

After these storms we mostly helped people in Loreto, but after one particularly bad hurricane, I put together a group of men who replaced the roofs on several buildings at a Christian drug rehabilitation center in Santa Rosalía. The men who helped came from various parts of Baja, some from as far south as Cabo San Lucas (about a ten hour drive from Santa Rosalía) and as far north as San Quintin (also about a ten hour drive). I put this team of men together because in our area of Mexico (and perhaps throughout the country), many people would be less likely to assist a facility for addicts or criminals when other people needed help. And everyone who joined this team not only wanted to help those living at the center, but also show everyone (especially the churches) that the love of Christ should be shown to all without discrimination.

Helping meet the needs of the English-speaking community

For several years, we had been concerned about the spiritual needs of the English-speaking people in Loreto, even though our main focus had been on the Mexican people.

So in January of 2009, we started hosting Bible studies for English-speaking Christians in our home, and we had pot-luck dinners for them at our home every couple of weeks as well. I created a website to keep everyone informed about these and other activities we organized.

Our activities for the English-speaking community had varying attendance because these people were not in Loreto all year long: some came for a couple of weeks, others for several months. But we pressed on, and in 2012 we put on our first Easter Sunrise Service. Twenty-six people attended. The next year, almost eighty attended, and people started pressing us to start a church. But how could we do more? We were away one or two weekends each month with our Health Fairs, so it was not possible for us to start and pastor a church.

In 2015 we had more help with our Health Fairs (by people who could manage without me), so we announced to the eighty-four people who had attended that Easter Sunrise Service that we would be starting English Worship Services the following Sunday. The restaurant where we would meet was called The Backyard, so we called our little church "Sunday in The Backyard".

Some English-speaking people in Loreto lived there all year long, but most were there for only one to six months. Conducting these services from November through April or May made the most sense, as this is when most Americans and Canadians are in Loreto, so our English church in Loreto began on my birthday: April 5, 2015.

A microfinancing program

In the fall of 2015, we became involved in a microfinancing program for women in Loreto. Mimi and

Ted Kaplysh had been coming from the United States to spend their winters in Loreto, and Mimi was involved as a volunteer with an organization called Get HOPE Global, which she had been sharing with a few people in Loreto.

The nonprofit organization had been active in countries in Africa and the Far East, helping impoverished women to get out of prostitution and start a respectable business to support themselves and their children, and helping women who were struggling with their small entrepreneurial businesses become successful. The course is based on biblical principles, and the classes are held one night a week for sixteen weeks, after which the class meets biweekly for the remainder of the year for counseling and encouragement, while their loans are being repaid. This support and training has a remarkable 96 percent success rate.

Mimi wondered if such a program and microfinancing opportunity could be offered to some of the women in Loreto. A meeting was held at one of the churches, and about thirty women attended. Ten of them showed an interest in signing up. Mimi had to return to the United States, and that is where we came into the picture. Lorraine and I had both been invited to attend the first meeting, and we encouraged one of the Christian women we knew to take on the responsibility to teach this course. Silvia agreed, and we agreed to assist her in every way we could.

I began to coordinate things in Loreto for Get HOPE Global in January 2016. At the start of the program, seven women signed up, but one moved away. The other six took the classes and applied for loans. All benefited from the course and paid back their loans in the time allotted, giving us a 100 percent success rate.

On February 15, 2017, we held our first Get HOPE Global Celebration Dinner with the six women receiving diplomas; all with gold, silver, and bronze seals on them depicting their true success in four areas: class attendance, success in starting their own personal savings program, timely repayment of loans, and how well they applied the lessons they were taught to their business.

Sharing our lives

I have recounted all these activities to show that for us, being missionaries was not just putting on outreach programs. Rather, it meant living with and sharing our lives with the people around us—and taking care that we always did things in such a way to show our respect for them while helping them.

We have tried to put into practice what we have found in the Scriptures: "Therefore, as we have opportunity, let us do good to all people, especially to those who belong to the family of believers" (Galatians 6:10) and "In the same way, let your light shine before others, that they may see your good deeds and glorify your Father in heaven" (Matthew 5:16).

This loving and sharing way of life brought us close to the people in Loreto, and to many others throughout Baja Sur. They are our brothers and sisters, even our children and grandchildren in the Lord. They are our family.

But it wasn't always easy

It is easy to look at the outward appearance of things and conclude that everything is going well—without difficulties, without stress, and without personal cost. But that was not the case for us.

We had financial concerns, and personal decisions had to be made. We often had just enough money to meet each month's needs. I have been known as a penny-pincher because I have always tried to be careful about how we spent the money we have, and I was always trying to get the most for my money. From my perspective, I was simply careful; but from another point of view, we made some sacrifices by not having some things, or not having things as quickly as we may have liked.

Worry and stress are common for all of us. But, throughout our lives the Lord has shown us that we really never needed to worry about anything. Everything that we thought might have been bad for us actually turned out to be pointing us in a good direction—because we were obeying Him.

Stress came whenever I tried to manage things as I best knew how, rather than *letting the chips fall where they may.* A better way of saying that is to let God do whatever He wants without knowing the outcome. This is what *living by faith* is about. So I learned to listen to the Lord constantly (by reading His Word) and talk things over with Him (by praying). I learned not to challenge Him, but rather to accept His direction about where to go, and obey His instructions about what to do—even when I did not know what the results would be.

I learned to *commit to Him everything needed* to do the job, and the protection required to keep us safe. I expected Him to be faithful to all His promises, and He was. After all, the Lord Jesus Christ has the Master Plan, which includes the finished project, all the big things that will be done along the way, and the smallest details that will bring everything together. He knows what is best and desires only the best for us. He will direct everything and everyone accordingly, and He has.

In other words, I had to *learn to be at peace* when I could easily have thought that everything was out of control. I had to find joy (His joy) when I could have become discouraged. All of this I discovered early in my life, and I learned throughout my life what it really means to *live life by faith.* I truly believe this is the secret to living the best life possible, and why we have seen so many blessings in the ministries we have been privileged to be a part of.

Learning to *live by faith* is a life-long process, and in that process we had times of stress—because we did not always know the outcome of some of the problems we faced, and it was difficult to simply accept some situations as being under God's control. (None of us are perfect, although we are getting better—this should be every Christian's testimony.)

One of those situations developed at the church we had been attending regularly and had helped so much. About three years after we moved to Loreto, the pastor of that church (the same one who had caused trouble for the other pastors at the Pastor's Fellowship Meetings) started causing us problems.

We had done so many things for the people in this church and for the pastor's family, but this pastor still believed we were not giving enough to them. They were of the mind-set that Americans in general have more of everything than they need, so the people in the church had the right to demand more and more things from us.

We loved these people, and tried to partner with them, but tensions started to rise. It seemed that they were more interested in improving their personal well-being than anything else (this I believe was their problem in a nutshell).

Something had happened in that church that we did not know about at the time. A few years before we had moved to Loreto, a man named Ricardo, who had been a member of this church, was driving a small truck to Tijuana with the pastor and his wife with him. Unfortunately, he fell asleep while driving, and there was an accident. Ricardo and the pastor's wife received only minor injuries, but the pastor suffered head injuries and amnesia set in, which resulted in a change in personality. He became very nervous when in crowds or in front of people, so much so that he could no longer be the pastor of their church. So his wife took it upon herself to take on the leadership of the church, and became recognized as its pastor. After the accident, Ricardo believed it was his responsibility to help her as much as he could in the church and around her home.

When we started attending their church and helping them as much as we did, Ricardo had a problem with it (unbeknownst to us), and his upset increased when we started bringing things down from San Diego for the pastor and her family. Ricardo was feeling that his efforts and the help he was giving were being minimalized by what we were doing.

Ricardo was a deep-sea diver and fisherman, and about three years after we moved to Loreto, the motor on his boat stopped functioning and could not be fixed. I shared his need for a replacement motor with a few of our supporters, and a man in San Diego purchased a good used motor for him. We then drove to San Diego and brought it back—a wonderful provision, we would all agree. But this new pastor said that Ricardo needed to give a tithe on this gift to her church. This was a hardship for him because he didn't have the money, and he resented us for having gotten the motor for him.

Shortly after Ricardo received the motor, the pastor and her husband went to the United States for a couple of months. During their absence, Ricardo was doing the preaching in the church, and he decided that he would like to stop fishing and become the full-time pastor. But a few people left the church during this time, and, rather than believe these people had left because of his preaching, he told the pastor when she returned that they had left because I had told them to leave. While this was not true, it brought to a head the feelings the pastor had against us.

Not knowing Ricardo's desires or his feelings, and not understanding why the pastor was becoming upset with us, we brought in an impartial third party in an effort to resolve whatever the issues were. But Ricardo's words were accepted to be true because he had a long-standing relationship with the pastor.

While all this was happening, the pastor at Vision Church, a new church in Loreto, asked if we could come and help start a Home Bible Study ministry for them as a way to interest new people to come to their church. Then three different English-speaking people during each of the following three weeks asked us if there was a church in Loreto that conducted services in English, so we brought them to Vision Church. After those three weeks, we were certain that the Lord was telling us to make this our new home church in Loreto.

What an ordeal to go through. We could have asked why the Lord used something so difficult to make this move clear to us, but we trusted that the Lord knew what He was doing or allowing.

A couple of years later, Ricardo and his family also left the church they had been so active in and started to attend a different church in Loreto. Then a couple of years after that, they were commissioned by the new church they were attending to go and start another church—a church reaching out primarily to the indigenous men and their families who had come to Loreto for construction jobs.

From the time we left our prior church, we had made it a point to forgive Ricardo for what he had done, even though we had not fully understood everything. In fact, we not only forgave him, but also continued to develop a true friendship with him and his family, so much so that they became our dearest friends in Loreto. So when Pastor Ricardo and his wife, Chayito, started their new church, we helped them from time to time with the construction of the building, gave them a generator (there was no electricity in the neighborhood where their church was), and took our Health Fairs to their church several times, helping them reach out to people.

So a stressful time became a blessed time, because we trusted God through it and obeyed His directions.

It reminds me of the message in Psalm 37 (my own abbreviated paraphrase):

> "Don't worry. Don't be envious of those who do you wrong. Rather, trust in the Lord, be content with His ways, and He will give you the desires of your heart. Commit your ways to the Lord, trust Him, delight yourself in Him—then He will make things turn out for the very best. Be sure to rest in the Lord, keep quiet (don't try to defend yourself), be patient, don't fret, and refrain from getting angry. Instead, keep expecting the Lord to bring about blessings through that which you are going through. Then you will be able to stand strong, enjoy peace, and receive those blessings He has intended for you."

Over the years, many things could have caused me much worry and stress, but I disciplined my mind and spirit to overcome that temptation. The Lord always looked after our financial needs as well as our personal needs. We have faced times we would have preferred to avoid, but looking back, we can see the Lord was in control. We could easily have questioned some difficult situations, as we did not have the privilege of seeing the benefit; but since He is Lord, we learned to trust Him and never give up (see 2 Corinthians 4:1–2).

Conditions requiring medical attention

It is natural for people to question God and argue with Him. We want to have control of our lives, and every detail of them, if possible, and it is not natural for us to give someone else the reins. Therefore, when we are called by God to go to another country—a poorer country—it is easy to have some concerns. Let me share the most obvious.

Upon being called to Mexico, these thoughts came to mind: *What about health issues? Are there illnesses and diseases that we might be exposed to? How can we avoid or prepare for them? If we do get sick, will there be doctors and hospitals that will be able to help us? Will they be well educated? What will we do if we have an emergency?*

But the answer was really quite simple for me. We had personally experienced so many times when the Lord had looked after us, so I really had no reason to be concerned. We did not, however, overlook making some wise decisions, like getting and maintaining our inoculations. But really, it boils down to whether or not we believe that the Lord can and will look after our personal needs.

When we moved to Mexico in 2004, we had no medical insurance because the premiums were over $1,000 per month. However, the following year we found some Christian organizations in the United States where the members cost-share the price of medical expenses. We joined one of these programs in the summer of 2005, and we were members for five years. The monthly cost was only $145 per month for both of us. What a great deal when compared to the medical insurance premiums we could not afford.

In 2006, I started having problems with my prostate. While my PSA test had been normal for years, I was having problems with urination becoming slower and slower. Dr. Robles, our doctor-friend in Loreto, suggested I have a yearly ultrasound of my prostate, which would allow a doctor to compare the ultrasounds and view if the prostrate was enlarging.

When I was in Tijuana in February that year, I had an ultrasound done and took it to another doctor-friend there. He said that my prostate was indeed enlarged and recommended having it removed when I was coming north through Tijuana the coming summer.

The following Monday, we returned to Loreto and invited Dr. Robles to our home, and I showed him my ultrasound. He immediately asked if he could use our phone, and when he returned to the living room, he told me, "Your operation is scheduled for this coming Friday."

"Just a moment," I said. "Why so soon? Who will be my surgeon, and which hospital are we going to?"

He explained that he had just spoken to the best surgeon for this kind of operation, and that we would be going together to Tijuana. When I questioned the method of surgery, he said it would be a new laparoscopic technique.

I was a little overwhelmed, so I excused myself from the living room, went to my office, and did a quick search on the internet to find out more about this type of surgery. I then asked Dr. Robles how many operations this doctor had done, because from my research this method of laparoscopic surgery had only been being done for about two years in the US. He again used my phone, and the surgeon told him that he had performed this surgery over ten thousand times—with 100 percent success—so I agreed to have this operation performed later that week.

On Tuesday, I started the two-day drive to Tijuana, with both Lorraine and Dr. Robles with me. We went to the surgeon's office on Thursday morning, and he explained just how he was going to do the operation: he would insert one small tube containing a camera, a very small knife, a pincher-type instrument, a cauterizing tool, and a vacuum, and the prostate would be removed with suction. He went on to explain that he could do all this without causing me any pain, and together we would watch him doing it all on a television screen beside my bed in the operating room. I would be awake for the surgery, and he would even provide me with a videotape of it.

Dr. Robles exclaimed, *"I told you he was the best... They don't even do this surgery this way in the United States yet. But not to worry, he has successfully done many surgeries this way."*

Next, I went to a cardiologist at the newest public hospital in Tijuana. There I was told that I had the first stage of an enlarged heart, but that this would not interfere with the surgery. Dr. Robles again said not to worry, and that he would help me deal with that after the operation when we were back in Loreto.

On Friday morning, I was checked into a first-class private Tijuana hospital where my surgeon performed all his operations. Both Lorraine and I were impressed. The surgery proceeded without any problems, although it did take longer than expected, and I enjoyed watching everything on the TV in the surgery room. My prostate was completely removed, something that surprised my doctor in the United States, but I have had no problems at all.

A year later, Lorraine needed her gallbladder removed, but Dr. Robles had moved to La Paz. We called him anyway because a few years previously he had coordinated everything for people from the United States who wanted first-class surgeries done in Tijuana, Mexico, with the best surgeons available. So he came up to Loreto and we again drove to Tijuana so she could have her gallbladder removed.

Both of these operations were performed for less than five thousand dollars each, much less than they would have cost us if we had them done in the United States. Our decision to have them performed in Mexico was not based upon cost, however, because we were members of the

Christian cost-sharing organization that would cover most of the fees in both countries. Rather, we made our choice to have them in Mexico because we believed the Lord had brought Dr. Robles into our lives. He had become a really good friend, and we had come to trust him as a doctor.

In fact, I trusted him so much that I was willing to do things with him that I would not likely have done without him. After my prostatectomy, he suggested that we start running together. I was apprehensive because I had been told when I was a teenager that I had a heart murmur and that I should not do any excessive exercise. But he said he would be running with me and that he would make sure I did not overexert myself. He also wanted to give me a few regular injections of some kind of new medicine, which I believe was some kind of human growth hormone. He said that in three months my heart would be back to normal. So I trusted him, and we started running. Later testing showed that my heart indeed returned to its normal size.

In 2008, I made an appointment with an ENT Doctor (another friend the Lord had brought into our lives in Mexico) because my hearing was diminishing. He told me I needed hearing aids and provided them to me at his cost. What a blessing, because the Christian medical cost-sharing program we were members of would not cover them.

In 2010, Lorraine and I became eligible to become members of a Medical Insurance Program in Mexico, so we discontinued our membership in the Christian cost-sharing organization. Joining this economical insurance program was a good decision. There was no copay or deductible to pay, and they provided excellent care. In addition to emergency medical services, this program included a doctor visit once a month to make sure we were keeping well, most of the medicines we needed, blood tests every six months, all other tests that needed to be done, appointments with medical specialists, and any surgeries we might have needed. So overall we were very pleased with this medical insurance program.

On May 28, 2012, Lorraine and I had driven back to Loreto from Santa Rosalía, where we held a couple of days of Health Fairs in the Prison there. We stopped at a restaurant in Loreto to have lunch with Dr. Malé Gutierrez and her family, before they drove on to their home in La Paz. But after we enjoyed our meal together, I suddenly slumped down in my chair. I had stopped breathing.

Malé tried to revive me, but she could not. My friend who owned the restaurant called for an ambulance, which arrived quickly. The paramedics checked me over and then took me to the hospital. I was examined, given four liters of electrolytes intravenously and some other medicines, and released three hours later—without any real explanations.

I was feeling better the next day; but a little uneasy about not having been told what had happened to me. I thought I should call Dr. Jill Cottel, my doctor-friend in San Diego, and explain to her what had happened. She suggested that I come to San Diego and have a few tests done, but I hesitated because I did not feel up to driving two full days to get there. The next day, my pilot friend Bill Neail phoned and said that he would be flying down the next day to take me and Lorraine back to San Diego for the tests Dr. Cottel wanted me to have done.

In San Diego I was seen by a cardiologist Dr. Cottel recommended, and various tests were performed over the following three days. The diagnostic conclusion was that I did not suffer a heart attack, rather my body just collapsed from trying to handle five things at one time: exhaustion from the physical work I had done the week prior, emotional excitement from how well things had gone in the Prison, food poisoning from what I had eaten the night before, dehydration from not drinking sufficient electrolytes, and sleep apnea.

So I was told how to manage things better, and that I needed a CPAP breathing machine to use each night.

I then went to the Mexican Medical office to see my friends there and to thank them for their prayers. I explained what the doctors had told me, and they said that a CPAP machine had just been donated. They did not know what they should do with it, so it was put on a shelf—apparently waiting for me.

On Mother's Day 2016, I had a detached retina and an emergency operation was required. I could not fly to the United States—there was no time to do so, and the altitude would have been a problem—so that wasn't an option. Rather, we called an ophthalmologist in La Paz we knew from a few years before, and then took the bus to see him.

The doctor saw me without any delay and called a retina specialist he knew, who said he would see me in half an hour. So we took a taxi to his office, and he arranged for the operation to be performed as soon as the operating room was available, which was to be later the following day. Then they had a cancellation so my operation was brought ahead a few hours, and the surgery was performed within forty-eight hours from the time of the detachment.

In late June we were in San Diego, so I made an appointment with an ophthalmologist I knew just to have things looked at, and she told me the procedure that was done in Mexico was done very well.

I have taken the time to recount all of this to show how well we have been looked after in Mexico. The Lord brought wonderful people into our lives to help us in our times of need, and in many cases they came into our lives before we even knew we would have a need they could help us with. The Lord also supplied things we needed, without us even having to ask for them. We have every reason to praise the Lord, and to tell you that there is no better life that can be lived than to listen to the Lord and obey whatever He tells you to do.

PHASE THIRTEEN

Changing Ministry Focus in Loreto

For the past couple of summers, during our travels to San Diego and north to British Columbia to share with our friends, supporters, and family all that had been happening in and around Loreto, we believed the Lord was preparing us for the next phase in our lives.

On June 24, 2016, Lorraine celebrated her seventieth birthday; on April 5, 2017, I celebrated my seventieth birthday; and on October 28, 2017, we celebrated our fiftieth wedding anniversary—a significant milestone. We had known for a while that the time was coming for us to make some changes. She and I realized that we do not have as much energy as we did when we first moved to Loreto over thirteen years ago, and that we had ongoing health concerns that needed to be addressed.

One concern was my hearing deficiency. Even with the use of the best hearing aids on the market, I have difficulty hearing what people are saying in some situations, which can result in some confusion and frustration with communication. This was not what I wanted, nor did I believe this was beneficial for the advancement of the Kingdom of God.

So I had been feeling led to respect the fact that we were getting older and would continue to do so, and our capacities would continue to diminish with time. I was also involved in so many ministries that it became difficult to manage and coordinate things without any problems. Therefore, the time had come to make some adjustments—in particular, to look at what was most frustrating and most physically challenging.

In the spring of 2016, we started to hold some of our Health Fairs on Friday and Saturday instead of on Saturday and Sunday. This allowed me to return to Loreto to conduct the English worship services on Sunday. When our Health Fairs were on Saturday and Sunday, I still returned to Loreto but left Lorraine in charge. In 2015, Steve Crews came and assisted with four of our Health Fairs, and in the first part of 2016 he came and assisted with three. This was a tremendous help when I was not there on Sundays, and this was much appreciated. So with a few adjustments, we were able to conduct the Sunday worship services and continue to hold our Health Fairs.

But then, in 2017, Steve was not able to come, so it became more difficult for me to do both the Health Fairs away from Loreto and the English worship services in Loreto. I continued to make all the advance arrangements with the churches for our Health Fairs, and to conduct the advance training programs, and continued to manage the set-up the day before and run the actual Health Fair each Saturday. But after the Health Fair was over for that day, I returned to Loreto to lead the English worship services, leaving Lorraine in charge.

But there were times when the generator or the dental delivery equipment would break down, and no one knew how to quickly repair them. Lorraine was also left with the responsibility of packing everything up after the Health Fairs were over. While she had help, some of the local men did not like taking instructions from a woman. So getting everything packed correctly so the trailer would not sway from side to side going down the highways was difficult.

These problems, I believe, were putting a bit of a damper on the great time we'd had at the Health Fairs, and were possibly diminishing the glory that God should receive.

So after re-evaluating everything, I decided that we had to make a change: we would not continue putting on the Health Fairs in churches so that we could conduct the English worship services in Loreto.

Health Fairs—taking on a more defined focus

In January 2017, we were asked to come to La Paz to meet with the director and the captain of the larger State Prison there. A couple of years prior, they had to bring in the riot squad to quell what could have been a real disaster in that prison. The new director, knowing a little of our work in Santa Rosalía Prison, said to us, "We know our methods (to control and retrain the inmates, and change them so that when they leave the prison they will become beneficial contributors to society) aren't working, and I believe you are able to help us bring about the changes we need. Will you please consider bringing your group into this prison and conducting your Health Fairs here?"

The focus of our Health Fairs shifted from being church outreaches to being held in the prisons. It was a bit humbling to think that God was leading us into such a task, but it brought joy to our hearts at the same time. Government officials were admitting that their methods were not working and were requesting our help. We knew God was opening doors for the love of Jesus and the message of salvation to enter—and God had chosen us to be His instruments to bring about these blessings and the change these men desperately wanted. *WOW!*

So from March 30 through April 1, 2017, a team of twenty-three volunteers conducted our Health Fair in the La Paz Prison—nineteen Mexican volunteers (four doctors, four dentists, and eleven general helpers), two Canadians, plus Lorraine and me.

At the conclusion of our third day, I spoke to a group of about two hundred inmates, standing with guards on the opposite side of a chain-link fence. "When we make something, we either fix it or throw it away if it doesn't work correctly. God is doing the same with us. He has created all of us according to His purposes, and because we have all done many things wrong, He has made a way to fix things. We've been given a choice: to accept God's fix-it plan or be thrown away. That's right! God will fix you, if you want Him to, or at the end of your life, He will throw you away."

I pointed to a Bible. "It's all written down for us in this book. If you'd like a copy so you can read all about it yourself, just ask us for one when you come to get the gift bags we have for you today. In these bags are toothpaste, a toothbrush, soap, and a washcloth. They were put together by people in the United States who love God, and who love you, just as we do. That is why we're all here today, to show you that even though you're here in this prison, you're still loved by God, by us, and (pointing to our group of volunteers) by our friends here in Mexico, the United States, and Canada."

I then asked the men to form a line to receive these gift bags, and to receive a New Testament or Bible if they asked for one. But the men continued crowding together and pushing up against the fence, not wanting to form an orderly line. The guards yelled at them without success. (Clearly there was a lack of respect between the inmates and the guards, and I could see that the guards actually feared the inmates.)

I calmly asked the guard to unlock the gate and let me go in with the men, and he reluctantly did. I then spoke gently with many of the inmates, just as I had long ago with the autistic children on my bus route. I told them that we loved them and had sufficient items for all of them. I helped them form an orderly line, and the men calmed down and lined up without incident. As I returned through the gate, some of the guards looked a bit stunned.

So the desired changes were beginning to happen. Over those three days, in a prison with over seven hundred men and fifty-five women, more than two hundred and fifty inmates requested and received New Testaments or Bibles; over one hundred Gospels of John were also given out; and over fifty inmates prayed to receive Jesus Christ as their Lord and Savior. This was an unprecedented blessing. The guards might have wondered how I was able to get the men in an orderly line, but I know it was only by God's power, because I certainly did not plan ahead of time to do what I did. After a wonderful three days there, we made plans to return the following November.

We plan to return to the prison at least twice a year and involve as many Mexican Christians from La Paz as possible. It is also my dream to start some training for the staff and guards to remove their fears and help them learn to respect everyone, including their inmates. I believe that the love of Jesus and the message of salvation will dissipate the debilitating fears that the guards have toward the inmates, and create an environment of care and order in the prison. Something to pray about.

What happened during those three days made it much easier to understand that the Lord was leading us to discontinue our Health Fairs in the churches and focus more on what we could do in the prisons in La Paz and Santa Rosalía.

Ministry to Pastors and churches

Although we had discontinued our Health Fairs in churches, we did hold an occasional class about diabetes. Why about diabetes? Because the World Health Organization had released that diabetes was the leading cause of deaths in Mexico, and it was predicted by 2050, that half of Mexico's population will suffer from diabetes unless the people become better educated and make the necessary changes to their diet. These classes also gave these churches a similar evangelistic opportunity in their communities, while being less taxing than the Health Fairs.

We also decided to continue ministering to the local pastors and evangelical churches in Loreto, even though we would no longer be bringing our Health Fairs to the churches. We will continue to loan chairs and tables, encourage them to hold evangelistic outreaches, and help them show evangelistic videos in their churches and communities, as they desire.

We will also continue to offer free paperback Gospels of John, New Testaments, and Bibles to the people who start attending these churches, as well as sell imitation leather Bibles, large print Bibles, Study Bibles, Bible dictionaries, commentaries, Children's Bibles, and Bible school correspondence courses.

We will continue to have a supply of free reading and distance glasses available for those who need them, and continue to assist pastors who have serious medical concerns with their respective financial needs.

Opportunities for ministry continue to come our way. In 2016, one of the local pastors wanted to begin a meal program for the children around his church. This would not only meet a physical need but also be an evangelistic outreach to the children and their families. We encouraged him and started to support him financially in this outreach, but have been careful not to make him dependent on us. We occasionally give him some of the funds from the offerings at the English church to show there is cooperation between the two churches, and we sometimes provide gifts that he can give to the children.

English church in Loreto moves forward

When we moved to Loreto, our attention was on making inroads into the Mexican population and assisting local pastors in any way we reasonably could. We did not go out of our way to make friends with Americans or Canadians who were living in Loreto, but instead spent our time making friends with the Mexicans.

Then a couple of people who did not speak much Spanish came to us asking if we could at least have a Bible study with them—in English. This eventually led to our "Sunday in the Backyard" services; first at a restaurant and now on our own patio. Our involvement with the English-speaking community has expanded. On Tuesdays we meet at a local coffee shop for a time of fellowship, and at night we conduct home Bible studies. Lorraine helps lead a women's Bible study on Wednesday mornings while I meet with some men at the coffee shop, and every other Thursday some of the church members go to a local restaurant or have a pot-luck dinner at someone's home.

We hope to continue doing all these activities, both to encourage the English-speaking Christians in their faith and to do what we can to encourage others into a relationship with Christ.

In His Hands

PHASE FOURTEEN

Looking Forward to Next Year and Beyond

Lorraine and I have driven north through California, Oregon, and Washington and on to British Columbia each summer since moving to Loreto, to report to our supporters how the ministries have been going. This took us about six or seven weeks in the beginning, which did not allow us much time to rest (or to have a vacation), but we were not complaining. Then we were given a small travel trailer, so we started taking a week's vacation on the way back to Loreto.

Over the years, we determined it would be good to take a little more time—driving fewer hours each day—and take a couple of weeks to relax. Our government pensions allowed us to take the extra week or two, and we really appreciated that. But we still found the heat and humidity in Loreto to be difficult to deal with when we returned in August. One year we left Loreto a little later in June and returned in mid-September.

I recently went to a cardiologist because I was having occasional discomfort when under stress. He ordered blood tests, an electrocardiogram, an echocardiogram, and a nuclear stress test. The following day he told me, "Everything looks normal *for your age*" (whatever that means). "And there are a couple of things you need to watch: You should not overexert yourself because you have a mild irregular heartbeat and leaky heart valve. You will also need to take blood pressure medication and watch your diet—no more red meats and other foods that would be difficult for your kidneys to process—because they are not working 100 percent and you could have difficulties down the road."

So I found out that I was not as young as I used to be. That was difficult to hear, as I have always applied myself 100 percent to whatever I did. So following my doctor's suggestion, I became more conscious about what I was eating. And we did take a little more time away from Loreto during the summer of 2016, and plan to do so in 2018 and in the years following. However, I was still working almost every day, not taking any mini vacations during the year, and not doing much exercise. So I will need to make some additional changes in the coming years to make time to take better care of myself.

Our financial support

Some have asked if we will continue to need financial support, so let me say this: we have always believed that those giving to our support were doing so to support the ministries we have been involved in—and we believe we have been good stewards of the funds received.

Our added summer vacation time is funded by our CPP and Social Security Pensions, and our non-vacation time is funded by those who support us in our ministries.

So, while there have been some changes with our involvement in certain ministries, we continue to appreciate the financial support and prayers for everything we are currently involved in, and the ministries we plan to continue.

Our home in Loreto

Our home in Loreto is not currently on the market, but that is not to say that we would not sell it if the right buyer were to come along. If we do sell our home, our plan is to rent a house in Loreto so we can continue with the ministries here.

If we find that spending our summers in our small trailer gets difficult, then we may consider buying a small home or possibly a condo in the United States, (homes in Canada have gotten quite expensive). We would likely consider buying in Southern California or Arizona because it would be closest to Loreto.

Writing another book

Some have asked if I will be writing another book. I have a second book almost finished. I also have a third book I am working on, and am thinking about some related subjects that I would also like to write about.

My second book will be titled *Chosen to be on the Team and in the Game*, and it is all about how to achieve *the best life possible.*

In John 10:9–11, Jesus said, "I am the gate; whoever enters through me will be saved. They will come in and they will go out, and they will find good pastures. The thief comes only to steal, and to kill, and to destroy; but I have come that you may have life, and have it to the full— *the best life possible.* Remember always: I am the Good Shepherd" (my own abbreviated paraphrase).

The problem is that most people do not experience what these verses describe. In fact, many people do not know what it really means to be *saved*, and how this should affect their lives. Instead, they spend too much time trying to just survive in this world, and lose many good opportunities to *have life to the full*, as Jesus said.

I hope this book will answer a lot of questions that people have. It will be an easy read yet designed for personal growth, and written in a building-block style. A summary and questions at the end of each chapter will assist the reader with their personal growth, and space will be given for personal notes.

The third book I am working on is a thirty-day devotional focusing on several Psalms, to help people discover and develop for themselves a meaningful life—a life filled with purpose and joy—to bring more enthusiasm and excitement into their lives.

At the end of each chapter, space is given for the reader to write down the discoveries they've made from the Psalm focused upon that day, as well as space to write additional personal notes. This inspiring book will be titled, *More Exceptional Days.*

PHASE FIFTEEN

Concluding Thoughts From My Heart

I want to say that I would not be where I am today, or have been able to do everything I've done throughout my life, if it were not for loving people who have helped me along the way. Their expressions of love kept my focus in the right direction. The counsel people gave from the Word of God ensured that I was doing what God directed, and the financial assistance we received made possible the ministries we've been a part of. And the prayers of hundreds of people, some I am not even aware of, helped us overcome the many challenges we faced. This is why we have so often referred to all these people as our Partners in Ministry. Lorraine and I have really not done anything alone, so I want to say, "Thank you so very much," to every one of you!

If you have been having difficulties in your own Christian life and not been able to understand why, or if you have just not experienced the joy and success you felt you should have as a Christian, then I encourage you to read the Appendix C.

I trust that, as you have read this book, you have learned more about who I am, some of the difficulties I have faced and overcome, and some of the wonderful ministries I have been privileged to be a part of. I am sure you can see, as I do, how God was very much involved in orchestrating everything. It was often hard to understand what was taking place, and easy to believe it was not for our good. But looking back now, we can see God's hand in everything, and come to the conclusion that everything is good when we have placed our lives *in His hands* (See Romans 8:28-32; Ephesians 2:10).

Ever since I discovered that my name, *Donald*, means "world leader or world changer," I thought, *God must have things predetermined to happen in my life that will influence the way other people live.* From that time on, I believed God had a special calling for me.

Has this happened? I believe it has. At various times in my life, I've been involved in ministries in Canada, the United States, Western and Eastern Europe, and Mexico. Through God's direction, some of the people I have had the opportunity to influence have become missionaries in other parts of the world, and others have traveled throughout the world. And who knows what effect all these people have had upon people in the countries they either now live in or have visited (See Jeremiah 1:5; John 15:16; Galatians 1:1, 13–24; Ephesians 2:10).

At the end of our lives, despite what the majority of people believe, it is not the man with the most toys who wins or the one who has done more good things than bad. The most important factors in life are not what company we own, what we have done, who we have worked for, or what programs we were a part of, but how obedient we have been to God. He has created you and me for a purpose—His purpose—and we will stand before Him on Judgement Day and give an account of how well we have lived our lives according to His purpose.

So as you look at your life today, realize that we cannot expect to be blessed by God if we are not doing what He wants us to be doing. This requires that we have a good relationship with Him, which can only happen on His terms, through the work of Jesus Christ and the acceptance of His offer of salvation. It also requires that we give up selfish control of our lives, determine that we will live up to our created purpose, make Jesus Christ the Lord of our lives, and constantly be listening to Him and obeying Him.

As you look back over my life, I trust that you have seen that *it does not take a special person* to do what God requires. I am not any special person, yet I have been privileged to take part in many ministries. I believe there is no better life than to live according to His plan, and there is no better reward than to be shown for all eternity the incomparable riches of God by Christ Himself (see Ephesians 2:4–10). It will not always be easy, and you will experience struggles and disappointments like I have. I hope you see that you are not alone in these struggles— everyone you will meet has them—and that God is always faithful through them. So I encourage you to put your complete life *in His hands* today, if you have not already done so—and then you will experience firsthand what it is like to live *the best life possible* (see Romans 12:1-2). Step into His plan today, if you have not already done so. You too can be *a world changer!*

APPENDIX A

Sharing the Message of Salvation

One of my greatest desires in life has been to help people who say they are Christians to actually know if they are truly a Christian according to what is said in the Bible. Assurance of salvation is what most people want to know. Then I try to help these people become more active in sharing their faith in meaningful ways with those in their spheres of influence—their families, neighbors, friends, and coworkers.

A couple of years ago, in the state prison in Santa Rosalía, I was speaking to about two hundred and fifty inmates at the conclusion of three days of Health Fairs. My subject was "Why is evolution being propagated in our societies today?"

I said, "Evolution is being taught so that people accept the lie that the universe was not created by God."

Then I asked, "Do you know why they would want to teach evolution, when there is more physical evidence to support creation than there is to support evolution?"

"The answer is simply this," I said. "(1) If we accept evolution to be true, then we'll be able to believe that God doesn't exist. (2) If God doesn't exist, then there will be no God to judge us at the end of our lives. (3) If there is no judge to face when we die, then we can live our lives any way we want!"

"So evolution is being taught and propagated to give everyone the license to live as selfishly as they want, and to not feel guilty about doing so. And so all sorts of evil and promiscuous lifestyles must not only be tolerated—they must be accepted by everyone as wholesome and valid. So that is the way the world is going, and their justification for it is that God does not exist—evolution has proved it, they say."

"*But ...* if God did create us (and there is a lot of evidence showing He did), then He must have had a purpose for doing so. And, if you believe the evidence, then you know that you and I are here today because God had a plan and purpose in mind. Therefore, the question that will automatically be asked of you and me by God at the end of our lives will be, *'Did you live your life according to My plan and for My benefit? Or did you just live your life any way you wanted?'*"

"This is what God will ask you when you stand before Him on Judgement Day. So it's your decision: you can believe what evolution teaches, or you can accept what a lot of evidence shows. When making this decision, keep in mind that there is more evidence for God having created the world, than it all coming about due to some evolutionary process." (If this is something you struggle to believe, or have difficulty with when talking with others, read through the articles and resources available through the Institute for Creation Research at www.icr.org Also there are several other resources noted in Appendix B that can be a great help to you).

I went on to explain that I had brought a book for them that they could read to learn the truth—one that would explain to them how they should live their lives. "This book," I said, pointing to the Bibles on the table next to me, "also explains that God knows all about each one of us—the failures we've each had, and the problems and penalties that must logically follow."

"*But ...* this book also tells us that there's a way to live our lives that will be acceptable to God, so no matter what we've done in the past, we can still pass the test at the end of our lives when we face him as our Judge. It all begins with us individually accepting a special pardon that He has to offer to each of us, and then He gives us a second chance."

"It's all written in this book, and it's really quite simple. You can all accept this special pardon! But you can only receive it on God's terms, and you must do what He requires—and that is perfectly reasonable, right? So, you need to read it for yourself. I'm not going force you to do anything, but if you would like to have one of these books, please come forward and take one from the table."

That day, after 250 men heard this message, 220 men took the Bibles they were offered. They were excited to hear the truth and wanted to be able to stand before their Judge at the end of their lives being acceptable to Him, rather than being rejected by Him. They wanted to read all about it.

You see, as I told another group of inmates another time, "We must all understand that God (in some respects) is no different than we are—or we could say we are no different than He is, keeping in mind that we were created in His image. Let me explain: If we make something and it doesn't work as we intend, then we will fix it or just throw it away. In this regard, God is doing the same thing with each of us. He has created each of us for His purposes, and because mankind is not living as He intended, He has implemented a plan to fix us. But if we are not receptive to His plan of salvation, then at the end of our lives, He will have no other option than to throw us away. So let's look at what God has to say about how He wants to fix us. It's all written down for us in that book."—pointing at the Bibles on the table. The day I spoke to these men this way, about 100+ men came forward to pick up Bibles.

What I have just shared with you is a great way to open up a conversation with anyone about how we individually need to accept Jesus Christ as our personal Savior.

Let me now share with you an easy method I've developed to continue talking with people about the message of salvation. First, you have to keep in mind that the topic of salvation is really a group of subjects. You will find this easy to remember, because each subject is under a letter heading, and, just like in the alphabet, A comes before B, and B comes before C, and so on. So each subject to discuss is followed by another related subject.

Also, it is critical that your listener has a complete understanding and acceptance of what has been presented to them under the A heading (accepting the authority of God) before going on to talk about what is under the B heading—believing the Bible—and so on with each subject.

The problem is that many Christians have tried to discuss the subject under the C heading—the need for Christ—before there is an understanding and acceptance of God's authority (as noted under the A heading), and the Bible being the only reliable means today of communication from Him (as noted under the B heading). So even though people have prayed to receive Christ, they have not become true Christians. They have recited a prayer, but did not fully understand all that salvation entails. Therefore, they did not receive Christ into their lives; and a few days, weeks or months later they will turn their backs on Christ, believing that He cannot help them. How tragic! And this happens all the time, because the person sharing Christ with them was in a rush to have them say a prayer. You see, it really is not the reciting of a prayer that saves a person. Rather it is their understanding and acceptance of all of the terms regarding salvation that is vital to receiving Christ into their lives.

Often this problem begins when a person does not understand why they need to be saved. Most people believe that God will look at all the good things they have done in their lives and overlook a few bad things. However while this may seem rational, it does not make this belief true.

The fact is that the miracle of salvation is achieved only by hearing the Word of God, understanding and believing what it says to be true, and then trusting Jesus Christ and His work on the cross to have procured salvation for us; and then—and this is crucial—making Him the Lord of our lives. In other words, turning our lives over to His absolute control, allowing Him to do with us as He alone pleases, and promising to obey His every desire. This is what will make a person a true Christian.

Here's the danger: We must avoid helping people become simply and only 'believers'—because we have been told that even the demons are believers (see James 2:19), and they most certainly are not Christian.

Rather, we must take all the time necessary to help people understand and accept the whole truth—the full plan of salvation. Only then will they be able to truly trust Jesus and decide with all their hearts to accept Him as their Savior. They must then be willing to put their own interests aside and be willing unequivocally to obey Him in every regard—something they are then willing to talk to others about (see Romans 10:9–10). This is what it means to make Jesus the Lord of your life.

Getting to this position is not easy for most people. Your listener will begin by evaluating and weighing the Truth against their own personal desires and what they have felt was the truth. We must help them come to the position where they realize for themselves that there is only one Truth. Then they must begin to respect God—not their personal interests—as being most important in their lives. We can help them come to this position by sharing a testimony from our lives about what it means to have Jesus as our Lord.

When will we know they have really decided to move in this direction? When they finally stop this 'weighing process' and decide that Truth can only be found in God's Word, the Bible—then and only then will they be willing to go with God; and then and only then, should we move onto the next subject in our presentation of the plan of salvation.

Jesus concluded His life here on earth by giving us the responsibility to not just share the good news with people, but to bring people into the disciplined life as disciples of His. Jesus explained that this requires us to teach people everything that He taught, and for the triune God to also be working in their lives. It is not something that only we do or that only God does. God's part is explained in the being born again process (see John 3:1-8); and our part is to help people along until they become a completely and irreversibly changed person—a disciple of Jesus (see Matthew 28:19-20).

So we've been given a responsibility. It is called the ministry of reconciliation, and it is to help bring people into relationship with God and to thereby become new and different people (see 1 Corinthians 5:17–20). Jesus called this process being 'born again' (see John 3:3-8). This is not just giving people a tract or sharing with them a concise version of the gospel. It is teaching the whole truth. So let's be careful to carry out this responsibility fully and dutifully, but also to do so with all the love and care it requires to be successful (see Matthew 10:16; Colossians 4:3–6; 1 Peter 3:15).

So don't be in a hurry. Be patient—explain to them only what they need to know one step (or subject), at a time—being sure not to overlook something important in the process. Do not be dismayed if it takes days or even months before your listener is ready to move to the next step. Our job is to present the truth to them—one bite at a time. Then we must give them time to digest what they have been told, and at the same time allow the Holy Spirit to do His work in their lives—and we will know the Spirit is doing His work when they acknowledge they have understood and have accepted what we have presented to them, and they want us to tell them more.

In John 3, Jesus told Nicodemus that everyone who wants to enter the Kingdom of God must be born again. It is interesting that Jesus used this illustration of birth to talk about those who will enter heaven and those who will not. Jesus refers to this spiritual life as "eternal life" because this new life is dependent not on how good we live our lives, but rather dependent upon the Spirit of God when He comes to live in us.

Let's look at the context of birth. Birth is always proceeded by conception, and conception is proceeded by foreplay. Bear with me, because I believe this answers many of the questions that we all have. We can look at the discussions we have with people this way: before a person becomes a Christian there will have been discussions between two people—one has the seed of life and the other does not; one presents the truth and the other argues the point. And so it goes on, until the seed (the truth) is planted in the recipient's heart (see Romans 10:11–15). From that moment on, the seed starts growing to the point of maturity when it can be born. The life that is in the seed is the Holy Spirit, and it is He who causes the growth, the maturing process, and the birth (spiritual birth), and the life (eternal life) that follows.

Now let's go back to what our part is in this process. We present the truth to people, and they argue point after point, until they finally understand and accept what we have presented to them. Then we go to the next logical subject, and they argue this point by point until they finally understand and accept what we have presented to them. This process will continue, like a farmer who is preparing the soil for the seed to be planted, after which the germination and growth process is always up to God (it does not matter if we are talking about tomatoes or our spiritual lives). The germination and growth processes, and also the reproductive process that follows, require God to be doing what only He can do. But we are called to be His farmers, preparing the soil and planting the seeds.

Our responsibility is to share the good news with everyone and to make the most of every opportunity. We are Christ's ambassadors. He has given us the ministry of reconciliation, and we are to help people become disciples of Jesus Christ by teaching them everything that Jesus taught. For that reason, we must study the Scriptures to carry out these responsibilities, and be careful to do everything in a loving manner (see Luke 8:4–15; Ephesians 5:15–17; 2 Corinthians 5:17–20; Matthew 28:18–20; 2 Timothy 2:15; 4:2; Colossians 4:3–6; 1 Peter 3:15; 1 Corinthians 13:13; 1 John 4:11–5:13).

As you talk with people then, do not overload them with information, or rush them to reciting a prayer. Rather, give only as much information as they are able to understand. Afterward, they will be able to hear and understand more information. In other words, gently work the soil and carefully plant the seed, then water it. They must understand and accept it all step by step, making all the appropriate decisions as you proceed. Presenting the gospel is not really just having people make only one decision. So be careful not to do things in a rushed or a slipshod way. To do so is not honoring to God, and not beneficial for the people we share the message of salvation with.

As you will see the first truth is foundational, and the second truth is foundational to truth three and all of the truths we will look at following. And similarly each truth or subject is a step or a link to the next, as you will see.

10 Steps to sharing the Message of Salvation with all of your friends

An effective explanation of the Gospel — taking people from no faith up to a level of understanding that will help them to make the best choice in life. When a person has this information it is simply rational to accept that Jesus Christ spoke the truth; he has the answers to life that everyone is looking for. and to believe that Jesus is the only way to our Father God.

J	Jesus	
I	My Inspiration	
H	Heaven, or it'll be Hell	
G	God will always be Good to	
F	Fellowship — you will never be alone	
E	The right decision let's you enjoy your Eternity	
D	Declare your Decision, because one day it'll be too late	
C	Christ Jesus — the Savior — the only one who is able to save us	
B	The Bible — it's the only reliable communication that we have from God	
A	Accept the Authority of God — there is no one else who has any higher authority	

This second illustration shows us how to get from one side of a canyon to the other—from this world to heaven.

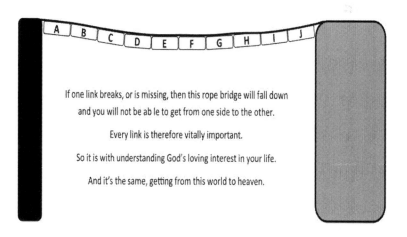

A B C D E F G H I J

If one link breaks, or is missing, then this rope bridge will fall down and you will not be able to get from one side to the other.

Every link is therefore vitally important.

So it is with understanding God's loving interest in your life.

And it's the same, getting from this world to heaven.

Steps for Sharing the Message of Salvation

Starting... = <u>A good introduction</u>
- This is critical to every presentation.

Step 1 – A = <u>Accept the **AUTHORITY** of God</u>
- There is no one else of higher authority.

Step 2 – B = <u>Believe the **BIBLE**</u>
- It is the only reliable communication from God.

Step 3 – C = <u>Consider **CHRIST** Jesus</u>
- He is the Savior we all need, and the only one who can save us.

Step 4 – D = <u>Declare your **DECISION**</u>
- Our free will requires us to choose our destiny.

Step 5 – E = <u>Enjoy your **ETERNITY**</u>
- It is a fact that there is life beyond the grave, and the decisions we make now will determine where we will spend eternity.

Step 6 – F = <u>**FELLOWSHIP**</u>
- You are not alone. The right way to live, according to God's intended purpose for our lives, is to be in fellowship with Him and others.

Step 7 – G = <u>**GOD is always GOOD**</u>
- God did not create anything with a bad start, nor is His purpose and plan for our lives anything but for our <u>Good</u>.

Step 8 – H = <u>HEAVEN</u> or <u>HELL</u>

> – There are only these two options at the end of our lives.

Step 9 – I = <u>INSPIRATION</u>

> – You and your life should always be an inspiration to everyone around you.

Step 10 – J = <u>JESUS</u>

> – Everything comes full circle—back to Jesus Christ.

Starting your presentation

The people you talk with should be able to see that you are different by your lifestyle, realizing that you have something they do not have—the answers to life.

However, while they are seeing that you are different from them, they may not be so bold as to admit this difference, so you might start your discussions with people by opening the door and explaining things this way: "You may have seen that I live my life a little differently than most people you may know ... that I have a love for almost everyone ... that I have a joy that most people do not have ... that I have a peace and strength that allow me to face the struggles that life throws my way ... and that I have a positive outlook when considering my future. Would you like to know why? Would you possibly like to have what I have, what makes me the different kind of person that I am?"

Before you think this is a little too bold or self-promoting, read Romans 8:1–20 and take time to meditate on it.

Here are a few starting points you should help others to see:

1. We are different from others because we are "no longer under condemnation". Praise God, we are "in Christ Jesus"!

2. We are different from others because we are "free from the law of sin and death."

3. We are different from others because we are no longer "powerless."

4. We are different from others because "we have our minds set on the Spirit", not on "what the flesh desires," and as a result we are governed by "life and peace."

5. We are different from others because we are no longer "hostile to God," by not submitting "to His laws," and not able to "please God."

6. We are also different from others because "we belong to Christ."

7. We are different from others because we are "led by the Spirit of God."

8. We are different from others because we are no longer living in "fear."

9. We are different from others because we have been "adopted into the family of God", and we are able to and do call God, "Abba Father" (Daddy).

10. We are different from others because we are now "co-heirs with Christ" and we will one day "share in His glory."

11. We are different from others as well because we consider whatever sufferings we face here and now in this world, are "nothing in comparison to the glory that is to come".

All of this explains why you are different, and the people around you should see some of this by the way you live your life.

We also read here that, "All of creation waits in eager expectation for the children of God to be revealed." In other words, your neighbors, your friends, your relatives, and all those around you are wanting to know that you are a child of God—so tell them!

Now I encourage you to read Galatians 5:16–25 and meditate on what is said there.

Here are a few important points you will see:

1. We are different from others because we are "walking in the Spirit".

2. We are different from others because we are "not chained to the flesh," always trying to "gratify" its longings.

3. There are only two lifestyles, and they are in conflict. We are different from others because "we are not living in sexual immorality, impurity and debauchery; idolatry and witchcraft; hatred, discord, jealousy, fits of rage, selfish ambition, dissensions, factions and envy; drunkenness, orgies, and the like."

4. We are different from others because we are living a life characterized by "love, joy, peace, forbearance, kindness, goodness, faithfulness, gentleness and self-control."

5. We are different from others because "we are living by the Spirit" and being "led by the Spirit."

So let's share the good news with others about how they too can have this same kind of life – one step, or one subject at a time … A, B, C, D, E, F, G, H, I, J.

As you read the following, watch how each step leads to the next—how each subject must be fully understood and accepted before moving on to the next.

A – Authority

Sharing the message of salvation must begin with helping people understand that there is only one Truth, and thereby helping them to accept God as their Supreme Authority in every regard. If people do not have this as their foundation in life, they will never understand or be able to accept Jesus Christ as their personal Savior.

Our responsibility as "Christ's ambassadors" (2 Corinthians 5:14–21) is to help people believe that God alone is to be *the authority* in our lives—the only one to whom we can look for the answers to life, the only one whom we must trust, and the only one from whom we will obtain truth and wisdom. It is only on this solid foundation that we can help people obtain eternal life and build a successful life in this world.

So we must begin with this basic fact—Almighty God does exist, He alone is Supreme, and we need to respect this truth.

Unless people believe God exists, and He is who He declares Himself to be, then there is no value in trying to tell them about His love for them. (Actually to do so may be harmful.)

So we must be careful, because if we try to explain anything about God, (for example His love for them), before they are willing to accept God as their authority, they will filter what we say with their preconceived ideas about Him—and will not be able to reconcile the truth with their ideology, and will come to erroneous conclusions. This has been the reason why so many people have rejected Christ as their Savior, because while they have heard the truth, they have passed it through their filters and have not been able to accept the plain truths about God or what He can do for them. The truth is not the problem—the filters are the problem. So until we help people get rid of those filters, they will not (and cannot) see the truth, understand the truth, or accept the truth.

Jesus put it this way in Luke 18:17: "I tell you the truth, anyone who doesn't receive the kingdom of God like a child will never enter it" (NLT). The NIV says "like a little child." What Jesus was saying is this: A young child does not have any preconceived ideas—their minds at this early age have not yet been twisted by hearing and believing lies—their minds and hearts have not yet been muddied by falsehood. A young child does not have these filters yet—filters that come as people tell them about evolution, for example, and other lies about God, and what they should believe or not believe.

The apostle Paul states, "The wrath of God is being revealed from heaven against all the godlessness and wickedness of people, *who suppress the truth* by their wickedness, since *what may be known about God is plain to them*, because *God has made it plain* to them. For *since the creation of the world, God's invisible qualities—his eternal power and divine nature—have been clearly seen, being understood from what has been made*, so that *people are without excuse*" (Romans 1:18–20).

I want to point out four things from these verses:

1. God has made it clear to us all that He alone is the Creator of everything.

2. God has made known to everyone His "eternal power and divine nature"—He has made it clear that He is the Supreme Authority.

3. God is not pleased with all of those who "suppress the truth"—those who tell lies about what He has revealed to us all.

4. God, the One who has created everything, will be our Judge—and when we stand before Him at the end of our lives, we will be "without excuse."

In other words, without the filters that come into place as we accept what the world teaches us, every person can look at creation and see clearly that it is God who has created everything, and instinctively know that God must have a purpose for everything. A person without these filters will also conclude that God must have had a purpose in creating them—and know that if they live their lives according to His will, He will bless them; and if they disobey God, they will not receive His blessings. In fact, they will know that at the end of our lives, God will be there to judge us all as to how we have lived our lives. They will know that if they have done what God wanted them to do in their lives, they will go to heaven and they will understand that those who were disobedient to God will go to hell. Their God-given unfiltered and untainted conscience tells them all of this to be true.

Paul tells us that we know all of this instinctively, simply by looking at what has been created all around us—by looking at everything without these filters.

So this is where we must begin our conversations with people:

> 1. We must help them to lay aside all of their preconceived ideas that have been based upon what others have told them.

> 2. We must help them rebuild their thinking by making the fact that God is the Creator of everything the foundation of their life.

> 3. We must help them understand and accept this account-ability factor—that God is both our Creator and therefore our Judge. He has created each of us for His purposes, and will at the end of our lives evaluate whether we have lived accordingly—and that our eternal destiny will be determined by this.

Therefore before talking with people about the love of God or salvation, we must discuss the subject of God being our Supreme Authority—helping them to look at the evidence all around them, without trying to filter God out (see Romans 1). They must come to accept God as the Supreme Authority in their lives—not their parents, not their university professors, not anyone who suppresses the truth about God—before you can talk to them about anything else.

When they have accepted this foundational fact, then we must help them understand that at the end of their lives, they will face God as their Judge—and He will reward them for the kind of life they have lived. They will go on to heaven if they have lived their lives according to their created purpose, or they will go to hell if they did not live up to what God expected of them.

People will try at this point to justify themselves, but we must bring them back to the fact that we do not have the right or ability to judge God. Rather, He alone has the right to pass judgment on the way we have lived our lives, and He alone is the One who can condemn us because He is our Creator.

Hebrews 11:6 says, "It is impossible to please God without faith. Anyone who wants to come to him must believe that God exists and that he rewards those who sincerely seek him" (NLT). And Hebrews 11:1 tells us, "Faith is the confidence that what we hope for will actually happen; it gives us assurance about things we cannot see" (NLT).

With these two verses in mind, we must help people place their trust and faith in God. In life we all trust certain things and certain people—this concept should not be hard for the people you talk with to understand.

Some questions you could ask them at this point are:

1. Do you believe God is the source of truth—the only truth?

2. Is God the one you are looking to for your answers to life?

3. Is God now the Supreme Authority in your life, or not?

4. Are you now willing to make God the one you will believe in and trust?

5. Are you willing to start building your life on a new foundation—making God the foundation on which the rest of your life will be built? Because only upon this solid foundation are we be able to obtain the best life possible—guaranteeing us a place in the Kingdom of God.

Without having people understand and accept God as their own personal and ultimate Authority, there is no value in moving on to discussing anything else about God or how to become a Christian.

In fact, if we do try to explain anything more to them, we will be encouraging them to become a judge of God.

1. They will start weighing the *real* truth against what they had thought up to this point as being true.

2. They will start evaluating God's true love against what they feel is fair.

3. They will decide that they want to maintain the control of their lives and do what they think is right.

4. They will condemn God for disagreeing with them.

5. They will condemn God for wanting to take control of their lives.

6. They will also condemn God for not accepting them on the basis of their good works, despite the fact that they have also lived sinful and selfish lives.

So I encourage you, be careful! Be wise! Helping people accept God as their authority is critical and primary.

This first step for anyone to become a true Christian is to understand and accept the authority of God in everything. There can be no one else trusted to tell us what to believe or what to do. Other people may help us, but their help must not be contrary to God's plan as disclosed in the Bible, and that is the introduction to our second step in presenting the message of salvation to people.

How will you know when they have gotten this far? How will you know when people are ready to go to step two? How will you know when they have made God their authority in life?

You may have to ask them, "Do you understand what we have been talking about? Do you agree that God is our Creator, and that He must have a plan for your life? Do you have any questions now that you have accepted all of this to be true?

At this point four things can happen:

1. They will likely start to ask you some additional related foundational questions.

2. They may ask you to give them some time to think about everything.

3. They may tell you they just are not ready to accept God into their lives.

4. They may ask you, "So what's next? How can I know what God's created purpose for my life is?"

If they are not at this point (#4), fully accepting what you have shared with them, respect that, and ask them if and when you can talk again about all of this.

If they are at this point (#4), then you can move on to telling them about the Bible—and it is only at this point that their hearts are going to be open to accepting all that God has in store for them. So be very sure they are at this point before moving ahead.

After they have accepted the authority of God in their life, then you can successfully start to build on this good foundation—just like when building a wall made of cement blocks, you can only install row two after row one has been successfully installed.

B – Bible

It does not help to tell people anything that is in the Bible until they accept that the Bible is the only reliable communication to us from God. Otherwise they will try to evaluate what the Bible says using their filters of preconceived ideas. They will then judge God on that filtered basis, and come to erroneous conclusions about what to believe or not believe—just as mentioned in the earlier section.

Therefore it is important to begin this step by discussing *why* the Bible has been accepted by us as being that reliable message and manual from God to us. If we neglect this part at the beginning of our presentation and go straight into what the Bible teaches, people will not understand *why* they should pay attention to what the Bible teaches. They may simply accept the Bible as only one possible revelation about God, and not see it as the *only* revelation from God. In other words, they will have no reason to obey its teachings.

It is important to explain: The Bible we have was written by forty different writers over a period of about 1,600 years. So many of these writers had no chance of knowing each other, or comparing notes on what they were writing. Yet the Bible has just one theme throughout, and no supposed contradiction has ever been proved. In fact, archeology has given much proof to us that the Bible is accurate, and has even proven the existence of many places and peoples that were thought to have never existed.

The Bible is an historical record of how everything came into being, how everything is maintained, and even how the development of humanity has taken place, from the very beginning of creation through to the ultimate future of mankind.

The Bible explains the sinfulness of mankind and its results as well as the only solution to our biggest problems. The Bible is therefore a manual from God on how to live life the only successful way. And the Bible gives testimonies over and over again of how people's lives have been changed and blessed through faith in God.

Thousands upon thousands of people living today, and millions upon millions of people throughout history, have entrusted their lives to the God of the Bible and have lived according to what the Bible has to say. They have proven by experience that God is faithful, and that what the Bible says can be relied on. In fact, many people throughout the centuries have believed its message and had their lives transformed as a result. Some have even died as martyrs, not wanting to recant their faith. Why? Because the Bible also has the promised blessings for life beyond the grave. And since God has proven Himself to be faithful and true throughout history, as disclosed in the Bible, there is every reason to believe that what the Bible says about the future will be true as well.

Before anyone can go on to understand anything about God, Jesus Christ, or salvation by faith in Christ, they must accept where such truths come from. If they do not accept that the Bible is the only Word of God, true and trustable, then they will forever have doubts. They will never be able to live the best life possible, and they will never know if they will be going to heaven when they die.

So please do not gloss over this crucial point. Before moving on, your listeners must have a clear acceptance that the Bible is today the only accurate communication to us from God. That does not mean they must believe and trust what the Bible states before reading it; that will come as the Holy Spirit works in their lives. But before you open and read any portion of the Bible to them, or disclose anything that the Bible states, they must understand that what the Bible says is the indisputable truth. (A person can reject the truth—that is their decision—but just because they might reject the truth, that does not negate the truth.)

If you try to go on to the next step without their acceptance that the Bible is true and worthy of reading, then they will try to compare what they read according to their preconceived ideas—and such comparison encourages a mistrust in God. So take your time, be patient, allow your listeners to ask questions, and do all you can to help them accept the Bible as the Word of God—before going on to tell them anything about Jesus Christ, God's love for them or the plan of salvation.

C – Christ

Until a person has accepted God as Supreme Authority in their lives and accepted that the Bible is the only reliable and truthful communication to them from God, there is no point trying to explain about God's love for them or anything about Jesus Christ. If you do go on before you should, they will use their filters of preconceived ideas to evaluate if what the Bible teaches is truly something from God that they need to obey. In other words, they will put themselves up as the authority in their lives with the right then to evaluate God—and this will encourage a mistrust in God—something we are wanting to avoid at all cost.

If you simply tell them God loves them, and that there is the promise of life in heaven after they die, they will be willing to pray any prayer and think they have done all that is necessary to guarantee themselves a place in heaven. And they will never experience the promise of a changed and better life, nor will they get to really enjoy the blessings of God. Therefore they will simply conclude at some point, "It didn't work! God cannot be trusted! I tried. I prayed the prayer." The sad thing is that this has happened with many people because someone rushed through explaining the message of salvation and quickly had them pray a certain prayer before they were ready, before they understood it all.

People are really only ready to move on with their discovery of personal salvation when they have accepted God as their authority and the Bible's teaching as truth.

Let me explain how to proceed through this section of your presentation of the message of salvation. Do not rush to talk about God's love, or that Christ is the only solution to our problems. At this point start with the teachings about Christ in the Old Testament and then in the New Testament (see Luke 24:13-35).

It is critical we begin this part of our presentation in the Old Testament, because it is there that they will learn the necessary foundational truths. We begin by reading about God creating the world and everything in it. We then see how God set out to continually reveal Himself to mankind in ever increasing ways, as well as how mankind was told how to live in healthy and successful ways. We read how over the centuries people have at times wanted to obey God's rules and regulations, and yet how at other times people have rebelled against God and suffered the penalties for doing so.

We tend to learn more from pictures, stories and history than we do through direct teaching. This is part of the importance of the Old Testament—we come to understand our sinfulness, and our need for a savior.

The purpose of the Law given in the Old Testament helps us become conscious of our sin, and that every person has this problem. In the Old Testament we read the prophecies of the Savior to come, and in the New Testament we read about Jesus Christ—the Savior that has come (see Romans 3:10-18, 3:19-20, 3:23-24, 7:7-25, 8:1-2).

As you talk about the stories and teachings in the Old Testament, and as your listener reads portions of it for themselves, they will begin to lay the important and necessary foundation in their understanding of God's purposes for humanity. They will also see how mankind has failed throughout history when they have rebelled against God, as well as how blessed people were when they followed God's instructions. These are important discoveries they must make as they begin to understand God's plan of salvation.

Before we talk to people about Christ, the Savior of the world, they must understand their own sinfulness and their personal need for a Savior. Otherwise they will only accept Jesus as a *good teacher*, and not much else. Only when they can fully grasp and understand their own personal helpless condition will they be glad to hear that God loves them despite their rebellion against Him—and that His love is not dependent upon how good a person is. Only then will they be thirsty and hungry for God. Only then will they be able to appreciate Christ and what He has done for them on the cross.

Therefore, when you come to this section in your presentation of salvation, do not rush to talk about God's love, or that Christ is the only solution to our problems. It must first really sink in that they are in a helpless and hopeless condition before they accept Christ's help. They must truly recognize and accept their own sinfulness, and understand the consequences they are facing as a result.

Quite possibly the best introduction to this part in your presentation will be to give the person you are talking to a copy of *The Story* by Zondervan or a copy of *The Daily Bible* by Harvest House Publishers. Both are selected readings from the New International Version of the Bible, printed in chronological order. These books will start the reader in the Old Testament and lead them correctly into the New Testament. It will be for them a discovery of how everything has happened from creation to the present, who we are and why we act as we do, and who God is and what He requires.

When they have this foundational understanding firmly in their minds, then we can share with them all about Christ—beginning with the Old Testament showing them how it is He who was promised long ago that would come and solve all our problems. Then we can move into the New Testament and share with them more about why Jesus came to earth, what He did throughout His life here, that on the cross He paid in full the penalty that is duly ours for the sins we have committed, and that He rose from the grave procuring for us the salvation we need, and the promise of eternal life.

When talking to people about Christ, we should not neglect to include related Old Testament teachings and prophecies. This is what Jesus did—and whose example is better to follow than His? I encourage you to read again Luke 24:13-35 where it says, "... beginning with Moses and all the Prophets, he explained to them what was said in all the Scriptures concerning himself ... then their eyes were opened and they recognized him ... They asked each other, 'Were not our hearts burning within us while he talked with us on the road and opened the Scriptures to us?'"

The goal of sharing this message of salvation with people is not so much to have them receive the blessings of God in their lives today, as it is for them to recognize Jesus for who He is, and then for them to find their place in the Kingdom of God and to fulfill what God has planned for them to do (see Ephesians 2:5-10).

It is at this point that you should take some time to reassess things in your own life. You cannot expect anyone you are sharing the message of salvation with to believe or do something you yourself are not fully compliant with. In other words, you must be practicing what you are seeking to explain to others, in order for them to be convinced of the truths you are talking about. So what is at the top of your priority list in life? What is your real focus? Are you fulfilling what God has planned for you to do?

If your purpose in life is to obtain God's blessings, you may become disappointed, because your focus should rather be on fulfilling God's purposes. Everyone wants God's blessings but we cannot expect them if the focus of our lives is on ourselves and our greedy desires (see Matthew 6:33). The truth is that His blessings are not an automatic gift or even a reward, but really the *by-product* of living our lives for Him. We must get our priorities in order!

Understand also that we have been adopted into God's family, and should not expect His blessings if we are not obedient to our Father's wishes. And how can we expect God to provide for all our needs and protect us from every danger (physical and spiritual; temporal and eternal), unless we are being obedient to Him—living our lives under His command and direction. We must therefore give up trying to hang onto the control of our lives, and allow God to do whatever He desires to do with our lives. In other words, you must make Jesus Christ the Master-Controller of everything in your life—making Him your Lord. This requires that you take on the position of being His servant, rather than thinking of yourself in any other way.

This might seem drastic—and it is when you think about it—and it all begins by making a big decision. And that is our next subject—the decision to make Jesus Christ our Lord and Savior, because this is what gives us entrance into the family of God, and being in His family is what guarantees us the family blessings and the family inheritance—eternal life.

D – Decision

When a person accepts the authority of God in their life, understands that the Bible is God's instruction book for them, recognizes their own sinfulness and the resulting consequences they are facing, and learns who Christ is and why He came to earth, then (and only then) can they make a decision to ask Jesus Christ to be their Lord and Savior.

Such a decision should not be based on the desire to receive God's blessings in their life, nor should it be to make sure that they will go to heaven when they die. Rather, this decision should be simply to express their recognition that God is their Creator, to express their desire to repent from their sinful ways, and to express their decision to live the rest of their life as God has intended, rather than simply for their own sinful desires.

This may sound like we are not focusing on our own personal fulfillment, but actually it is, because God's plan for our lives is really the best plan that could be designed for us. God is our creator; therefore to live life to its fullest would be to live life according to our created purpose. Make sense?

It is not necessary that a person pray a specially worded prayer; nor is it necessary that a person put up their hand at a meeting, or go to church and go to the front of a church at the end of its service.

What is necessary is that a person make a decision to change from being self-centered to being God-centered— and that they express their desire to change to God.

Therefore the prayer a person should make at this point should be a simple one—made in their own words. They should state first their deepest gratitude to God that He is willing to forgive them for all the wrong they have done, and thank Him for wanting to adopt them back into His family and give them a second chance to live their life according to His design and for His pleasure. Their prayer should then turn to focus on their promise that they will do all they can to be obedient to His direction, and do whatever He may ask them to do, each day for the rest of their life.

Becoming a Christian, therefore, is not just praying a simple prayer, and then continuing to live life as we wish. Rather, it begins by making one big informed decision and talking to God about it, and then making many appropriate decisions every day thereafter to live according to God's direction and desires.

Up to this point it may sound like becoming a Christian and living the Christian life only depends upon us becoming informed, and then having a change of heart and deciding to follow God's plan for our lives. In other words, it might seem like becoming and being a Christian depends entirely upon us and how we live our lives, when actually there is more to it. For us to be adopted back into God's family, and as a result become involved in the Kingdom of God, we must be 'born again'—this is what Jesus told Nicodemus (see John 3:3-8). In other words, we already have physical life, but to be a Christian we must have spiritual life—and this involves the Holy Spirit coming into our lives.

A Christian is also described as being a "believer" in John 3:14-18, 36, but this word means much more than simply accepting history as fact. It means putting one's whole trust in Jesus Christ as the Son of God, the One who died on the cross to procure salvation for us; instead of trusting any others, ourselves, or our works to gain approval or acceptance by God.

So becoming a Christian and living the Christian life involves a complete change of heart and the way we live our lives. It involves making several decisions—some we have already talked about.

1.   A decision to want to be told what the *truth* really is about life and how we ought to be living our lives.

2.   A decision to give God His rightful authority in our lives.

3.   A decision to accept the Bible as God's only reliable communication to us.

4.   A decision to delve into the Bible to find what God wants us to know, and to accept the truths laid out for us in the Bible.

5.   A decision to repent of our sinful ways and to start living according to God's plan.

6.   A decision to receive the pardon from God that is available to us through the death of Christ on the

cross. (A pardon provided is of no value if it is not received.)

7. A decision to obey God, no matter what He may ask us to do or where he may ask us to go.

8. A decision to start sharing with others in our spheres of influence, the good news about how they can be reconciled to God through Christ.

9. A decision to mentor others who accept this salvation through Christ, so they too may become disciples of Jesus Christ.

10. A decision to recognize the now indwelling Holy Spirit's involvement in our lives, and to live each day listening to and trusting the Holy Spirit to enlighten us, guide us, protect us, strengthen us, and comfort us.

11. A decision to be content with whatever God gives us to do and to have.

12. A decision to consciously set and maintain our focus each day on His Kingdom and on the return of King Jesus and not on our own selfish desires.

You may be thinking that this is much more than you had envisioned the Christian life to be about—that you will no longer be living for your own purposes and your own pleasures, and that you will no longer be in control of your own life.

Understanding that everything is all about God and His plans, rather than about how we can live life to the fullest, is hard for most people to accept. But the truth of the matter is that God created everything for His purpose and enjoyment. God created mankind because He wanted our companionship, and He had jobs for each of us to do in His Kingdom. But every man, woman and child have turned away from God to do as they have pleased—and we have suffered the consequences.

But God, in His mercy, has designed a way to bring us back into His plan. So Jesus Christ came into the world to redeem mankind, so that God's plans (plans that involve mankind), could be fulfilled.

We therefore have the option to be brought back into God's plan by accepting Jesus as our Lord and Savior. (We can refuse this option, and suffer the consequences—this is our individual choice.) By making the decision to lay aside our desires and to live as God intends, we can now share the message of salvation with others, so they too can fit back into God's plan. And, we look forward to Christ's return, so that God's plan can go on to the next stage...

When looking at things from eternity past, to eternity in the future, we can see that you and I are not the central focus in all of this. Rather the central focus of everything is God and His plan.

So the decision is yours—there is a choice to be made. Do you want to be included once again in God's plan? Then you must decide to forsake everything else and become a disciple of Jesus Christ—a disciplined and obedient follower (see Luke 14:25–33).

Before leaving this subject of decision making, I encourage you to take some time to review all the benefits to being one of Jesus' disciples that are listed in John 10:1-14. (In this passage Jesus refers to us as His 'sheep').

E – Eternity

You are now ready to show how God's plan for mankind from the beginning was not just to create everything, allow men and women to live their lives as they wish, and then for them to die (and that be the end, with no life beyond the grave).

Rather, God's plan is an eternal plan, and His desire is for each of us to become His children and to live with Him for all eternity. Your listener will have discovered this for themselves as you have walked them through these steps. I encourage you to share and meditate on John 1:1–33; John 3:12–21, 31-36; and Ephesians 1:3–12.

Explain how meditation involves truly thinking about what is being said, and then personalizing it. A great idea would be for them (and you, for that matter!) to write in a notebook all the things God points out to them as they spend time in meditation.

After meditating on the above verses, read and meditate on what the apostle Paul says to those who have turned their lives over to Jesus Christ in Ephesians 1:13–14.

Are they grasping the fullness of God's plan? Again, take the time to write down everything God is pointing out to you. Finally, read and meditate on the apostle Paul's prayer that follows in Ephesians 1:16–23.

F – Fellowship

God has not only laid out for us a little of His plan for all of creation and how it is all for His benefit, but He has also explained how we ought to live with Him (in His presence) and with each other here on earth. There is to be fellowship between us and God, and fellowship with other Christians. Here is where you encourage your listener to find a local body of believers—a church—where they can begin to fellowship.

The word *fellowship* refers to a group of people of equal status who share the same interests, have a unity of purpose, and work at doing things together as partners or as a group. Each partner values what they have, not only what they have individually but also what they have together as a group, because that is what holds them together. All partners in this group are loyal to the group and supportive of each other, and proud of their association. This is what is involved in being an individual in fellowship with others. Praise be to God for the fellowship we have with Him because of Christ Jesus! Let's now focus on building our fellowship with these new Christians and the place that each person has in the Body of Christ.

In his letter to the Ephesians, the apostle Paul described this fellowship as being a body. He then goes on to explain how we are individually unified into one organism (body or fellowship) by the Holy Spirit. He describes our individual responsibilities as given to each one by Christ, and goes on to explain the contributing purpose of each one to the other and to the whole. Then he emphasizes how important it is that we treat each other with love, and how important it is to maintain peace with each other in this fellowship (read Ephesians 4:1–16).

It is hard when thinking about fellowship to not also think about love, because the unity of fellowship is created and held together by this bond of love. Each participant in this fellowship possesses a supernatural love and a commitment to do whatever God asks of us (see 1 John 2:3–5).

What is this supernatural love? It is a love that motivates us and causes us to do things for people we normally would not do. It is a sacrificial love (see 1 John 3:1–18). In fact, this lifestyle of love is not only a characteristic of our lives, but it is a commandment that we are to keep throughout every day—and when we live this way, we have the assurance that we are real Christians (see 1 John 3:23–24). Your listener will begin to see this love in their own life, and give God the glory for it.

G – GOD is GOOD

God is to be Number One in our lives. He is the greatest and ultimate authority. He created us for His good purposes; nothing was created to turn out bad. God knows what is really good for us. Nothing He has planned is to harm us, but rather to bring us into our greatest position in life. We can trust God because God knows everything about everything, and He is in control of everything.

God is gracious and full of compassion. He is patient and loving, never pushing Himself or His ways on us. God showers grace on us, and He is always merciful, never giving us the bad we deserve because of our stubborn or rebellious ways; but ready to give us the good things we do not deserve, because He really does love each of us. In fact, God gives us good things every day of our lives: everything that is good comes from God.

Great is God's love and faithfulness (see Psalm 36:5, 57:9-11; 89:21-24, 33; 100:4-5; Lamentations 3:22-26). He always comes through when we commit our lives into His hands. You can encourage your listener to hold fast to this truth when the inevitable disappointments and heartaches of love come into their life. We often do not understand what His purposes are when we face various situations, but if we take the time to look back on what we've gone though, we can often see that God engineers things for our good (see Romans 8:28). How great is our good God—the only one true God.

H – Heaven or Hell…?

There are only two places people can go to at the end of their physical lives here on earth, and they are heaven or hell—to be living with God for all eternity, or to be existing without God (see Luke 16:19-31). The most interesting thing is that God has told us in His Word that He will not force us to go to either place, but He has told us there are only these two options. What is even more interesting is that God tells us that our destiny is completely up to us (see John 3:17-21, 36).

Encourage your listener to meditate on this. What will heaven be like? Think about it. God is there, and God is love. God is good. Therefore, everything we experience for all eternity will be done in love, and everything will be good. There will be no questions, no uprisings against Him, and no reluctance about following His instructions. There will be peace in every situation and with every person. There will be no sickness, no disease, and no sin. Nothing could be better!

What will hell be like? Think about it. God will not be there, so there will be the absence of love and all that is good. It is a place of condemnation and punishment (see Matthew 13:36-42; 2 Thessalonians 1:6-10; 2 Peter 2:1-22).

It is with this outlook of being one day in heaven with God that we can truly look forward to our future. It is with this focus that we can face every situation. It is with this reality that we are motivated to share the message of salvation with everyone around us. Your listener is sure to agree with you, now that they are also experiencing God's transforming power in their own life.

I – Inspiration

Your life should be an inspiration to everyone around you. Often we go through things in our lives just so those around us will see that our faith is real, that our God is trustworthy, and that the message of salvation that we have been telling them about is the truth.

God is wanting, willing and waiting to give us all a life beyond comprehension (see Ephesians 3:20-21; John 10:7-10). Many Christians try to live their lives in perfect order, appearing as though nothing is too difficult for them and wanting the world to believe that simply believing in Jesus will make all this possible for them too. However, I believe that attitude to be very short-sighted, and in some ways even fraudulent and erroneous.

The Bible is clear: the Christian life is not all about simply trying to do good things and believe the historical facts about Jesus to be true. Rather it's all about surrendering the ownership of our lives to Jesus Christ, giving Him the complete control of our lives, then listening to Him and obeying Him and allowing His Spirit to work in and throughout our lives. It is a life to be lived in faith, by trusting God in every way and for everything all the time, and thereby reaching out to those around us with the love of God (see Hebrews 11:1-12:2; Romans 6:3-14; 8:1-14; 12:1-21; James 1:22-27; 2:14-26; 1 John 3:17-24; 4:7-21; 5:1-12).

Some might say that living life that way would not be self-satisfying or much fun, and I agree; it is not all about satisfying our physical passions. However, I have proven throughout my life that there is no better place to be than where God wants me to be, and there are no better things to be doing than what God wants me to do. I have also proven throughout my days and years that life can be very satisfying and tremendously fulfilling when we put our lives *in His hands*. (This is why I have chosen this to be the title of this book.) I believe that everything I have been through, both the joys and the heartaches, are to serve as inspiration to others who are trying to live as I have—wholeheartedly trusting God for absolutely everything.

Your listener opened up to you initially because they saw something in you that was different—you were an inspiration to them. And now they will experience God's provision, protection and guidance and, in turn, become an inspiration to others as they share their own story and the message of salvation. Isn't God's plan wonderful?

J – Jesus

Everything comes full circle back to Jesus. We have looked at Bible verses where we have been told that He was the Creator of everything and that nothing was created apart from Him (see John 1:1–3). We have read that only Jesus has life and can give life, and that only He has the true answers to life (see John 1:4–5, 9–14).

We also read in the Bible that Jesus is the sustainer of all things and in control of all things, and that everything was created according to His plan and for His benefit. In fact He is not only the present controller, but He is also the future heir of everything (see Hebrews 1:1–4).

In John 3:35–36 we read, "The Father loves his Son and has put everything into his hands. And anyone who believes in God's Son has eternal life. Anyone who doesn't obey the Son will never experience eternal life but remains under God's angry judgment" (NLT). So the crux of the matter, the cornerstone of truth, the only Savior of mankind, is Jesus Christ.

We have come full circle. We began speaking about who is the authority in your life. Now, at the conclusion of this presentation of the message of salvation, we have seen that everything is in the hands of Jesus. At the end of the book of Matthew we read, "Jesus ... told his disciples, 'I have been given all authority in heaven and on earth'" (Matthew 28:18 NLT).

In his letter to the Philippians, the apostle Paul writes, "God exalted him [Jesus Christ] to the highest place and gave him the name that is above every name, that at the name of Jesus every knee should bow, in heaven and on earth and under the earth, and every tongue acknowledge that Jesus Christ is Lord, to the glory of God the Father" (Philippians 2:9–10).

So even those who reject Jesus today will one day recognize Him for who He really is: the only way to heaven, the discloser of absolute truth, and the only giver of eternal life (see John 14:6). Therefore, as you conclude talking with your friends about this message of salvation, it is important to stress that what you have been sharing with them from the Bible is the truth. If they choose to disagree, argue, or reject what the Bible states, that is a decision they are allowed by God to make. But nothing they say, disagree with, or argue against will negate what the Bible has stated to be the truth.

And the truth is that one day they must face Jesus as their judge (see 2 Timothy 4:1; Hebrews 10:29–31; James 4:12; 1 Peter 4:3–5; Jude 14–16). Today He can be their Savior, but one day that door will be closed to them (see 2 Corinthians 6:2; Revelation 3:15–20).

Finally, you must realize that all the explaining we can give them will never be enough. We must leave them with the message of salvation, clearly presented, and then let the Holy Spirt do His job of conviction and salvation (see John 16:7–13; 3:1–8).

I am sure, after you have taken the time to read all this and meditate on what is written in God's Word, that your question is, "Where do I start?" The answer is, start with the person next door to you—your neighbor.

Jesus gives us this instruction and summary:

> "Hearing that Jesus had silenced the Sadducees, the Pharisees got together. One of them, an expert in the law, tested him with this question:

"Teacher, which is the greatest commandment in the Law?" Jesus replied: "'Love the Lord your God with all your heart and with all your soul and with all your mind.' This is the first and greatest commandment. And the second is like it: 'Love your neighbor as yourself.' All the Law and the Prophets hang on these two commandments" (Matthew 22:34–40).

"One of the teachers of the law came and heard them debating. Noticing that Jesus had given them a good answer, he asked him, "Of all the commandments, which is the most important?" "The most important one," answered Jesus, "is this: 'Hear, O Israel: The Lord our God, the Lord is one. Love the Lord your God with all your heart and with all your soul and with all your mind and with all your strength.' The second is this: 'Love your neighbor as yourself.' There is no commandment greater than these" (Mark 12:28–31).

What does it mean to "love the Lord your God"—and to do so with your heart, soul, mind, and strength?

Love simply means to consider the other person (whether it be God or our neighbor) as more important than ourselves. We are to love them with everything we have, setting nothing aside for ourselves and holding nothing back for whatever personal reasons we may have. So regardless of what the cost to ourselves might be, we are to help them with their needs according to the abilities and things God has given us.

How do we *love* God? I believe to love God with my mind is to make God the primary factor when I am trying to reason things out, and when I am developing conclusions and making decisions. To love God with my strength is saying, "I will do whatever God wants with all I've got; I am 100% committed to His plan and program; nothing in my life is going to hold me back..." To Love God with my soul is to allow Him to control my conscience. And to love God with my heart is to become passionate about what He is passionate about.

God's need is for us to recognize Him as our Creator and that we were created for His benefit, and then to live our lives according to His plan that He has had for us since before we were created. We are to do all that we can to spread the good news of God's great love for all mankind, and His wonderful message of salvation with everyone around us. Now there are a myriad of ways to do this, and God has individually equipped each of us to do this in ways that He knows will work with those around us, specific to the part of the world that we are each living in and those we are in contact with.

The other question is, "Who is my neighbor?"

I believe this is a reference to everyone who is in our sphere of influence—our relatives, our friends, the people we work with, the people who live around us, and everyone we encounter every day of our lives. All these people have both physical and spiritual needs, and God's instruction to us is that we share all the blessings we have received from Him with these people. This is our responsibility, and this is God's will for our lives. This is living life *in His hands*.

As you share the message of salvation with others, you will not want to stop. Many people will likely reject you, but there will be some who will be so thankful that you have helped bring them into the family of God. You may be physically tired at the end of some days, but you will be spiritually exhilarated. You will be strengthened to carry on doing what you now know is God's will for your life, and you will know that you have found your purpose in life.

When living your life in this manner—*in His hands*— you will experience that close relationship with God you have been longing for. You will know that God really loves you, and that He is delighted with you. You will receive blessings from Him that you never dreamed of, and He will be close to you through all of your trials and disappointments. You will not have to worry about anything. He will be in control, providing everything you need and protecting you (see again Matthew 6:25-33; Ephesians 3:20-21).

So you see, you cannot work for a better boss, or be a servant under a better master. Living with Christ as your Boss, you will feel like clay in the Potter's hands, and He will be making some beautiful things through your life.

There really is no better life to be lived than *in His hands*.

The apostle Paul prayed for the Christians in Ephesus as recorded in Ephesians 3:14-21—let me echo that prayer for you right now.

I kneel before the Father, from whom every family in heaven and on earth derives its name. I pray that out of His glorious riches He may strengthen you with power through His Spirit in your inner being, so that Christ may dwell in your hearts through faith. And I pray that you, being rooted and established in love, may have power, together with all the Lord's holy people, to grasp how wide and long and high and deep is the love of Christ, and to know this love that surpasses knowledge—that you may be filled to the measure of all the fullness of God. Now to Him who is able to do immeasurably more than all we ask or imagine, according to His power that is at work within us, to Him be glory in the church and in Christ Jesus throughout all generations, for ever and ever! Amen.

APPENDIX B

Resources for Effective Evangelism

Believability of Creation by God:
- ❖ Scientific Creationism
    Author: Henry M. Morris
- ❖ Guide to Creation
    Author: Institute for Creation Research
- ❖ Guide to the Human Body
    Author: Institute for Creation Research
- ❖ Evolution and the Modern Man
    Author: Henry M. Morris
- ❖ The Case for A Creator
    Author: Lee Strobel

Evidence for the Christian Faith:
- ❖ The Case for Christ
    Author: Lee Strobel
- ❖ The Case for Faith
    Author: Lee Strobel
- ❖ Many Infallible Proofs
    Author: Henry M. Morris

❖ New Evidence that Demands a Verdict
  Author: Josh McDowell

Sharing Christ with Others Effectively:
  ❖ I Don't Have Enough Faith to be an Atheist
    Authors: Norman L Geisler; Frank Turek
  ❖ Making Your Case for Christ Training Course
    Authors: Lee Strobel; Mark Mittelberg
  ❖ The Way of the Master
    Author: Ray Comfort
  ❖ Evangelism in a Skeptical World
    Author: Sam Chan

Making Cross Cultural Ministries Productive:
  ❖ Mañana Forever? Mexico and the Mexicans
    Author: Jorge G. Castañeda
  ❖ When Helping Hurts: How to Alleviate Poverty
    Without Hurting the Poor and Yourself
    Authors: Steve Corbett; Brian Fikkert
  ❖ Walking with the Poor: Principles and
    Practices of Transformational Development
    Author: Bryant Myers
  ❖ Bruchko
    Author: Bruce Olson

APPENDIX C

Why Many Christians Lead Unsatisfied Lives

AND

The Surprising Solution...

I trust that you realize by now that I take the responsibility of sharing the message of salvation seriously, and I have written this book to serve as an inspiration to others to do as I have done and fully trust God for every aspect of their lives.

Some people have only known parts of my life and thought that everything must have always gone well for me. But they have only seen some of the wonderful ministries and relationships that I have been privileged to be a part of, and not the struggles and sacrifices made along the way. You have now seen that I have faced many challenges in my life—some which you may well be facing, and had not known before that I too have faced.

Some people will conclude that the Christian life has too high of a cost and is not worth the struggle. Or they have tried with all their might to live according to biblical principles, but just don't see any fruit in their lives.

This will lead them to wonder, as they look at their fellow Christians' lives, *What is it that should make a Christian different from other people? Because we all seem to act the same as others do who do not profess to be Christians. How will I be an inspiration to others when I don't see any difference in my own life?*

I believe that the root of this thinking causes people to reject Jesus and to reject those who follow Him. Some do it out of frustration and sheer exhaustion, others do it because they resent the time and energy given to a God they don't trust, and that they believe could have been better invested in themselves. Maybe this is how you feel.

Take a journey with me to the heart of the matter – it will not be easy. But if you will read and try to understand each of the areas addressed and apply these lessons to your life, you will definitely not be disappointed. Let's begin:

1. Unfortunately many people look at their lives and wonder why they have to go through certain difficulties when it appears that other people never deal with any problems.

Some people I know even believe life has been so unfair to them that they wonder if God really loves them.

Have you faced any situations or problems that no one knows about? Or maybe one or two people may know about those difficulties, but you've done well hiding these challenges from everyone else? During the week you live one kind of frustrated life, but on Sunday you put the best smile on your face and no one knows what your week has been like. Or maybe you go to work in the morning and have a difficult day, but you come home at night and do not tell anyone about it. Or possibly you have had some difficult situations to face in your marriage, but your friends will never know because you and your spouse try to put on a good show in front of others. Does any of this sound like you?

So as you look at others, do you say to yourself, *Well, they certainly haven't had to face any of these situations I've had to face. Just look at them. They always seem to have a smile on their face.*

Let me tell you not to be discouraged. I've been in all the situations described, and many times others have not known about them—and it has not been easy! Several times in my life, I've even considered committing suicide, but I have found solutions that have really helped me, and I believe they may help you overcome your problems, too.

2.   Unfortunately many Christians wonder why they do not experience the wonderful things that some other Christians talk about.

In John 10:14–20, Jesus says, "I am the Good Shepherd; I know My sheep and My sheep know me. They listen to My voice. They enter the sheepfold through the gate. They go in and out and find good pasture. I am the Good Shepherd, and I have come that they may have life, and have it to the full" (my own abbreviated paraphrase).

In the Christian life, few things happen automatically. Most things take place not because Jesus takes action, but rather because we take certain action. You see, Jesus is always willing to help us, but we must believe in Him, take the time to go to Him and ask for His help, and be willing to obey Him—no matter what He asks us to do. When we do everything this way (and I have proven this in my own life), then we will feel we are living a privileged, abundant life—"life to the full"— however not necessarily as defined by the world. You will know you have received—and are indeed experiencing—the blessings of God in your life.

I encourage you to read the history of three men who had to do three things—believe, trust, and obey—to receive the blessings of God. The first is about an unnamed man in Mark 1:40–42. Now read about Naaman (Luke 4:25–27; 2 Kings 5:1–14) and Nicodemus (John 3:1–12).

Do you see that they each had to *'believe'*, *'trust'* and *'obey,'* in order to receive the blessings of God?

The same is true for all of us today. We must "believe, trust, and obey" to receive the blessings of God in our lives. This does not mean just when becoming a Christian, as you have seen in the histories of these three men, especially the two men with a physical problem. They had to do something in order to receive the blessings of God. And in order to be willing to do what they were asked to do, they had to first believe that God would bless them if they did what they were asked to do. Then they had to trust the person who was talking to them and obey the instructions given to receive the blessings of God in their lives. None of this was a gift from God where they did not have to do something. There was a mind-set required, a certain amount of risk involved, and an obedient action to follow—and the action required was not what they would have chosen to do.

God wants you too to experience "life to the full", but it must be on His terms.

3.   Unfortunately many people in our world today who call themselves Christians will one day learn that they have never been true Christians.

In Matthew 7:21–23, Jesus said, "Not everyone who says to me, 'Lord, Lord,' will enter the kingdom of heaven. ... Many will say to me on that day, 'Lord, Lord, did we not prophesy in your name and in your name drive out demons and in your name perform many miracles?' Then I will tell them plainly, 'I never knew you. Away from me you evildoers!'"

If you are like most people, when you have read these verses, you have wondered, *How can I be sure that I am a real Christian?*

As we carefully look at the verses, it seems that one is not a *real* Christian by simply saying, "Lord, Lord." And certainly prophesying, casting out demons in others, or performing other miracles does not make a person a Christian. In other words, one does not become a Christian by simply praying a certain prayer, or by even being involved in church.

I encourage you to read, and re-read, the book of 1 John in the Bible. There are ten proofs mentioned there that describe a *real* Christian. Also, as you read, I encourage you to write down each of these proofs with its corresponding chapter and verse. Then as you review it, you can ask yourself if all ten of these proofs are true of you. If they are, then you are a *real* Christian and can be sure you will enter the kingdom of heaven.

However, if you do not see yourself measuring up to the standard in God's Word, then look again at Matthew 7:21: "Not everyone who says to me, 'Lord, Lord,' will enter the kingdom of heaven, but only the one who does the will of my Father who is in heaven."

4. Unfortunately many people have spent too long wondering, *What is the will of God for my life?* But while searching, they are doing next to nothing of spiritual value.

If you've ever asked yourself this question, I want you to go to the Appendix A in this book where I present a simple way to share the message of salvation and ask yourself, *Who is the authority in my life? Who am I listening to each day? Am I obeying God as He compels me to do all the time, or do I try to say to myself, 'That can't be God. It's just my brain trying to trick me to do something'.*

The second question to ask yourself is, *Am I reading the Bible each day, and asking God to show me something about Himself, something about myself, and something about what He would like me to do?* Or, dare I ask, are you trying to be in control of your own life—in other words, trying to ignore God or outright disobey Him? That may seem a little harsh, but ask yourself these questions. It will be a benefit to you to be honest with yourself.

There are no other options. You are either the Master-Controller of your life, or Jesus is the Lord of your life. You cannot have it both ways. You are one day going to enter the kingdom of God based not on just giving ascent to historical facts, but whether you have done His will or your will during your lifetime. Look at Matthew 7:21 once again.

I encourage you to now read Luke 14:1–33, where Jesus tries to explain in practical terms what all this means. He explained it first to the Pharisee, then to those who followed Him as well as to others in a large crowd. Take out a notebook and write down what the Lord impresses on your heart as you read.

As you read Luke 14:1–6, what popped into your mind? Now think about that thought a little longer, and ask the Lord to reveal to you exactly what He would have you do in light of what you have just read, then write that down. Do the same as you read Luke 14:7–14. Write down in your notebook what God is saying to you.

Next, read and think about what you should be writing down as you read Luke 14:15-24. The last set of verses, Luke 14:25-33 are important. They draw a conclusion on what you have been writing down. But don't get sidetracked by the last sentence, "...you cannot become my disciple without giving up everything you own." The problem is that many people have misunderstood what Jesus was teaching here. Consider what Jesus began with, "If you want to be my disciple, you must hate everyone else by comparison" (v. 26 NLT). Unfortunately, some translations do not include the tone of this sentence by adding the two important words *"by comparison"*. These words give us the context of this whole section of verses, so when it ends with the statement "you cannot become my disciple without giving up everything you own" (v. 33 NLT), we should reword it to get its true meaning: "you cannot become a *true disciple* of mine without giving up *the ownership of* everything you possess" (my own abbreviated paraphrase). Jesus was basically saying, "You need to understand the truth about what I teach, and also give up the ownership rights to your own life and all that you possess and make Me the Lord (Master-Controller) of your life. Then you will be My *true disciple*. When you do this (give up your ownership rights), then all that you possess will be used (not necessarily given away), as I direct you to further the Kingdom of God, and as you share the Gospel with others."

Now take out your notebook, contemplate what is said in these verses for a few minutes, and write down what God is saying to you.

5. Unfortunately many people do not look deeper into the crucial subject of doing the will of God. So let's dig deeper.

First, and most obvious, is the matter of what or who is controlling your life. Is it God, or the people around you? Are you disciplining your mind to rise above those who might be trying to control you? This begins not with looking deeper at the people or things that might be keeping you from achieving your best in life, but instead deciding in your heart and mind that you will listen to God and obey Him, no matter what He requires. In other words, will you give up your selfish control of everything in your life? Will you decide to agree with God, that He always knows what is best for you? Will you decide to give Him complete control and make Him the Lord of your life no matter what others might say or do?

Second, after making this decision to allow God to run your life as He wishes, you must listen to Him in order to know what He wants you to do. You will likely also want to discuss things with Him to obtain clarity—not really to complain to Him, but to simply get the assurance you need about moving in a direction that you might not have chosen if you were in control of your life.

Third, you must take action. God wants you to do things for Him. Read Ephesians 2:10: "We are God's handiwork, created in Christ Jesus to do good works, which God prepared in advance for us to do." Consider Philippians 2:12–14: "My dear fellow Christians, we must allow God who has saved us and is continually working on us, to bless other people around us, through the things we can do for them. This is His will and purpose for each of our lives. We must not grumble, complain, or argue with Him, like the world might do. Rather, you are to shine like the stars in the heavens—and you will, when you do what He has planned for you to do" (my own abbreviated paraphrase).

Fourth, we must have complete confidence in God, believing He really is in control of everything, trusting that everything we are doing is making a positive impact for Jesus in the lives of all those we are in contact with, being grateful for all the opportunities that come our way to bless others, and thankful for all His provisions and protection.

Now, you may be asking yourself, *But what exactly am I to do?* The answer is simple. Do not do the things that the Bible calls sinful; rather, do things that honor God. Take time to read 1 Corinthians 10:24–33; Galatians 6:9–10; Colossians 3:1–11; and Romans 8:5–13. Think about all that is being said in these verses, and I believe God will speak to you about what you should be doing with your life. (Again, it will be helpful to write down your thoughts in your notebook, even if they do not yet show you a complete picture.)

6.   Unfortunately many people think that to live out the will of God in their lives is just too difficult. I agree that it is not easy, but I also want you to know that it is really to live the best life possible — and it is possible for all of us to do.

When Jesus is not just your Savior, but also the Director of your life, and you are obeying His instructions, then you will be a blessing to others. You will feel at peace with God, you will have a joy in your life you otherwise cannot experience, and you will feel like you really are living out *the best life possible.* Your life will definitely be a very purposeful experience, with treasures in heaven to look forward to.

Consider the apostle Paul's testimony concerning what it meant for him to live out what God calls us to do: "We are hard pressed on every side, but not crushed; perplexed, but not in despair; persecuted, but not abandoned; struck down, but not destroyed. We always carry around in our body the death of Jesus, so that the life of Jesus may also be revealed in our body. For we who are alive are always being given over to death for Jesus' sake, so that his life may also be revealed in our mortal body. All this is for your benefit, so that the grace that is reaching more and more people may cause thanksgiving to overflow to the glory of God. Therefore we do not lose heart. Though outwardly we are wasting away, yet inwardly we are being renewed day by day. For our light and momentary troubles are achieving for us an eternal glory that far outweighs them all. So we fix our eyes not on what is seen, but on what is unseen, since what is seen is temporary, but what is unseen is eternal" (2 Corinthians 4:8–11, 15–18).

From Paul's perspective, life was hard, but he was able to live above his circumstances by keeping his focus on God's plan; therefore he never lost his ability to trust God or his compassion for helping others.

As Paul continues, he tells the Corinthians that we are *Christ's ambassadors*; we have the *ministry of reconciliation*—what a privilege and what a responsibility—to share with those around us the message that will bring people into relationship with God. We are God's coworkers (see 2 Corinthians 5:17–6:1). This is what it means to be living according to the will of God.

At the end of your life, despite what the majority of people believe, it is not the man with the most toys who wins or the one who has done more good things than bad. Rather, the most important factors in life are not what company you own, what you have done, who you have worked for, or what programs you were a part of, but how obedient you have been to God. He has created you and me for a purpose—His purpose—and we will stand before Him on Judgement Day and give an account of how well we have lived our lives according to His purpose.

So as you look at your life today, realize that we cannot expect to be blessed by God if we are not doing what He wants us to be doing. This requires that we have a good relationship with Him, which can only happen on His terms, through the work of Jesus Christ and the acceptance of His offer of salvation. It also requires that we give up selfish control of our lives, determine that we will live up to our created purpose, make Jesus Christ the Lord of our lives, and constantly be listening to Him and obeying Him.

I trust that you have been encouraged through reading my story. It is not the story of a popular TV personality, the pastor of a large church, some person telling you that they have a wonderful self-help program for you, or a person who has never faced any problems in life. Instead, it is the story of an average person who has believed God, trusted and obeyed Him, and as a result many people's lives have been blessed. I do not say this boastfully—rather praise be to the God of love and life who has worked in and through my life, and who has been directing everything—so that I might be another example of His handiwork (see Ephesians 2:4, 10).

Your life can be filled with peace, love, and joy—a life with everything you need provided, treasures included, and without any reason to be anxious about anything (see Philippians 4:4–9; Matthew 6:19–33).

You may find it hard to believe. Well, look at it this way: If one of the richest men on earth were your father, you would not expect or hope for anything less than what I have described, would you? Of course not. In fact, you would want everything in life to be good—and even if bad things would happen to you, that they could somehow be engineered to give you greater opportunities for better things. In those troubled times, you would want the best defender. In times of weakness, you would want the best help possible. In times of loss, you would want more and better replacements. Now isn't it true that all of this and more is exactly what you would want from your rich father? Well, the richest and most able person to help you with all this is your heavenly Father.

I am sure you are now thinking that I'm about to give you some kind of get-rich scheme or some kind of prosperity theology. But that is not the case. This book has been all about my life history, my experiences. And in many ways, I have lived life in all these ways. You have read my story. So I encourage you to read the following, and then trust God to do in your life what He really can do for you and with you. You will, in fact, come to experience *the best life possible—in His hands.*

So as you read the following verses, ask God to speak to you about what He would like to do in your life, and hold nothing back. Tell Him that you will obey Him, even when you cannot see the big picture—you will trust Him. Tell Him that you are tired of living life under your own management, frustrated that you have not been able to deal with many situations, and that you want to give Him rightful ownership of your life and let Him take total control.

After talking to God this way, read and meditate on Joshua 1:1–10 (a good introduction to the life that lies ahead for you, just as it was for those Israelites many years ago). Do not just read these verses, but take some time to really meditate on them. Think about what is written in each verse, personalize what is being said, and write in your notebook all the things God is pointing out to you.

Then read and meditate on Proverbs 3:5–6 (a good introduction to all the verses and chapters of wisdom that follow). Following this, read and meditate on John 10:1–16; Matthew 11:27–30; Psalm 37:3–5; and Romans 8:26–39.

As you now move forward, realizing that your life can be filled with peace, joy and love, you should not only focus on what you should be doing as you serve Christ but also how:

When we were born again (see John 3:5–8) through the Holy Spirit (see 1 John 3:24), we became a child of God; we entered the fellowship of God's family (see John 1:12–13; 1 John 3:1). God is love, and we therefore have this supernatural love by virtue of being in God's family—love runs in the family (see 1 John 4:7–13, 16). And Jesus said, "This is My commandment, that you love one another—just as I have loved you—and by this love you will prove to everyone around you that you are truly one of My disciples" John 13:34-35 (my own abbreviated paraphrase).

This lifestyle of sacrificial love is not something to be afraid of at all! Rather, this love carries us through every situation here on earth (including all kinds of trials and troubles), and it will one day take us on to our glorious eternity with Him (see 1 John 4:18; Romans 8:14–17; Matthew 10:28–31; Colossians 3:23–24; 1 Peter 3:3–9; 2 Corinthians 4:16–18).

This sacrificial love was first expressed by our Lord Jesus Christ. It was His love for us, and the eternal joy that motivated Him to endure all the sufferings He went through here on earth, and even during His death on the cross (see Hebrews 12:1–3; 1 John 4:19). The ongoing expression of this sacrificial love is up to us. We are to love others—not just care about them, empathize with them, or help them, but actually personally do our very best to help them in their struggles (see Ephesians 5:1–2; 1 John 2:9–11; 3:11–18). In fact, if we do not really love people as we should, then we are told that we cannot say that we are Christians.

Jesus said everything comes down to love—love for God and love for others—and it is this one thing that will show others which people are Christians (see Matthew 22:34–40; Mark 12:28–31; John 13:34–35).

Likely the biggest problem we face today in our society, as have people throughout history, is loving what money can buy for us—things and friends. Jesus gave His solution to us: set your priorities and serve just one master; don't try to love two things at the same time. You cannot love what money can buy for you and love God simultaneously. If you really do want what God has to offer—if you want to be a real Christian—then you must give up everything else. This is what Jesus told the crowds who were following Him. In other words, a follower of Jesus is not a real Christian, only a disciple of Jesus Christ is a Christian (see Matthew 6:24; Luke 16:13–15; Luke 14:25–33).

Consider this: A dedicated athlete will only achieve his or her desired results with diligent discipline and maintaining focus on the finish line and the reward and life that is to follow. This was exactly how the apostle Paul looked at his life, and why he was able to achieve so much during his lifetime. This is why the writer of Hebrews told us, after describing what faith really is and giving examples of many people throughout history who had accomplished so much for God (see Hebrews 11): "throw off everything that hinders or entangles ... Don't let yourself grow weary doing what God has for you to do ... and above all, don't lose heart" (Hebrews 12:1–3, my own abbreviated paraphrase).

We all struggle with our propensity to sin, and at times we stray off the path set for us. At these times we need someone to help us get up, get going again and refocus on the race, the finish line, and the life that is to come— eternal values instead of temporal values. This will not only involve bringing the things that are important to our attention, but it may even involve the Lord Himself disciplining us. He will do this because He loves us. He wants us to be successful, and to share His eternal treasures with us (see Hebrews 12:4–29).

But you may ask, "What is God's will for my life? What should I be doing? What is my part, my responsibility? How important am I?"

Before you jump ahead, let me remind you that it was Christ who chose each of us. He is the Head, the Master-Controller, and the Lord. In fact, He is the Creator, the Firstborn, and in Him everything is held together and kept functioning. Everything we have is because of Him (see Colossians 1:13–20; 2:9–10).

We are also told that there is nothing special about any of us, yet Christ has chosen us to be a part of His group of representatives in the world today, and in this group—the church (not referring to a building, but to His group of representatives in the world today)—we all have equal status (see Romans 3:9–18, 21–24; 1 Corinthians 12:12–13; Galatians 3:26–28). The only difference between each of the members is the gifts we have been given by God, which we are to use for the benefit of the other members in the group. None of those is more important than the other.

So whether you tend to agree or not, God says you are just as important as everyone else, so you ought never to minimalize who you are or what you can do, and never to consider your worth by comparing yourself with others— who they are, what they may be doing, or what they may possess (see 1 Corinthians 1:26–31; Ephesians 1:11–14; 1 Peter 1:9–10; 1 Corinthians 12:12–27; Romans 12:3–5).

Rather, we have individually been given tasks by Christ and therefore are responsible to Him, the Head, and not the other members (see Ephesians 2:10). Our relationship with God is only through Christ, and not in any way influenced by others; therefore our responsibility is not to please others or to boast about anything, but only to please Christ. He is to be our focus (see Colossians 2:6–10; Galatians 6:14–15; Philippians 3:7–14).

So our relationship is with Christ, but the practical activities we are to be involved in on a daily basis are to be with people within this group of chosen representatives. We are to love each other as noted, but how should this love be expressed?

At this point, I encourage you to take out a pen and paper, draw a line down the middle of the paper, and take all the time you need to read and then write down on the left side of your paper all the activities (expressions of love) that you can find in these passages: Colossians 3:11–17; Ephesians 4:1–3; 5:15–20; Philippians 2:1–5; and Romans 12:3–21.

Now on the right side of your paper, beside each action item listed, make personal notes about how well you are doing each one, and what improvements you could make. You will no doubt recognize that there is a lot you can do to be better at all of this—and that is part of growing in Christ. Do not be discouraged; just realize that with the help of the Lord, you will gradually become more like Him. That is the goal: to love others as Christ has loved you (see Ephesians 5:1–2).

We also have a specific responsibility to share the message of salvation with others so that more people can be added to the group. But as you now have come to realize, this is not simply and only information that is to be disclosed to others through some organized formula. Good communication skills are involved, and one must be living what they preach—they must be living a life of integrity for the message to be believed—and that is the goal: to help others understand the truth and come to the position where they too will believe in the Lord Jesus Christ (see John 20:30–31). So how do we get to this point of integrity? Consider the following: 1 Timothy 1:5; 2 Peter 1:2–11; Philippians 4:4–9; and James 1:22–25.

Last, the most exciting aspect of this is not what we get to do for the Kingdom of God, but with whom we carry out our responsibilities. I am not referring to working with other Christians rather than having to try to do things on our own. The most exciting aspect that I am referring to is working with Christ Himself. He has commissioned us and also said He would help us and never leave us (see Matthew 28:18–20).

By now you may see that your reason for feeling unsatisfied with your life is that you did not believe yourself to be significant in God's Plan—but you are, according to God's point of view, and that is what really counts. You should also see that joy comes from knowing that God is orchestrating your life, providing for you and protecting you, and having you make a significant contribution to the advancement of His Kingdom – because you are obeying Him, and therefore doing just what He wants. And as a result you will see others around you being positively impacted with the love of Christ you are expressing to them—this too should bring you joy. In fact, at this point you will find that there is no reason left to be dissatisfied with your life. You are making a significant and positive impact in the lives of others, and God is proud of you—you are "His masterpiece" Ephesians 2:10 (NLT).

As you look back over my life, I trust that you have seen that *it does not take a special person* to do what God requires. I am really just an ordinary person, yet I have been privileged to take part in many ministries. I believe there is no better life than to live according to His plan, and there is no better reward than to be shown for all eternity the incomparable riches of God by Christ Himself (see Ephesians 2:4–10). So I encourage you to put your complete life *in His hands* today, if you have not already done so—and then you will experience firsthand what it is like to live *the best life possible* (see Romans 12:1-2).

APPENDIX D

More about the Author and His Life

INTRODUCTION:

In this book I have selected some of the highlights of my life that I have felt were important to illustrate the message of my book. There are therefore many details that were not included in the book, details that you may be interested in. The following interview will draw your attention to many of them.

INTERVIEWER:

In your book you mention some things in your life that possibly you could explain in more detail. We realize that to give us context you might have to duplicate a little of what is in the book, but we shall be understanding of that.

QUESTION:

So let's start. In your book you give us very little information about your childhood. We'd like to know more, starting possibly with some background about your parents.

ANSWER:

Well, my mother was born and raised in Vancouver, British Columbia; and my father was born in Moosejaw, Saskatchewan but raised mostly in Vancouver.

My mother's parents immigrated to Canada when they were newly married and settled in Vancouver. They were from Bristol, England. My Mom had one younger brother, and he lived with his wife and family in Vancouver also.

My father's parents had a different background – his mother was born in Norway, although she and her parents lived mostly in Sweden. My grandfather on my dad's side came from Denmark; and both he and my grandmother immigrated to Canada before my father and his two older brothers were born.

My dad's oldest brother was a medical missionary—an ophthalmologist—and lived in Pakistan with his wife and family for many years before returning to Canada when his wife became ill with what was later diagnosed as Alzheimer's disease.

My parents were married shortly after World War II, and lived in Vancouver where I was born in 1947. We moved to North Vancouver after my brother was born – that was two years after me – and that is where my first sister was born. When I was in grade four we moved back to Vancouver – to live in the Kerrisdale neighborhood, and that was where my other two sisters were born. So I had one brother and three sisters – all younger than me.

Kerrisdale was a middle to upper class area of Vancouver – and it was there that I went to Point Grey Junior High School for grades seven and eight, and then to Magee High School for grades nine through twelve. We did not live in a luxurious home – it was a two story middle class type home, but nearby there were some very expensive homes. So there were some *snobby-type* kids at the schools I attended, as well as many average middle-class kids.

QUESTION:

You've shared some things in your book about your childhood, but I'm wondering, were you ever into sports?

ANSWER:

I played a little soccer and baseball in grades seven and eight, and I enjoyed doing some high-jumping too—and actually became quite good at it. However, my parents would not allow me to join any athletic teams because their games were almost always played on Sundays, and I was told we did not have enough money to buy the required sports equipment.

It rained a lot in Vancouver, so in gym class we would often be in the gymnasium instead of outside, and I loved playing floor hockey. We often had competitions in the gym, and one day I raced some guys up the climbing ropes to touch the ceiling and then slide back down—and I won. But I allowed the rope to burn into my leg, and I was not careful enough in treating the burn. It got infected and developed into wet gangrene. So I was home for a few days with my leg elevated with steaming cloths applied every few hours. In any case, I got over it and was back to school the next week, feeling very good about winning the competition.

When I was a maybe thirteen, our family doctor said that I had a heart murmur and therefore needed to be careful with strenuous exercise. So after that I especially tried to limit my involvement in activities that involved too much running.

QUESTION:

Did this heart murmur limit you in other ways? What illnesses have you had during your life? Were there any accidents that caused you physical harm? Did you ever have to spend time in a hospital, apart from that which you mentioned in your book?

ANSWER:

I just mentioned the rope-climbing that gave me wet gangrene—that was when I was in grade eight. I won't repeat what I have already mentioned in my book, (for example: about the prostate surgery I had, or my retinal detachment), but I'll mention some other incidents that happened.

When I was in grade five, I was hit broadside by a car. That was traumatic for me—but it was not the driver's fault. I had left home for school late that morning, and I was riding my bike through a narrow pathway with lots of high grass and weeds on either side. Then as I approached the crossing road in front of me, I didn't slow down as I should have to look for cars coming. So I was hit by the car, and thrown about twenty feet. I felt quite shaken up. But fortunately I only suffered a few scratches and a sore leg. Praise the Lord!

When I was in elementary school (I do not remember which year), I had my tonsils and adenoids taken out, and so that put me in the hospital for a couple of days.

I was not in the hospital again until 1968 when I had my appendix taken out. Now that was scary!

It happened one Saturday morning, just a few months after we were married, when I was working in my father's hardware store. An odd pain began to develop in my stomach and it kept getting stronger.

So I left work to go see my doctor, and as I was driving my car the pain got so bad that I started to speed and go through red lights. (Fortunately, there were no police around to stop me.)

When I arrived at my doctor's office, I almost collapsed in the reception area. The doctor came out quickly and determined that I needed to go quickly to the hospital. He explained the situation to the people waiting in the reception area, telling them that there was not enough time to wait for an ambulance, and asked if someone would volunteer to drive me. Thankfully, one man said he would, and when we got to the hospital, a nurse was waiting on the curb with a wheelchair. In the hospital I was immediately transferred to a gurney, quickly looked at by a doctor and wheeled directly into an operating room—as I remember. Later I was told by the surgeon that my appendix was removed, without it bursting—but it was very close to doing so. Again, praise the Lord!

A couple of months earlier I was out behind my parents' home with my brother and a friend of his. We were cutting down some large branches from one of the trees using an ax and a chainsaw. Steve, my brother's friend, was up in the tree working away with the ax, and when he wanted the chainsaw, he passed the ax to my brother. At the same time I lifted the chainsaw up to Steve. But I was not watching what my brother was doing. He swung the ax hard to put it into the trunk of the tree, so as not to lose it in the leaves at our feet. But instead the ax hit my left arm, and blood started to gush out.

I ran to the house and called for my dad. He came running, and when he looked at my arm, he looked like he might faint. He quickly ran back upstairs, (and later told me it was to take a tranquilizer). He then drove me to the local clinic, where I received a few stitches. It was not nearly as bad as it could have been, the doctor said. Praise the Lord!

In 2010, I had the cataract in my left eye removed—that was in a Mexican hospital, in San Quintin.

In 2015, I had the cataract in my other eye removed—that time it was in a hospital in San Diego—not because I had had any problems with the Mexican hospital, but since I had become eligible for Medicare in 2013 it seemed logical to have it done in the US.

Also shortly after going on Medicare, I had an ENT and Plastic Surgery doctor in San Diego check my hearing—because even though I was by then wearing hearing aids, my hearing was getting worse. Dr. Mehta operated on my right ear, removing the ear drum and the innermost bone (called the stapes). The removed bone was then replaced with a synthetic ear bone made of titanium, after which the ear drum was glued back on using fat from my ear lobe. Unfortunately, this remarkable surgery did not help as much as the doctor had hoped. But since then I have gotten some better hearing aids and they are helping—but still not as well as I would like. I am now on my fifth pair of hearing aids—each being a little stronger than the previous ones. (Why five pairs of hearing aids in such a short time period? Because my hearing has been diminishing more rapidly than normal)

So apart from these things I've really been pretty healthy. Oh, I've had pneumonia a couple of times during my life, and food poisoning four times–but only once in Mexico.

I think the only thing I've not mentioned is that in 2015 I was diagnosed with having arthrosis in my right big toe, and that makes walking and running difficult. But thankfully no arthritis as yet, which I understand is hereditary, and something that both of my parents really suffered with.

QUESTION:

What did you do on weekends while you were growing up, besides spending a lot of time in church on Sundays as you have mentioned?

ANSWER:

Aside from going to church on Sunday, most Sunday afternoons Mom and Dad rested, and for us children that meant either playing games together quietly or reading. Sometimes, not very often though, I remember Dad taking everyone for a Sunday-afternoon drive. On Saturdays, Dad was always at work, and my brother and I had chores and homework to do. After all that was done, then we were able to play with our friends.

As a teenager I often went ice skating or roller skating at the local arena. Sometimes I would bike to and around Stanley Park with my friends. Sometimes we would take the bus to Stanley Park with our girlfriends, and then rent tandem bicycles to bike around the Park. A couple of times we all biked from our homes to a friend's summer home in Deep Cove (about a two-plus-hour bike ride), water-ski all day, and then bike back home.

QUESTION:

I think we have a good understanding now about your childhood. Can you tell us why you went to Bible School instead of choosing to go on to University?

ANSWER:

I always struggled in school to get passing grades. I tried very hard, and studied long hours, but getting a 'C-' or a 'C' was my usual grade in every subject. My Mom tried helping me occasionally with my homework, when she was able to squeeze some time away from her other responsibilities, but my grades did not get any better. I did once get a 'B' in high school– that was in mathematics.

When I brought up the subject of college or university, I was told that my father felt that if he could do what he was able to do with an eighth-grade education, so could I. So I really did not get any encouragement to take any education following my twelfth grade.

In high school we took some aptitude tests, and a couple of other ones as well, to help us decide what career might be of interest to us and what field of work we might be good in. The results in my case did not demonstrate clearly what field or career I should pursue. All that these tests did show was that I would be probably be good in some field where I would be helping less enfranchised people.

For most of my high school years I knew God had something in mind for me to do when I graduated; I just didn't have any clear understanding or direction at that time. So I decided to go to Bible School–I assumed that my parent's would approve and not think of this as the same as going to 'college or university'. Also I felt certain that what I would learn at Bible School would help me in whatever field of work I might do in the future.

QUESTION:

Can you tell us about your wife, Lorraine—how you met and maybe a little about her life, and what it was that attracted you to her?

ANSWER:

I first met Lorraine Roberts just a week or two after arriving at Emmaus Bible School—it was also her first year at Emmaus. But we didn't start dating until the fall of 1966.

From the time I first met Lorraine, I saw her as a really beautiful girl that I'd probably never get to have a relationship with. And throughout my first year at Emmaus, even though there was another girl that I felt I was in love with, I was always enamored with Lorraine's smile and her personality. Lorraine was not conceited or flamboyant. She was *down to earth,* and as I got to know her better it was her desire to overcome the many obstacles she believed were in her life that also attracted me to her.

After the summer of 1966, I decided to return to Emmaus by train – from Vancouver to Seattle, and then from Seattle to Chicago. That summer had been a very difficult time for me as I mentioned in my book; and low and behold when I boarded the train in Seattle, bound for Chicago, Lorraine was there – on the same train. That was the opportunity I needed and I was bold enough to take the seat beside her. Then we started talking – in fact we spent most of our time over the following three days on that train talking and getting to know each other.

A few weeks after we arrived at Emmaus that fall, I got up the nerve to start talking with Lorraine again. Then over the following few months we spent more and more time together, and we became good friends. As our relationship grew stronger, so did our ideas for spending the rest of our lives together.

In April 1967, I gave Lorraine an engagement ring—actually it was a *promise ring* I had made from some bread-bag twist-ties. Emmaus Bible School prohibited students from getting married or engaged during the school year (September through early May), so she did not receive her real engagement ring until later that summer.

QUESTION:

You have shared things about Lorraine in your book, but can you tell us more? What was her life like before she met you? I'm sure that influenced your lives together later.

ANSWER:

Lorraine is one of three children in her family – she being the eldest. Her brother Glenn was born about a year after Lorraine, and he was followed the next year by her sister Nita. Shortly thereafter the family moved to Harriman, Tennessee – where her dad's family was from. They lived there for about a year, before moving back to the Pacific Northwest.

It was not long after her family had moved to Seattle that her parents were divorced – and she saw very little of her dad after that.

When Lorraine had completed grade ten, her mom took her three children and moved to Coquitlam, British Columbia, Canada – where her grandmother was living. They all enjoyed their time while there, but returned to Seattle the following year.

So Lorraine and her family, while moving from here to there and back again, had their many struggles. Lorraine's mom suffered for many years from undiagnosed Narcolepsy. This not only made it very difficult for her to raise her three children, but also made things difficult for her while working at Boeing, and while working later at the University of Washington. Lorraine being the eldest child, did her best all of her teen-age years (and a few years before as well), to carry out many of the responsibilities at home when her Mother was not able to do everything the way she would have really liked.

QUESTION:

Can you tell us about the time from when you both got engaged until you were married, and how that impacted your lives together all these years?

ANSWER:

In May 1967, after completing two years at Emmaus Bible School, Lorraine and some other students went together to visit Washington, D.C. and the surrounding areas, before joining an Outreach Team in Salt Lake City, Utah; while I returned to Vancouver to work in my father's hardware store, and to live with my parents in Tsawwassen – a suburb of Delta, close to Vancouver.

In August, Lorraine returned from her summer travels and lived with her grandmother in Coquitlam and got a job in Vancouver. So we were both commuting each day into Vancouver for work; and often I would drive Lorraine to Coquitlam after work, and then drive back to Tsawwassen – we spent a lot of time commuting back and forth.

During this time of our courtship, we thought everything was coming together as well as could be expected. We enjoyed each other's company, and we were working out many practical details. So I told my parents that Lorraine and I were planning to be married the following spring, which would give us several more months to get to know each other even better, as well as adequate time to prepare for our wedding.

But in late September my parents told us that a spring wedding was simply out of the question because my mother had become pregnant, and at that time it was improper for a pregnant woman to be seen in public, especially at such an important event as a wedding. So we were advised that it would be best to just get married the following month; therefore we chose the date of our wedding to be October 28, 1967.

I thought, *'In the future when people ask, "Why did you both get married when you did?" I'll have to answer, "I may be the only one who had to get married because my mother was pregnant."'*

So the rush was on – we only had a few weeks to plan our wedding. Therefore our focus changed from developing and strengthening our relationship to becoming more concerned about our financial status. Both Lorraine and I had really just started working full-time, and neither of us had any savings, so we had to look very carefully at both of our incomes and our expenses. This became then the basis for making many of our decisions, and that was good. But it also became the preoccupation of many of our discussions, and that, in retrospect, was not so good. Because instead of discussing or doing other things that would have helped us get to know each other much better, we became obsessed with many immediate practical decisions. The long-term result of this was that the foundation of our marriage, our relationship and our friendship was a tendency to look at everything from practical perspectives, rather than developing a passionate love for each other. This affected our whole lives together, and made many things somewhat difficult for us.

QUESTION:

So you have now been married for a little over fifty years, and I am sure it has not always been easy. Can you tell us a little about what challenges you have faced, and how you both were able to overcome those obstacles?

ANSWER:

Let me start this answer by mentioning two little challenges we had early on in our marriage. Just a couple of weeks after we were married I found the toothpaste tube all crumpled up. So I showed Lorraine how to smooth out the tube by sliding the hard end of her toothbrush along the tube and then rolling up the end, making it tidy and nice looking.

A week or so later, I got frustrated when I found the bar of soap in the bathroom sitting in water on the side of the sink. So I bought a small plastic disc with little spikes on one side of it and pressed that into the bar of soap, so that this plastic thing would be on the bottom side of the soap—keeping the soap from becoming mushy—when it sat in this insert on the side of the sink. I thought this was an ingenious idea. But a day or two later I found the soap in the same place on the side of the sink, but with the plastic side up, instead of being on the bottom of the soap – and the soap was again mushy. So in my upset, I explained to Lorraine, *"See this little round piece of plastic that is now on the bottom of the soap? It is to be like a boot, not an umbrella! So when you are finished using the soap, please make sure it is on the bottom of the soap when placing it beside the sink!"*

I mention these two incidents to point out that Lorraine and I really did approach many things in life differently; and while trying to work out our differences may have sounded a bit humorous, that was not always the case.

Not only did we both have different perspectives about how to deal with many things, I, unfortunately, almost always thought that I knew what was best—and this superior attitude made it very difficult for us at times. You may ask, "Why did you feel that way?"

First, I believe it was because we did everything *the right way* when I was being raised—so I was told. My mother's parents had come from England and my father's parents had come from Denmark and Sweden—so almost everything was done in a well-organized manner, and done in a way I was told was, *the proper way*. This instilled into my mind that I had learned *the right way* and *the proper way* to do everything, which was the way I had been taught at home as a child.

Also Lorraine and I had come from very different backgrounds:

1. I was raised by both my mother and father. However, Lorraine's parents were divorced when she was very young, and so she was raised only by her mother. Lorraine therefore did not have the opportunity to understand the role that a father should have in a home, and she also never saw the relationship a mother and father should have with each other as husband and wife.

2. Lorraine's mom suffered from Narcolepsy (as mentioned earlier), and as a result Lorraine's mom had difficulties at work and at home. Therefore many of the household chores fell on Lorraine's shoulders, she being the eldest child in her family. This naturally caused her to become a strong and somewhat controlling person.

3. When Lorraine's mom got upset with her for any reason, she got slapped across the face. In my family, when I did something wrong, I was told, "Go up to your room, take down your pants, lie on your bed, and your father will be up in a moment," and a few minutes later Dad would come in, take off his belt, and whip me a few times. So discipline was done in different ways in each of our families as we grew up.

4. Lorraine's mom was not able to ever own her own home, and could only afford to rent older

homes in poor neighborhoods. My parents always owned and lived in nice homes, in good neighborhoods – even though they were not wealthy by most standards when I was living at home.

5. Lorraine's mom never owned a car, while my parents always owned their cars.

6. Lorraine grew up with very few toys. In fact, she never had a bicycle until I bought one for her when she was thirty-seven years old. But I got my first bicycle when I was seven years old.

7. Lorraine's mother's family had come over from France (sometime in the seventeenth century), so most of her family attended a Catholic Church, although Lorraine's mom had stopped going to church. Lorraine therefore did not grow up going to church, although there was still this Catholic environment in her family. However in Lorraine's mid-teens she did start to go to an evangelical church – that is where she heard about Emmaus Bible School. I, on the other hand, was raised all my life in an evangelical church.

For all these many reasons, blending our different ways of looking at everything was difficult.

When we got married, Lorraine saw everything as she had when she was growing up in her home with her mom, brother, and sister—and she did her best to do everything from the viewpoint of being in control, being the self-sufficient and independent woman she had grown up to be. However, when we got married I believed that it was my responsibility to lead and direct our home.

So for almost all of our lives together we have both struggled trying to reconcile our differences.

That said, we both always looked at things from a practical perspective. Seldom did we spend money on things we thought we really did not need. We never, unfortunately, got to a place where we did things solely from a romantic perspective. I realize that may sound dull and boring, and at times it probably was, but we never gave up. There were times when we were tempted to do just that—get divorced—but we didn't.

QUESTION:

Sorry to interrupt, but why didn't you get divorced? What was it that held you both together?

ANSWER:

Yes, there were a few times over the years when it became extremely difficult to work things out, so the threat of divorce did come up. But we had made a commitment to each other when we got married, and that commitment was to spend life together no matter how difficult things might become.

It was not only our commitment to each other that kept us together, but our commitment to the Lord Jesus Christ as well. We knew that He had a plan for our lives, and that plan was for us to do everything together. So that is what we have tried to do, and while it has been a struggle to work many things out, we have always tried to do what was best for our family, which was the motivation we have had from the time we first met each other.

QUESTION:

Can you tell us a little about your three children, and maybe what challenges you faced raising them, how you faced those challenges, and how your children are doing today?

ANSWER:

First, let me say that our children's lives are their lives, and I would not want to say anything that might take their deserved glory away from them, or say anything that might in some way make life difficult for them. In other words, we are very proud of each of our children—Jason, Deborah, and Nathan—even though we did face some challenges while raising them. But isn't that true for every family?

In any case, I am glad to report that not one of them has had a problem with drugs or alcohol, or is carrying on in a lifestyle that might cause us some embarrassment. Also, I am very pleased that despite the many struggles that Lorraine and I have faced, and the faults we've had as parents (and I realize that no parent is perfect), we are proud to tell you that they are each doing well in their own way. They have each had to face some challenges in their lives (not identical ones – we all have face different problems at different times), but again I am glad to report that they each seem to be overcoming those challenges. So in different ways, we are proud of each of them today.

We saw each child to be very different from the other while they were growing up. They each had different personalities and different strengths. Jason, the oldest, probably had it the hardest because we were new at parenthood when he came along; and Nathan, being the youngest, probably had it the easiest. In fact, when he was working in youth ministries, he asked us one day, "I'm having difficulty identifying with some of the kids who are struggling in their homes, so can you tell me why I was never spanked as a child?"

That was an easy question to answer actually, and to answer it I said, "Imagine yourself in a field with a fence around it, and that you've been told not to climb the fence and go outside that field. So every day there was a choice to be made: to learn and enjoy as much as possible within the fenced area, or to distrust us and test us by climbing over the fence to do other things. And Nathan, you chose to never climb that fence. You were happy accepting these limits, so you were never spanked; however, your brother had a difficult time while we were building the fence (so to speak), so he did get spanked from time to time. As for Deborah, she climbed the fence a few times and also got spanked."

"Let me explain further", I said. "The fence was there for a purpose, and even though we knew there would be some wonderful things outside the fence, we also knew there would be many problems that could be encountered if you went beyond the fence. So really, the fence was there because we loved you and Jason and Deborah, and we wanted the best for each of you, and did not want you harmed in any way."

We raised our children on Biblical values and teachings, and tried always to live by example, never expecting them to *"do what I say, not what I do."* That is not to say we were perfect examples. But we did always try to do what we thought to be best for our children.

In the early days of our marriage, there were very few books on marriage or child rearing available. However, we did find one book that gave us some insights; and one of the subjects discussed in that book was how to discipline your children. The verse in Proverbs 13:24 was mentioned: "Whoever spares the rod hates their children, but the one who loves their children is careful to discipline them." So I took what today would be thought of as a somewhat strict approach to helping our children accept authority and learn obedience. However I never did go overboard with spankings.

In 2 Timothy 4:2–4 it states, "Preach the word; be prepared in season and out of season; correct, rebuke and encourage—with great patience and careful instruction. For the time will come when people will not put up with sound doctrine. Instead, to suit their own desires, they will gather around them a great number of teachers to say what their itching ears want to hear. They will turn their ears away from the truth and turn aside to myths."

So we were careful to raise our children on Biblical values and teachings. We did what we believed was best for our children, and most times during their childhood years that was understood and accepted—despite the struggles Lorraine and I were having in our marriage and in discovering our roles as parents. In any case, we loved our children dearly as we raised them and love them dearly as they are today.

QUESTION:

You have told us on other occasions why you have written this book, and we understand you hope that people in general will come to a better understanding of how God can and will use *average* people for His purposes and for His glory. But tell us, what is your deepest hope for the people who have known you best during your lifetime, as they read this book?

ANSWER:

I guess my hope is not only that people will come to understand and appreciate God's interest in our lives more, but also that those who think they know me will come to understand *me* more. I do not mean to understand more about what I have done in my life, but more about the *inner me*—what has made me think and act the way I have throughout my life.

You see, we usually try to understand a person by the works they have done, and many times we want to judge them according to some moral standard. But by simply taking this approach, we rarely come to understand what it is that has made a person the kind of person they have been or become—or shall I say, what it is that has made them live their life as they have, or even act the way they did on a few occasions.

So the question then becomes, what were the things in my life that affected me and caused me to develop the way I did, and then later to be the kind of person I have been?

There are many things that influence a person as they grow up—that mold a child into the person they will become. The place (country, and neighborhood, etc.) where one is raised has a big impact on a child. But I believe parents have the greatest influence, especially in a child's early years. I believe it also makes a difference if a child is raised by both parents living at home, or if a child is raised by only one parent. Then of course there is what their parent or parents taught them, and what kind of values were passed on to them. Another huge influence on a person's development is how their parents treated them as children, and how they saw their parents treat other people, as well as how they treated each other.

Friends that a child makes and keeps also play a significant role in a person's development. Economic conditions that a person goes through in life is a big factor. Then it goes without saying that a person's education and their work experiences also have a lot to do with what makes a person think the way they do and do the things they do.

In other words, it is all of this and more, that when understood, helps us to appreciate someone for who they are, or have become.

Therefore, a person should not be judged solely on the basis of what they have done or accomplished in life. But to be fair to anyone, we must also take into consideration all of these contributing factors as well. For example, I believe many people misjudged my father. Had they understood what made my father the kind of person he was, they would have been able to look beyond some of his faults and appreciate him for the person he truly was—or at least for the kind of person he wanted and tried to be.

So one of my hopes is that everyone reading this book, especially those who have been closest to me throughout some portion of my life, will learn what has gone into making me the person I am; as well as learn how blessed and used by the Lord a person can be when they turn their life over to Him. And for those who may have not known me as well as they had thought, I hope they will now be able to look beyond some of my faults and be able to understand and appreciate the person I have tried to be.

I also hope that this book will help every reader who believes themselves to be *'just an average person'*, to understand that God uses *'ordinary people'* who will be obedient to Him, to do wonderful things to bless the people around them, and to bring glory to God.

QUESTION:

You have told us so much about your life, both in your book and in this interview, and I sense that you have learned a lot from what you have done throughout your life. If you were to have the opportunity to do it all over again, what would you change? Have you ever asked yourself, *Could I have done more?* or *Could I have done things better?*

ANSWER:

That certainly is a very important question and worthy of much consideration. But quickly, I would have to say two things.

First, I would like to have been less selfish. By that, I mean I wish I would have given more freely to others in need when I had the ability to do so, but instead (and I am speaking of early on in my life) I held back, choosing to worry about whether I would have the financial resources to meet my own needs.

In more recent years, experience has shown me that when God nudges us to do something, or when He urges us to give of ourselves in some way, He will always meet our needs. In fact, He will provide even more than we need, so we will be able to do more the next time He brings us an opportunity to help others.

This is what 2 Corinthians 9 is all about—this chapter is often misunderstood and preached on incorrectly. The point the apostle Paul was making is that when there is a need before you, give joyfully what you can, knowing that God will not only meet your needs but will also give more than you need—not for some personal gain or so you can become wealthy, but so you will be able to help more people to a greater extent the next time.

I have learned that if you want to do more and/or bigger things for the Lord, start supporting others in need, even in a small way, and He will expand your ministries as a result. I encourage you to read this chapter again to understand its context, and then meditate especially on these verses:

> "God is able to bless you abundantly, so that in *all things* at *all times*, having *all that you need*, *you will abound in every good work*. ... He who supplies seed to the sower and bread for food *will also supply and increase your store* of seed and will *enlarge the harvest of your righteousness*. You will be enriched in every way *so that you can be generous on every occasion*, and through us your generosity will result in thanksgiving to God" (2 Corinthians 9:8–10, emphasis added).

Second, I must mention that I would have spent more time in preparation for what the Lord put before me to do—more time in His Word, and more time studying to become fluent in Spanish, for example.

Thank you for taking the time for this interview

I am sure that all we have talked about will help the readers of your book to know and understand you in a deeper way, and truly understand what it means to be committed to the Lord, and what the results of such a committed life can mean for them.

About the Author

Donald Gordon Karsgaard

Don was born on April 5, 1947, in Vancouver, British Columbia, Canada, then became a naturalized citizen of the United States and more recently received his Permanent Resident status in Mexico.

Don began his career in youth ministries, and became a pastor before becoming involved in ministries in Western and Eastern Europe. Don has also been involved in business management and sales, and even for a short time was University Professor of Law.

Don lives with Lorraine, his dedicated wife of fifty-plus years, in Loreto, B.C.S., Mexico where they have been missionaries for fifteen years and impacted the lives of about twenty thousand people.

Don is a practical Bible teacher and makes himself available for various speaking engagements and other short-term assignments.

You will find more about Don on his website—where you will also find information about his other books. You may also contact Don through his website:

www.Donald-G-Karsgaard.com

Coming Soon...

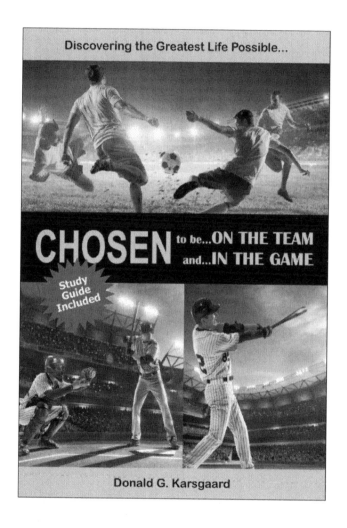

Are you not sure if you can be significantly used by God to bless others? Let me tell you: you can be used by God, and God will bless you in the process. God, our Creator, knows what is best for each of us. He not only has a general eternal plan for all His creation, but He also has a significant contributing individual part planned for each of us to play.

When you understand God's plan, you will appreciate Him in ways you never have before. When you discover God's specific plan for your life and start living it, you will experience the best life possible.

Have you been winning or struggling in this game of life? Sadly, many people have tried to be good and to help others, but when tempted by this world and all it has to offer, they have simply given up on God. Then while enjoying the pleasures of this life, they have discovered that they still feel empty in their soul. They feel cheated; the world has not given to them what they believe they are entitled to.

But do not give up! The meaning to your life can still be found. You can still find the way to have your life filled with joy. You can still be a person of significance. So do not stop searching. Do not throw in the towel; it is still early in this game of life. You may have been thinking that you have been in the penalty box. But the good news is that you have another chance; you are now being called back into the game.

Sure you have questions, such as, 'How do I get started? So..., "trust in the Lord with all your heart; do not depend on your own understanding. Seek his will in all you do, and he will show you which path to take" Proverbs 3:5-6 (NLT).

Another question you must face is, "How good a player will I be?"

This book will help you become the great player you can become, and it will give you some valuable insights and instructions on how to overcome your questions, your fears and many of the struggles in your life. This is not a self-help book or a book on psychology, but it certainly has a lot of powerful concepts in it—some you may have never considered before. When you read this book and apply the principles presented, I can promise you that you will discover and experience for yourself how to become a real success.

I encourage you to reserve your copy of the first edition of this most-inspiring book. I am sure this book will be a wonderful help to you, so go my website today.

www.Donald-G-Karsgaard.com

May God bless you richly!

In His Hands

In His Hands

In His Hands

Made in the USA
Middletown, DE
23 April 2019